The Violent Workplace

The Violent Workplace

**P.A.J. Waddington,
Doug Badger and Ray Bull**

WILLAN
PUBLISHING

Published by

Willan Publishing
Culmcott House
Mill Street, Uffculme
Cullompton, Devon
EX15 3AT, UK
Tel: +44(0)1884 840337
Fax: +44(0)1884 840251
website: www.willanpublishing.co.uk
e-mail: info@willanpublishing.co.uk

Published simultaneously in the USA and Canada by

Willan Publishing
c/o ISBS, 920 NE 58th Ave, Suite 300
Portland, Oregon 97213-3786, USA
Tel: +001(0)503 287 3093
Fax: +001(0)503 280 8832
e-mail: info@isbs.com
website: www.isbs.com

ISBN-13: 978-1-84392-168-4
ISBN-10: 1-84392-168-5 Hardback

First published 2006

British Library Cataloguing-in-Publication Data

A catalogue record for this book is available from the British Library

Typeset by GCS, Leighton Buzzard, Beds
Project management by Deer Park Productions, Tavistock, Devon
Printed and bound by T.J. International, Padstow, Cornwall

Contents

'To Jamie'

Preface

As I was writing this text on behalf of my collaborators and myself, an incident occurred in the university hall of residence of which I was the warden. A student resident had returned a week before term began without giving prior notice and in any event the hall was occupied by a conference. When the porter explained that the student could not be admitted to the hall, his father, who had transported him and a car-load of possessions, became agitated. Such was his agitation that the hall secretary summoned me, but by the time of my arrival the resident and his father had left. The porter found it rather amusing and speculated that the father was likely to direct his anger towards his son for bringing him on such an unnecessary jaunt.

Three days later I was in my study when the phone rang. Again, it was the hall secretary's alarmed voice asking me to go to the hall foyer where the resident and his father had returned and were now engaged in an altercation with staff. As I walked into the foyer I could hear the father's raised voice and saw him standing directly in front of the young man who is the deputy hall manager. He was making a stabbing gesture towards the deputy's chest with his right hand. The deputy drew attention to my arrival and the father glanced briefly in my direction, but returned his attention to the deputy. I asked what the problem was and the father turned and angrily said 'That's no way to speak to me! "What's the problem?"!' He then explained that on the previous visit he and his son had been led to believe that his son could return on this day, but now he had learnt that his son would have to pay an additional daily rent for occupying a room during what remained of the vacation. Well, 'explained' hardly does justice to the spluttered and incoherent string of allegations that fell from the father's lips. As he spoke, the father started to use the same jabbing gesture that he had earlier employed when addressing the deputy. I placed my hand over his and gently lowered his arm to indicate that I was not willing to allow him to continue making this gesture.

The conversation with the resident's father was proving fruitless and since he was not the 'contracting party' I said that I would talk to his son, who stood quietly a few feet away. He repeated that he and his father had been told he could return later in the week, but no mention had been made of an additional payment. However, before this conversation could progress much further the father interrupted and he was becoming progressively agitated. After uttering a few angry complaints about the management of the hall, the father declared that he and his son were leaving. They began walking towards the exit and I followed a few feet behind. The father turned towards me and asked rhetorically, 'Who do you think you are? A bouncer?' He then threatened to 'have me' if I laid a hand on him. As he went through the exit he declared that if he saw me in the city where he lived he would 'have me'. As they drove away, the car paused near the entrance and the father glared towards the foyer.

Anticipating that the father might complain about his and his son's treatment, I instructed all the staff who were present to write down exactly and fully what they had seen and heard. For the remainder of the day, this incident was recalled, analysed and condemned by various members of staff. One of them who had been on the margins of the incident came to see me in tears, for it evoked feelings from her previous employment. Staff were distressed and angry. They felt traduced by what they regarded as the unfounded allegations hurled around so freely by the resident's father. They reassured me that they had done nothing to foster the false impression that the resident and his father harboured. They speculated about the father's motives and what he might do.

The following day news was received that the father had indeed contacted a central office in the university regarding the incident. Whilst he had generally complained, he had been more concerned that his son should not be discriminated against because of his altercation with staff. A few days later when all students returned for the beginning of term, the father approached the porter who had witnessed the earlier episode and thanked him for 'everything you've done' for his son. Just a brief interlude in paradise!

It is incidents such as this that are the focus of this book. The reader may well ask why such commonplace behaviour has devoured the attention of a criminologist, a forensic psychologist and a senior social work lecturer. At the outset of the research on which this book is based, it was not our intention to focus on such incidents. Our concern had been aroused by the burgeoning of workplace violence and its apparent concentration in certain occupations, most notably the 'caring professions' of health care, mental health and social work. It was our aim to explore fully the experience of being exposed to such violence and understand the meaning that victims gave to it. What we discovered in the course of fieldwork was the mundane reality of workplace violence: clients, patients, customers, suspects and their respective companions become occasionally angered by what they consider poor service or injustice. They express that anger by raising their voice, making complaints and allegations, perhaps uttering more or less specific threats. Rarely, the incident will result in some physical contact that may amount to an assault.

If physical violence is relatively rare, why do such incidents merit examination and analysis? Whether physical injury is caused or not, employees – like the porters and administrative staff of the hall of residence – often find such episodes deeply disturbing. Staff in the hall of residence remained agitated for the remainder of the day in which the incident occurred. There was apprehension among some staff about what would happen if and when the father returned to bring his son to begin the academic term. Long after the incident had occurred staff recalled and discussed it. For me, what had hitherto been an academic curiosity became an experiential reality.

In the pages that follow we will show the breadth of what is described as 'workplace violence': from life-threatening incidents and serious physical injury to angry expressions of annoyance. We seek to analyse the experiences of those we interviewed; to understand the meanings that they gave to those experiences; and to consider the implications of our analysis for practice and policy. We believe that this will challenge common misconceptions – misconceptions that we shared when we embarked on this venture.

Of course, we could not have done any of this without the willing cooperation of our interviewees and the organisations who granted us access. Preserving anonymity and confidentiality precludes us from identifying those to whom we owe so much, but they know who they are and we hope that if they read this book they will feel that we have done them and their experiences justice.

We *can* thank the Home Office for funding this research and the Nuffield Foundation, who also provided funds to assist with the analysis of the unexpectedly large volume of material that was generated. We hope that they will conclude that we have given value for money.

I wish to thank my two collaborators. Professor Ray Bull has been at the forefront in developing the methodology – cognitive interviewing – without which this research could not have been conducted with the depth that I believe we achieved. He steered the fieldwork and ensured its 'quality control'. Doug Badger has been a valued colleague of mine for many years at the University of Reading; without his help access would have been very much more difficult and his grasp of the realities of social work practice proved invaluable to the analysis of results. Needless to say all three of us jointly accept full responsibility for what follows.

P.A.J. Waddington
The University of Reading
September 2005

Chapter 1

Discovering workplace violence

The breadth of the problem

Writing in 2002, Wells and Bowers observed that 'The growth in the literature has been quite marked, from 32 articles in 1988 to several hundred today' (Wells and Bowers 2002: 231). Citing Paterson and Leadbetter (1999), they describe this as the 'rediscovery' of work-related violence. Since 2002 there has certainly been no abatement in the output of publications. Not only has this concern increased in recent years, it has done so throughout the world: in the United States and Canada, the United Kingdom, Europe and Scandinavia, Australia and New Zealand. Not even Iceland (Aromaa 1994) or Turkey (Uzun 2003) is immune, nor has the Third World escaped (Isotalus 2002). The 'international community' has also been stimulated into expressions of concern and analyses of the problem with the European Union (European Agency for Health and Safety at Work 2003, 2002; European Commission 1998; Smulders *et al.* 2001; Wynne and Clarkin 1995); International Labour Organisation (Chappell and Di Martino 2000; Curbow 2001; Hoel and Einarsen 2003; Hoel *et al.* no date); and World Health Organisation all commissioning research and producing weighty reports.

Matching this worldwide breadth of concern about workplace violence is the spectrum of workplaces that are affected. Of course in almost any location where people gather together there is the prospect of violence and aggression. In the United States the phrase 'going postal' is used to refer to those occasions when workers kill and injure their workmates in a dramatic outburst of violence (Giga *et al.* 2003a). Whether this is because of the stress under which postal workers perform their duties in the United States (as the American Postal Workers Union claims) is another matter (Denenberg and Braverman 1999).

However, there are some occupations that do seem unduly exposed to workplace violence. First among them are the public services: health care springs readily to mind (Gerberich *et al.* 2004; Gerberich *et al.* 2001; National Audit Office 2003a, b; Rippon 2000). Emergency medicine has acquired a reputation for the threat of violence to which its practitioners are exposed (Foust and Rhee 1993; Gillespie and Melby 2003), but the problem extends well beyond this field. As Winstanley and Whittington found, 'contrary to expectations, Accident and Emergency (A&E) staff did not report the highest level of physical assault for either single or for multiple incidents' (2004: 8). Mental health is one of the most perilous callings because psychiatrists and nurses are caring for patients some of whom are deeply disturbed (Coyne 2001), but the elderly can also be disturbed and those who care for them also suffer comparatively high levels of workplace violence (Eastley *et al.* 1993; Freyne and Wrigley 1996; Gates *et al.* 1999a, b). Likewise, the staff of drug and alcohol dependency clinics are also exposed to a section of the population who suffer emotional and psychiatric disturbance and the staff suffer violence as a result (O'Connell *et al.* 2000). Elsewhere, health care workers may find themselves dealing with people in particularly stressful circumstances, such as intensive care and high dependency wards (O'Connell *et al.* 2000) or midwives (Nursing Standard 2005; Shepherd 1997). The 'workplace' of some medical staff may not be a hospital or clinic, but in the community. Coyne cites evidence that health visitors and district nurses are at high risk (Coyne 2001). In Australia the homes that such community health practitioners visit may be very isolated and leave the health care worker particularly vulnerable (Denton *et al.* 2000; Tolhurst *et al.* 2003). Surprisingly, perhaps, pharmacists are unusually exposed to violence (Isotalus and Saarela 1999) because they are involved in three of the highest-risk activities: dealing with people; handling money; and dispensing drugs (which, according to one report, places them more at risk than any other occupation [*Chemist and Druggist* 2004]). Many readers may be even more surprised to learn that occupational health nurses (Findorff-Dennis *et al.* 1999), nephrologists (Hlebovy 2000), radiographers (Healy *et al.* 2002) and dentists (Pemberton *et al.* 2000) also suffer from violence at work. In health care, it seems, there is no hiding place.

Whilst considerable attention has been paid to health care, it is not alone among the public services in being exposed to the ravages of violence. Teaching is an occupation that has come to be associated with violence from parents and schoolchildren, some of them very young indeed (Gill and Hearnshaw 1997; Leyden 1999). Less prominent, but no less deserving of attention, are social workers (Brown et al. 1986; Bute 1994; Dunkel et al. 2000; Littlechild 1995; Norris and Kedward 1990; Rowett 1986; Rowett and Breakwell 1992; Thompson 2004), some of whom have suffered serious injury and even death in the course of their professional work. Equally hidden are occupations like environmental health officers (Journal of Environmental Health Research 2002) who, like social workers, may sometimes seek to correct the unhealthy practices of their clientele. More surprising is the appearance of local authority officers generally (Kedward 2000), housing officers (Thornhill 2000), librarians (Farrugia 2002) and even construction project negotiators (Construction Law 2000) and 'women planners in Scotland' (Illsley 1997) among those who suffer violence, but apparently they do.

It is not only the public services that suffer the blight of work-related violence; so too does the private service sector, for instance bank staff (Rogers and Rogers 1997) and many in the retail sector generally. Hotels, catering, pubs and bars and tourism (Gilbert et al. 1998; Guerrier and Adib 2000; Hoel and Einarsen 2003) all suffer elevated levels of violence, presumably because of the consumption of alcohol by their clientele. Another 'at risk' group of workers are those in the performing arts, especially 'dancers, particularly those employed in "exotic dancing" such as stage dancing, table dancing and lap dancing' (Giga et al. 2003b). Likewise, attention has recently been drawn to sex workers (Barnard 1993; Campbell and Kinnell 2001; Church et al. 2001; Kurtz et al. 2004).

To summarise, we have become aware throughout the world that workplace violence is commonplace. This is not a problem that afflicts only a few, but seems to plague the workforce as a whole.

The scale of the problem

If work-related violence is commonplace, how severe a problem is it? There is a substantial literature on how workplace violence afflicts specific occupations, but no profession has been more thoroughly examined than health care. The authoritative National Audit Office recently summarised the available data on violence directed at health care workers.

In 2000, the Health Service Report in its survey of 45 NHS trusts found that 81 per cent had experienced an increase in the number of violent incidents reported in the year to April 2000, and that on average incidents had risen from 1,200 to 1,400 incidents per 10,000 employees.

In 2001, a United Kingdom Central Council for Nursing and Midwifery report, *The recognition, prevention and therapeutic management of violence in mental health care*, based on responses by 839 staff found that three quarters of nurses had been physically assaulted during their career and most had been subjected to violence on at least six occasions.

In 2002, the Royal College of Nursing published the results of its *Working Well* survey covering a random sample of 6,000 nurses. Fifty-five per cent of respondents were working in NHS hospitals, of which 43 per cent reported that they had been harassed or assaulted by a patient/client or the patient's relatives in the past 12 months, with 32 per cent subjected to physical assault.

UNISON's annual membership survey in the health sector showed a rise in the number of staff reporting incidents of violence from 34 per cent in 2000 to 41 per cent in 2001.

The Health and Safety Executive found that physical assaults to NHS staff were the third greatest cause of accidents that resulted in more than three days absence…

Out of 34,000 NHS acute trust staff and 6,544 ambulance trust staff who responded to recent staff surveys, 29 per cent and 50 per cent respectively had personally experienced violence and aggression in the previous 12 months. (National Audit Office 2003b: 9)

Clearly, amongst health workers the problem is endemic and serious. It is also a problem that continues to worsen despite government targets designed to reduce the scale of violence and aggression.

The same report cites two national surveys conducted by the Department of Health:

Their 2000–2001 survey identified 84,214 reported incidents of violence or aggression, an increase of 30 per cent over 1998–1999. Our 2001–2002 survey showed a further 13 per cent increase (to 95,501 reported incidents). (National Audit Office 2003b: 2)

To the reports of the National Audit Office can be added other independent and authoritative reports from Incomes Data Services

(2000), the American Psychological Association (Vandenbos and Bulatao 1997) and European Foundation for the Improvement of Living and Working Conditions (Cooper *et al.* 2003), all of which endorse the view that workplace violence is a serious and growing problem.

Workplace violence is serious not only for the victims, but also for those responsible for the workplace. In Britain and most other developed countries employers are responsible for ensuring the health and safety of their employees and must assess the risks to which workers are exposed and take all reasonable measures to eliminate or diminish them (Croner Employment Digest 1997; Health and Safety Executive 1996; Kloss 2003; Roach 1997). This is a costly obligation in itself, which if not properly discharged can result in hefty legal damages and loss of reputation for public and private institutions.

> In August 2002 a community trust was convicted under the Health and Safety at Work etc Act 1974 following serious assaults on two support workers by a patient. The trust was fined £12,000, and HSE was awarded costs of over £14,600. (National Audit Office 2003b: 45)

As European-wide research points out, the cost of workplace violence is not confined to legal compliance; they extend to problems of recruitment, retention, absenteeism and poor work performance (Cooper *et al.* 2003; Hogh *et al.* 2003). The National Audit Office report estimated that workplace violence and aggression constituted 40 per cent of all health and safety incidents, the direct costs of which amounted to £60 million per annum. As they go on to point out:

> While a minor incident may not incur much in the way of direct costs, it can nevertheless result in low morale, a less efficient and effective approach to duties, affect the morale of other staff and require some training or new equipment to avoid a repeat. The more staff are exposed to violence and aggression the greater the impact. (National Audit Office 2003b: 45)

They continue by citing a Royal College of Nursing study that found that 'nurses who had been assaulted or harassed showed poor psychological well-being and were more likely to consider leaving their job within 12 months than nurses who had not been harassed or assaulted' (National Audit Office 2003b: 2).

Moral panic?

It seems clear that workplace violence is a serious and worsening problem, but the sceptical researcher is obliged to ask whether this is a justified conclusion (Mullen 1997). The concept of a moral panic was devised by criminologists to account for those circumstances in which public concern arose in connection with problems that did not justify the anxiety they provoked; for instance, the battles between 'mods and rockers' that supposedly erupted in British seaside resorts in the 1960s were blown out of all proportion by hysterical media coverage and exploited by 'moral entrepreneurs' (Cohen 1972; Goode and Ben-Yehuda 1994).

There are reasons for caution with respect to workplace violence, for here too there are signs of media exaggeration. Reviewing the literature on violence directed at health care workers, Coombes remarks that 'the tone is often alarmist, for example "Why nurses are more at risk than these bouncers"' (cited in Wells and Bowers 2002: 231). To this example one might add such headlines as: 'Violence at work: the brutal truths' (Crabb 1995); 'Work zone or war zone?' (Ryan 1997). The *Nursing Standard* quotes an MP who spent a night shift in A&E as saying:

> I knew that violence and abuse towards staff was an increasing problem but I was not aware of just how frightening this could be in reality. It is quite incredible that nurses who come to work to fulfil their role as dedicated healthcare professionals are subjected to this sort of treatment. (Simmonds 2002: 20–21)

Such depictions of working life are routinely published in magazines such as *The Nursing Standard, Nursing Times, Social Work Professional, Police Review,* and also escapes into the public domain. For instance, the *Daily Telegraph* asserted that nursing is a 'dangerous' occupation (Fletcher 1997). Fictional portrayals of hospital life or policing in the broadcast media emphasise violence, no doubt because of its dramatic appeal.

Even the National Audit Office report is not immune to such hyperbole. A montage of press cuttings reproduced in one of their reports contains the following under the banner headline 'Shocking Facts of Life in A&E':

> A male deputy charge nurse was talking to a female patient in A&E. He felt she was becoming hostile so stopped the conversation and walked away. The patient followed and punched him in the face. (National Audit Office 2003b: 16)

Of course, behind such headlines lie real victims: 'between 1974 and 1987 Bute estimates that five social workers were killed in the course of their duties and three others were severely injured' (quoted in Norris and Kedward 1990). It was media pressure surrounding these tragic but exceptional events that seems to have provoked Sir Norman Fowler (then Secretary of State for Health and Social Services) publicly to commit his department to seeking a remedy (Norris and Kedward 1990).

The level of media attention that has focused on workplace violence has not done so spontaneously: 'professional organizations, health trades unions and the government have pursued the issue on behalf of members/staff' (Wells and Bowers 2002: 231). For instance, the Royal College of Nursing (Royal College of Nursing 1993, 1994, 1998a, b) and United Kingdom Central Council for Nursing (Gournay 2001), the British Medical Association (2003), British Dental Association (1997), National Association of Probation Officers (1989), the TUC (Gallagher 1999a, b) and unions like UNISON (1995, 1997) and NUPE (1991) have all been active in pushing the issue of workplace violence up the policy agenda.

Even more crucially, government departments and agencies have advanced the cause. The Health Services Advisory Committee of the Health and Safety Commission conducted a survey of 3,000 health care staff (Health Services Advisory Committee 1987) and found that 1 in 200 had suffered a major injury at work requiring medical attention during the previous 12 months, and more than 1 in 10 had suffered a minor injury needing first aid. In 1998 Industrial Relations Services conducted a survey of the provision for staff in respect of dealing with violent episodes.

The Department of Health has been particularly active. The National Audit Office recalls:

> Two initiatives, launched in October 1999, have been key to tackling the growing concerns about the level of violence and aggression in the NHS: the NHS *zero tolerance zone* campaign, which had the support of the Home Secretary, the Lord Chancellor and the Attorney General was aimed at increasing staff awareness of the need to report, assuring staff that this issue would be tackled and informing the public that violence against staff working in the NHS is unacceptable and would be stamped out; and *Working Together, securing a quality workforce for the NHS*, required NHS trusts and health authorities to have systems in place for recording incidents using the standard definition...and set targets

for reducing violence and aggression by 20 per cent by 2001 and 30 per cent by 2003. The targets were subsequently incorporated in the *Improving Working Lives* standard, launched in October 2000, which all acute, mental health and ambulance trusts were required to put into practice by April 2003. (National Audit Office 2003b: 2)

The Parliamentary Public Accounts Committee (2003) has expressed concern and so too have the Scottish Executive (2004) and Local Government Management Board (1991).

Inevitably, perhaps, the health and safety 'lobby' has actively promoted the importance of the issues of workplace violence, not only through official publications (Health and Safety Executive 1996, 1997), but also propagated through the bewildering array of health and safety publications: *Safety and Health Practitioner* (Brennan 2001; O'Connor 2000; Weadick 2001); *Safety Management* (Home Office Violence at Work Survey 2001); *Occupational Health* (Occupational Health 2001); *Health and Hygiene* (Golding 2000); *Safety and Health* (Graham 2000); *People Management* (*People Management* 1998; Crabb 1995); *Personnel Today* (*Personnel Today* 2001); *Director* (McCurry 2000); *Labour Studies Journal* (Declercq 2000); and many others. All of this has been designed to raise awareness, but from the perspective of 'moral panics' it might be interpreted as the actions of 'moral entrepreneurs' spuriously arousing anxiety.

The British Crime Survey (BCS) has allowed a less partial and partisan analysis of work-related violence, for almost alone this survey does not focus on discrete occupations, but is able to compare the broad spectrum of work (Budd 1999, 2001; Upson 2004). The first glaring contradiction between the BCS and the picture painted by the generality of discussion on workplace violence is that work-related violence is neither as prevalent nor increasing as many commentators would have us believe.

> The risk of being a victim of actual or threatened violence at work is low; the 2002/03 BCS indicates that 1.7 per cent of working adults were the victim of one or more violent incidents at work...
>
> The number of incidents of violence at work has fallen by 35 per cent from the peak of 1,310,000 in 1995 to the current level. (Upson 2004: 1)

Secondly, those relatively few occupations that do seem to be unusually exposed to violence are headed by those for whom relatively little concern is expressed in the extensive literature reviewed above, namely those in the field of security and control. It is true that the police have attracted sympathy, especially following high-profile incidents in which officers are seriously injured or killed, and this has encouraged the 'officer safety' agenda within the police service. However, one hears much less about prison officers who likewise suffer the depredations of criminals and those employed in the field of private security, such as 'bouncers'. As Hobbs and his colleagues have pointed out, 'doorstaff' (as they are euphemistically described) are at the forefront of controlling alcohol-fuelled excess (Hadfield *et al.* 2001; Hobbs *et al.* 2002, 2003; Lister *et al.* 2001; Winlow *et al.* 2001, 2003). Compared with these professions, other public servants have relatively violence-free working lives. Moreover, some of the occupations that have attracted public attention – for example, the teaching profession – are not prominent among those most exposed to violence, suffering no more than many other occupations (Budd 1999, 2001; Upson 2004).

'Violence'?

Apart from these substantive questions there is, buried in the literature on workplace violence, a crucial conceptual and methodological issue – the meaning of 'violence'. The common connotation of 'violence' is physical attack, but this has been expanded by researchers, campaigners and official bodies to embrace a much wider spectrum of disagreeable interpersonal experience that has had the effect of greatly inflating the apparent incidence of 'violence'.

Surveys conducted among particular groups of workers revealed worrying levels of exposure to violence and alerted official bodies to the scale of the problem. But these surveys rely upon respondents' reports of incidents to compile their estimates. Whilst the sophistication of these surveys appears to vary greatly, all of them ultimately ask the same question: has the respondent experienced an act of violence in the course of their work? But what is 'an act of violence'? Does it require that an aggressor physically attacks the respondent or simply threatens to do so? What if the violence is not directed against the respondent, but the respondent witnesses its use against a third party? Suppose an aggressor simply becomes angry and the respondent fears that they might convert that anger into physical attack. Does that qualify?

Historically, workplace violence was narrowly defined to include only physical assault or homicide that occurred at the workplace. The general tendency now is for definitions to widen the scope over time in parallel with the greater public and professional awareness of the problem. Thus in some circumstances the understanding of what constitutes work-related violence has been expanded to encompass forms of aggression such as verbal threats, abuse, harassment, any assault or threat that cultivates psychological harm, personal or motor vehicle theft and self-directed harm. (Harvey *et al.* 2002: 42)

The BCS disaggregates physical attack from threats and intimidation and has discovered that the latter are far more common than the former (Budd 1999, 2001; Upson 2004). Yet, complying with official received wisdom, the BCS insists upon bundling both elements together to create a global estimate of the extent of violence. The European Commission, too, defines violence as 'any untoward incident where staff are abused, threatened or assaulted in circumstances relating to their work, involving an explicit or implicit challenge to their safety, wellbeing or health' (1997).

Researchers also use a variety of expansive definitions of 'violence', including:

The intentional infliction of harm on one person by another, resulting in *psychological* and/or physical injury (Spokes *et al.* 2002: 200, emphasis added)

...a continuum of behaviours from verbal through to physical and sexual assault, while bearing in mind the impacts of these behaviours on the professional in terms of emotional and physical injury (O'Beirne *et al.* 2003: 178)

...the term 'aggression' will be used and defined as 'any form of behaviour directed towards the goal of harming or injuring another living being who is motivated to avoid such treatment' (Whittington 2002: 820)

verbal violence (Brennan 2001)

The project director of the authoritative and influential Violence Research Programme of the Economic and Social Science Research Council admitted that: 'Despite an assumed, almost self-evident core, "violence" as a term is ambiguous and its usage is in many ways moulded by different people as well as by different social scientists to describe a whole range of events, feelings and harm' (Stanko 2003:

2–3). She continues, citing Brubaker and Laitin (1998), 'The problem of defining violence is not that there is no agreement on *how* things are to be explained; it is that there is no agreement on *what* is to be explained, or *whether* there is a single set of phenomena to be explained' (p 427, emphasis in original). Stanko seeks to make a virtue out of such ambiguity:

> I suggest that what violence means is and will always be fluid, not fixed; it is mutable...
>
> I would even go so far as to suggest that it is only through fluidity of definition that we can think creatively about disrupting violence as a social phenomenon. (2003: 3)

Others regard such 'fluidity' as a handicap to effective action. Having noted 'a lack of consistency of view' among their sample, Harvey *et al.* note that this 'has implications for policy formulation relating to both the defining of violence and in devising staff education and training which makes the nature of violence and its consequences and remedies a real issue' (2002: 48). If people mean different things by the term 'violence' this obscures our grasp of the problem. Reflecting upon inconsistencies between their own research and that of the Health Service Advisory Committee, Winstanley and Whittington comment:

> All these results may indicate differences in interpretation of physical assault. A&E staff may be less likely to classify incidents as aggressive and therefore reported fewer experiences.
>
> Alternatively, the frequency of physical assault in A&E might have inured staff to aggressive incidents so that fewer were recalled. (Winstanley and Whittington 2004: 8)

The experience and meaning of violence

The task of our research and this book is to try and illuminate these possibly varied meanings of violence by examining in detail what personnel in high-risk occupations actually experienced during a violent episode. We do so not by investigating only one occupation, but a range of those that have been identified as particularly exposed to violence: the police, Accident and Emergency hospital staff, social workers (occupied mainly in child protection), and mental health professionals (both medical and social workers). In doing so, we pay heed to Stanko's observation that

> Four elements are crucial in grappling with the meanings of violence: (1) the act itself; (2) the relationship of the participants to each other; (3) the location of the act; and (4) the outcome or the resultant damage. (Stanko 2003: 11)

In the following chapters we will consider what the violent actions were, who committed them, the context in which they took place, and the different impact that such violence had upon different victims. Before doing so, we need to explain how we obtained the information upon which these accounts of violence are based.

Chapter 2

Researching workplace violence

Introduction

This chapter is the one that many readers skip in books of this kind. It promises a dreary and self-justificatory account of how the evidence upon which the rest of the book rests was produced. Yet, it is the most important part of any research project, for unless the empirical basis is sound, the grand edifice that follows might be erected on insecure foundations. This is no less true here, for what follows in the rest of this book are descriptions of violent or hostile encounters that were not directly witnessed by the researchers. We are obliged to take on trust what interviewees have told us. Why should we trust them? This is a methodological issue that goes to the very heart of social science scholarship.

To spice things up a little, this chapter will not only describe the methods used in this research, but also set out a prospectus for the application of a particular research technique. The research reported here can be considered not only as an inquiry into an important social and policy issue, but also as a demonstration exercise in the use of this technique for research purposes. The technique in question is 'cognitive interviewing' and we believe that it offers scholars tremendous opportunities for recovering accurate and thorough descriptions of people's experience through interviewing them. However, it is a technique that refuses to fit in to widely accepted methodological categories; indeed it challenges those categories.

'Gimme the facts, man, just the facts'

Those old enough to remember the 1950s American television series *Dragnet* will immediately recognise the instruction that weekly fell from the lips of its central character, Joe Friday. Armed with the facts of what witnesses had experienced, he and his partner tracked down the felons on the mean streets of Los Angeles. But cops – fictitious or real – are not the only ones who rely upon witnesses telling them 'the facts'; so do scholars. Some facts can be observed directly in experimental laboratories or through structured observations in field settings. To be sure, methodological issues remain and we will return to some of these later. However, there is a clear distinction to be drawn between the transparency and rigour that can be achieved by these highly structured methods of data collection and reliance upon interviewees' recollections or reports.

Interviews: remote sensing for the social sciences

Despite its evident weaknesses, researchers are condemned to rely upon interviewing for much of the evidence upon which they erect their theories. This is because, firstly, some events are simply hidden from view. This is an acute problem for criminologists because much delinquency is perpetrated privately. For instance, there is very little realistic prospect that domestic violence or police malpractice could often be observed directly. If researchers are to study such issues at all, then they are virtually compelled to rely on accounts given by participants. Secondly, many events in which researchers are interested occur so infrequently and/or unpredictably that it would require a massive research enterprise to net a sufficiently large number of them to support any generalisations. For instance, Worden (1996) analysed direct observations of 5,688 police–citizen encounters during 900 patrol shifts in 60 neighbourhoods selected from three cities representing different regions of the USA. The yield from this vast observational endeavour was that 'Whilst they were observed…officers used no more than reasonable force to restrain or move a citizen in *thirty-seven* encounters. In *twenty-three* encounters, officers used force that the observer judged to be unnecessary or excessive; in three of those, officers hit or swung at citizens with a weapon' (p 36, emphasis added). In other words, the proverbial 'bang for the (research) buck' can be meagre indeed if we are compelled to rely on direct observation.

Pragmatism dictates that researchers must rely upon reports from third parties if they are to obtain information upon which they can build social or criminological theories. They actually do so routinely and *successfully*. The victim survey has transformed criminology (Stanko 2000). Before this research tool became widely used, criminologists had speculated about the 'dark figure' of crime. They had imagined that many criminal offences went unreported to the police; that a hefty proportion of those that were reported went unrecorded by the police; and that those offences that survived this filtering process created a distorted picture of crime. The relatively straightforward expedient was not to rely upon official statistics, but to gather the evidence directly from victims. Thus, the victim survey approaches a random sample of the population, each member of which is presented with a list of common criminal offences described in non-legal language, and asked whether they have suffered any of them in the recent past; if so, details are then taken of the offence, offender, response of the police, and so forth. The result was to confound popular assumptions and corroborate criminological theory: officially recorded crime is a small proportion of the crime that is suffered by the population and does indeed create a distorted picture of the problem (Hough and Mayhew 1983).

What is important for our purposes is that this criminological triumph is based upon the *reports* of numerous interviewees who tell the crime survey that they have indeed suffered victimisation. How do we know that they have? The short answer is that we don't know; we are obliged to *trust* our interviewees. We console ourselves by reasoning that whilst some individuals may falsely answer the interviewer's questions, these aberrations are likely to cancel each other out in a large-scale survey. We recognise that certain kinds of crime, such as sexual offences against women, may be systematically under-reported and methodological innovations are made to negate any embarrassment that might impede accurate reporting (Myhill and Allen 2002). Yet, no matter how dedicated and rigorous researchers have been, the fundamental problem remains: if an interviewee reports that they suffered crime in the past, how do we know that their report is accurate? If this is an issue in a methodology as relatively straightforward as the victim survey, then it is even more acute in other areas of research.

Remote sensing: an analogy

It is necessary now to digress, albeit briefly. Extravagant pretensions to the scientific status of social research in the past have made contemporary social scientists wary of drawing analogies with scientific practice. It is not our purpose here to slavishly imitate what scientists do, but this does not mean that we cannot learn anything from science. When it comes to remote sensing there is much to learn, for this is routine in science. Name your science and you will find that it relies very largely, if not exclusively, on some form of remote sensing. The spectrograph that tells astronomers about the most distant objects in the universe; the scanning electron microscope that shows the microbiologist the structure of cells; the orbiting satellites that inform meteorologists about the atmosphere; even the humble thermometer all convey information that is not amenable to direct observation. Like the social scientist who relies on the interviewee to report what has happened, our colleagues in the natural sciences rely upon devices that *mediate* between the phenomenon under research and the researcher who gathers the data. There is, however, a crucial difference: whereas social scientists are obliged to trust the interviewee, natural scientists do not blindly trust their instruments.

Look into the night sky and you will see points of light of varying brightness – planets, stars and nebulae. How can we tell which of them is nearer or further away than any other? We cannot rely on their apparent brightness alone, for some objects might emit vastly more light than others and thus shine more brightly even though they are much further away than other objects that are intrinsically dimmer. One answer is to employ simple geometry to triangulate the distance to the object. The object is viewed at one day in the year and the angle at which it is viewed is recorded. Exactly six months later, when the Earth has rotated through its orbit of the Sun to a position directly opposite the location when the first observation was made, we repeat the exercise. We have a baseline of known length (twice the solar radius) and the angles that enable us to calculate the triangle this forms with the object, and thereby we calculate its distance. What this simple illustration tells us about remote sensing is that it relies on sound logic and evidence. We can trust triangulation to estimate the distance of astronomical objects because it is supported by geometry and proven in the mundane reality of constructing buildings. As Pawson remarks:

> The very objective of measurement is to incorporate and embody within an instrument principles derived from theoretical science. Instrumentation is a branch of engineering, and engineering is nothing other than application of the laws, theories, hypotheses and principles of theoretical physics. (cited in Ackroyd and Hughes 1992: 59)

One need not be dazzled by the ingenuity of astronomers. Archaeologists do much the same when they excavate ruins of long-forgotten civilisations. The layering of habitation provides a record of the past. The nature of the artefacts recovered will reveal the era in which they were created. This, of course, is not geometry and lacks its certainties, but it still relies on clearly formulated theoretical underpinnings supported by robust evidence. Whilst we might invest less trust in archaeological estimates than we do with astronomical distances, we nonetheless have good reason to trust the archaeologist.

What good reason is there to trust the reports of interviewees in social research? In his highly-influential (but apparently only partially understood) critique of *Method and Measurement in Sociology,* Aaron Cicourel (1964) concluded that there was no good reason. He cogently argued that beneath the apparent scientism of survey methodology lie foundations of culturally-specific commonsense knowledge. When the survey researcher formulates a question, this is not analogous to the calibration of a scientific instrument, it is grounded in shared cultural knowledge. As ethnomethodologists and conversational analysts were later to itemise (Heritage 1984), the language that we all use has embedded within it cultural assumptions and many expressions are 'indexical'; that is, they stand for much more than their ostensible referent. For instance, the description of a person as 'retired' or 'streetwise' conjures up a whole world of meaning. If questions and answers are to be intelligible then interviewer and interviewee need to inhabit that same cultural world of meaning. It is perfectly possible for the interviewer and interviewee not to share the same assumptions without knowing it, for whilst they use the same words those words conjure different meanings in each of them. This has led to researchers attempting to reduce the 'social distance' between interviewers and interviewees by matching them according to race and gender. However, this serves only to illustrate the problem, for Foddy argues that applying Festinger's theory of social comparison processes

> ...means that it can be predicted that respondents will be under psychological pressure to give answers that they think are normatively acceptable to the interviewer when they perceive the interviewer to be socially similar to themselves. It also seems reasonable to hypothesise that the questions themselves will have a tendency to make researchers and respondents define one another as social equals when they deal with general normative issues that can be seen to be of equal concern to all social groups in the researcher's and respondents' community (e.g. matters of

hygiene or social morality). In such situations the question threat that is generated will be reduced if the threat of being socially rejected is reduced.

...Fear of being socially rejected can be reduced either by increasing the psychological distance between the interviewers and respondents or by ensuring the respondents' answers are anonymous. (Foddy 1993: 121)

In other words, there is as much reason to support shrinking social distance as there is for increasing it! Indeed, much of the advice offered to interviewers on how to conduct interviews amounts to little more than commonly understood interview etiquette. The impact of such advice on the accuracy and thoroughness of interview content is largely untested. As Ackroyd and Hughes remark:

It is not self-evident, for example, that the establishment of a 'warm and trusting relationship' will necessarily get the respondent to tell the truth. It seems plausible to argue that it could, just as likely, result in the respondent avoiding potential conflict and controversy, offering instead blandness and deceptions designed to maintain conviviality. (Ackroyd and Hughes 1992: 113)

Accounts

If social scientists cannot be truly scientific, at least they can be honest and admit that their evidence is little better than that gained by anyone else. This relativism received impetus from research on how people give 'accounts' (Scott and Lyman 1968). This challenged the idea implicit in much survey research that the 'correct' stimulus would inevitably elicit an 'appropriate' (that is, true) response. Accounts are constructions influenced by the context in which they are offered. Sykes and Matza (1957) had suggested that delinquents availed themselves of a repertoire of 'techniques of neutralisation' or excuses for their delinquency. There was no reason to believe that what was true of delinquents was no less true of interviewees generally. The interview is a social encounter and methodologists had long been aware that the quest for social desirability was likely to lead interviewees into constructing more, rather than less, acceptable opinions, views and accounts of their own actions, especially if those opinions, views or actions were at all contentious.

What beckoned was the fog of relativism and into that fog many have disappeared. From this perspective (if there is perspective in a fog) no account is superior to any other. In other words, there is no truth, only a range of accounts, any of which we may or may not believe for any particular purpose. However, this creates enormous theoretical and practical problems. Theoretically, it means that since no account is superior to any other then the research that supports this conclusion is as fallible as any competing view. To claim that delinquents or sex offenders construct accounts designed to neutralise their offending behaviour is itself simply an account that enjoys no superiority to any other. So why then vest so much in it? In practice researchers have not adhered to this relativism. How could they when it undermines their own endeavours? Practically, the view that no account has superiority has immense implications for criminal justice. Not only does it mean that any pretensions collapse that the criminal justice process might have to establishing guilt or innocence, but so too do any claims to miscarriages of justice, or abuse by state agents. When the Macpherson Inquiry was told that Stephen Lawrence and Duwayne Brooks were attacked by a gang of white youths, this was taken by very few as simply one among many potential accounts of what happened that fateful evening. On the contrary, it was deemed to be true and its truth gave it superiority. Indeed, the fact that some police witnesses questioned whether Stephen's murder was racially motivated was itself regarded by Sir William Macpherson as evidence of 'institutionalised racism' (Macpherson of Cluny *et al.* 1999).

In other words, those who inquire into events are not genuinely agnostic about the veracity of the accounts they produce. Even when relativising the accounts of others, we reserve to ourselves the mantle of truth. The issue then remains: how can we establish accurate and thorough evidence from interviews?

Why we *can* trust interviewees

Whilst the developments described above were leading many in the social sciences down an epistemological cul-de-sac, advances elsewhere offered hope, for cognitive psychology replaced behaviourism as the dominant theoretical paradigm in that discipline (Davies and Thomson 1988; Kohnken *et al.* 1999; Memon and Bull 1991; Milne and Bull 1999; Py *et al.* 1997; Tulving and Thomson 1973). At the heart of this paradigm is the humanistic assumption that people are actively engaged in making sense of their environment. The methodological implications of cognitive psychology are also to reject the simple stimulus–response model: people do not cease to actively make sense of the world when they enter an interview. But instead of leading to the fog of relativism, cognitive psychologists have sought to understand how cognitive processes can be exploited for methodological purposes. In other words, although the quest continues, science is replacing etiquette as a guide to interviewing.

Nowhere has this been more successful than in devising techniques for recovering memories of past experience, for this is an area of cognitive psychology that is well developed. Memory and recall are no less active cognitive processes than any others. This is of the utmost importance for research methods, because if we can understand those processes well enough, then we can use that knowledge to engineer methods for enabling interviewees to provide good-quality recall of events. Whilst this may not allow us to compete with the astronomer's use of geometry to estimate distance, it might raise social research methods to a level equivalent to that of archaeologists. In other words, interviewing (at least insofar as it is designed to elicit recall) can now rest on well-formulated theoretical foundations, instead of the shifting sands of supposition and speculation.

The key to this transformation in the interview is the mnemonic. Like many crucial theoretical concepts this is both simple and familiar, not least to anyone who has been required to memorise information by rote. For instance, police in Britain are taught the GO WISE mnemonic to guide them through the legal procedures for stopping and searching those they suspect of committing offences.

> **G**rounds: the officer should explain clearly the legal basis of his or her suspicion
> **O**bjective: the officer should explain for what they are searching
> **W**arrant: the officer should show his or her warrant card if not in uniform
> **I**dentification: the officer should identify themselves by name
> **S**tation: the officer should say at which police station he or she is based
> **E**ntitlement: the person stopped is entitled to receive a copy of the record of the stop and search.

'GO WISE' is easily remembered and then is used as a cognitive trigger to unlock each of the words for which it stands, and this in turn assists recall of the required actions. 'G' stands for 'grounds', which means explaining the basis of suspicion and leads the officer to say, 'I'm stopping you because you fit the description of someone…'. This is not rocket science: students have relied on mnemonics for generations.

Understanding these cognitive processes allows psychologists not only to devise techniques and stratagems for memorising information, but also to devise methods to enhance recall of the past that was not spontaneously remembered. Mnemonic triggers exist whether or not they are consciously created as learning devices. What differs is that the idiosyncratic mnemonics of each respondent need to be encouraged.

The craft of the cognitive interview

It is the process of discovering and using those cognitive triggers that is central to cognitive interviewing. Here we find unexpected synergies with styles of interviewing that sociologists and other social scientists have long described as 'qualitative'.

Qualitative interview methods reject the proceduralism of methods that seek to elicit accurate and truthful responses by consistently delivering the same stimulus to the respondent (Foddy 1993). Proceduralism works in natural science where the phenomena studied do not actively engage with the world in which they reside: the same measurement techniques applied to the same object will yield the same results repeatedly. This is what is meant by reliability, and embedded within it is the stimulus–response model. Qualitative interviewing methods correctly recognised that this could not be applied to human beings, who, they insisted, *did* actively engage with the world around them, including the social encounter of the interview. Applying standardised procedures, such as always asking the same questions in the same order, would not quell the interpretative strategies of interviewees but might impose an alien frame of reference on the interviewee. Thus, the watchword for qualitative interviewing (indeed for qualitative methodology in general) has long been 'flexibility': being able to *respond* to the interviewee.

The good news is that this advice was sound. When recalling past experience, the 'frame of reference' of the interviewee is their system of mnemonics. The interviewer cannot possibly know what those mnemonics are and neither will many interviewees. The cognitive interview is a process of mutual exploration in which both parties wander around the interviewee's cognitive terrain, discovering mnemonics that point the way back to the past.

In this endeavour what the interviewer *abstains* from doing is as important, if not more important, than what they actually do. Nothing is more destructive of recall than breaking the link between mnemonics and their referents. If an interviewee appears to wander off the subject, they may be doing no more than taking the 'scenic route' to the past.

Better that than a more direct route that terminates in a roadblock! So, interruptions should be avoided. This entails abandoning prepared prompts and follow-up questions, because these are unlikely to be in tune with the mnemonics of the interviewee. Moreover, mnemonics are not fixed cognitive structures, but are fragile links. Interruption can easily break those links and once broken they are unlikely to be restored. So, the most important technique for the cognitive interviewer is to remain silent. (Incidentally, it is also one of the most difficult when the interviewer is itching to know something in particular.)

Beyond that abstinence there is much that the interviewer can do to assist the interviewee in recalling the past. First, the interviewee should be given *licence* to recall fully. Sociologists who have studied accounts are correct (obviously so) in observing that people tailor their accounts for the purposes in hand. We do not expect the same response to a casual greeting 'How are you?' as to the same inquiry from a physician. Whilst different accounts may be equally fit for their respective purposes, this does not mean that they are all equally valid. People normally edit the extent of their recall because of their estimation of what other parties want to hear – 'It's a long story, but ultimately comes down to this.' However, if the other party (in our case the interviewer) makes it clear that they desire – indeed *need* – to know every minute detail of some past event, then they give licence for the unedited version. Tell the interviewee that you, the interviewer, want to 'be there', experiencing what they experienced as if present at the scene, and the account that is 'fit for purpose' is comprehensive and thorough.

The provision of an unedited account entails trust in the interviewer on the part of the interviewee. They must be convinced that they will not suffer adverse consequences; that their anonymity will be preserved and confidentiality maintained. The social skills of the interviewer in placing the person at their ease are crucial. The theoretical justification for creating the 'warm and trusting relationship' that Ackroyd and Hughes (1992) view with intellectual scepticism lies in the need to discourage editing out anything that the interviewee thinks might cast them in a bad light.

Because providing unedited accounts is an uncommon experience, the interviewer can assist the interviewee by techniques designed to encourage mnemonic linkages. Central to this is 're-instating the context' in which the event took place. Suppose that you have mislaid something that you need to recover. A good strategy for finding it is to close your eyes and recall where last you remember having it. If possible, actually return to that location, but returning to the location in your imagination is a good substitute. Close your eyes and recall what you were doing at the time; who else was present; what you could hear, touch and smell. Do this and you are 're-instating the context' and enhancing thereby the likelihood that you will recall that in the middle of performing one task you were momentarily interrupted by another and placed the mislaid object in an otherwise unlikely place. This is exactly what cognitive interviewers do at the commencement of an interview: they ask the interviewee to close their eyes and to imagine the scene; to look around it in their imagination; to recollect what had happened previously; to recall what they could see, hear, touch and smell at the time. In doing so, the interviewee creates for themselves a rich field of mnemonics that aid recall.

The most common mnemonic is narrative – time links events in recall as it does in reality. So, the interviewee is invited to provide an unedited and uninterrupted description of what occurred. Meanwhile, the interviewer notes down any apparent gaps or aspects that require clarification. Once the interviewee has completed their initial account, the interview takes the form of a series of iterations in which the interviewee is invited to elaborate their recall. Inevitably this becomes a dialogue between the interviewer and the interviewee. Typically, each iteration commences with re-instatement of context. Interviewees may be invited to draw maps or plans of the scene partly to inform the interviewer, but also to enable them to recall the spatial arrangements in which the event occurred.

Certain techniques enable interviewees to create mnemonic linkages, one of which is to capitalise upon memory and return to those moments and aspects that are most memorable to the interviewee. For instance, if an individual is particularly prominent in the interviewee's memory, then the interviewee can be invited to tell as much as they can about that individual. They might be invited to close their eyes and imagine the person as they saw them at the time of the incident, and then to describe them. The description might commence with the person's most prominent features. In one of our interviews it was a man's hands that the interviewee found the most memorable feature, and from this prominent feature the interviewee reconstructed their recall of the person in question. Recalling the most memorable person present may enable the interviewee then to recall others as they remember how this person behaved to those around them.

Another technique is to reverse the narrative and ask interviewees what occurred immediately *prior* to a significant moment in the incident. This inhibits skipping over important detail because narrative linkages carry recall too readily from one moment to the next. This technique also reduces the likelihood that in recalling events interviewees will merely rely on their mental script of what usually happens rather than what happened in that specific situation. Interviewees can also be asked to state what other people present at the scene would have witnessed from their vantage point and which the interviewee also witnessed but has not yet recalled. This technique must be used with caution and interviewees should be clearly instructed not to concoct events that did not occur. However, it has been found that this change of perspective can unlock memories because it encourages the interviewee to use multiple mental pathways to access memory.

It will be immediately apparent that cognitive interviewing is far from being a passive process of recording recall. It is an *active* dialogue between interviewer and interviewee in which recall is *constructed*. This produces nervousness in some, for active construction is misconstrued as meaning fabrication and invention. This reaction confuses process and content: the value of the interview lies in the content of the recall, whereas the process is the means of obtaining that content. The aim is to reconstruct the interviewee's experience of the past and like any construction enterprise it is active – pieces of the puzzle need to be put together – which benefits from the assistance of others. The fact that the interview is a joint enterprise does not entail that it must be a distortion. What matters is whether jointly the interviewer and interviewee arrive at a narrative that is valid.

Does it work?

There are three criteria that must be met for cognitive interviews to be regarded as valid: completeness, accuracy and lack of confabulation. Completeness appears a simple matter: accounts containing fewer gaps are superior to those suffering more gaps. Of course, no account is likely to be utterly complete; the pattern of the wallpaper in a room will figure rarely in accounts of social encounters. The criterion is relative: cognitive interviewing claims to produce *more* complete accounts than alternative methods. Implicit within this criterion, however, is relevance, to which we will return shortly. Accuracy also is straightforward: cognitive interviewing is superior to the extent that it is relatively error free. Confabulation refers to the insertion into accounts of details that were not witnessed. This arises from the desire of interviewees to provide a seamless narrative and results in them inferring what *must have happened* rather than restricting themselves to recalling what *did happen*. Again, for cognitive interviewing to be superior it should minimise this tendency.

So, how does cognitive interviewing actually perform? It has mainly been applied and assessed in a forensic, rather than academic, context (Milne and Bull 1999). This is important, because it means that cognitive interviewing has been obliged to satisfy the most exacting standards. It has done so in two ways: experimental and practical. Experimentally, incidents have been staged, independently recorded, and then witnesses independently interviewed about the incident using various methods, including cognitive interviewing. The accounts yielded by these interviews are then compared with the recording and their respective levels of completeness, accuracy and absence of confabulation assessed. On this basis cognitive interviewing outperforms alternative methods, including hypnosis.

The second test is practical: law enforcement officers have used cognitive interviewing techniques to elicit from real-life witnesses of crime evidence of what occurred. That evidence has been found to be sufficiently credible that it convinces the courts. Moreover, in the course of many investigations evidence that independently corroborates the accounts elicited by cognitive interviewing comes to light (Cutler *et al.* 1987; Fisher *et al.* 1989; Hollin 1981; Memon *et al.* 1994; Py *et al.* 1997). More recently, research on cognitive interviewing has concentrated upon its utility with particularly problematic witnesses, such as children, and ensuring that investigators use the techniques effectively in real-life situations (Cherryman and Bull 2001; Geiselman and Padilla 1988; Memon *et al.* 1995; Memon *et al.* 1998).

It is rare indeed for social research methods to be tested by such stringent methods and against such exacting criteria. The success of cognitive interviewing in meeting these challenges has been so comprehensive that it now is recommended worldwide as the preferred method of witness interviewing. At the same time, it may be objected that interviewees in a social research project are not witnesses in a legal process. Indeed so: what normally passes for evidence of past events in social research falls far short of the evidential standards required of witness testimony and is hardly ever subjected to the scrutiny that witness testimony is likely to receive during a trial. On the other hand, those who feel that they have suffered violence and threats are directly equivalent to witnesses and if social researchers can have confidence that their methods satisfy the rigour of criminal justice procedures, then why complain?

There is, however, one respect in which forensic witnesses and social research interviewees do differ. Victims and witnesses of crime may be assumed to have a vested interest in cooperating with law enforcement agencies in detecting offenders. They are likely to accept searching questioning about unpleasant events. Are participants in social research as willing to cooperate? This probably depends upon the nature of the research and it will be for the reader to judge whether the quality of interview evidence obtained in this research is sufficiently detailed as to justify the use of the technique. As researchers we were struck by the richness of the data available to us.

Criminal justice professionals and researchers should have a common interest in obtaining complete, accurate, and non-confabulating evidence. Cognitive interviewing satisfies that requirement because it – unusually among social research methods – rests on solid theoretical and empirical foundations.

Meaning

There is a further difference between forensic and research uses of cognitive interviewing that emerged during this research. It has already been explained how cognitive interviewing relies upon context re-instatement as a means of unlocking recall of such events. What has been omitted so far is that one element in context re-instatement is to invite the interviewee to recall how they *felt* about what they are recalling. Feeling dread in the pit of one's stomach or elation are very effective mnemonic linkages to what circumstances prompted those (and other) emotions. Interviewees usually have little difficulty in recalling the people or events that produced such feelings.

For forensic purposes this is where the interest in subjectivity ends. The fact that an interviewee felt dread or elation has no evidential value. But for research purposes what interviewees felt and thought is of the utmost relevance, especially when dealing with threat and intimidation where the overt behaviour of the threatening person may not amount to much. There is little need for the interviewer to prompt interviewees to elicit their feelings; in our experience they are available in abundance, embedded within the events that are described.

Like others who have recently probed individuals' experiences of violence (Lee and Stanko 2003), the aim of this research was to discover the *meaning and interpretation* given to the events by those who had suffered them. In so doing, we sought to probe the quality of the experiences that lie behind the bold figures found in surveys. Like Edgar and his colleagues (2003), we agree that

> The chief benefit of approaches based on personal accounts of events is that these methods honour the person's individual perspective on their experience. (p 75)

Second best?

Even if we have convinced you that cognitive interviewing is superior to other currently available forms of indirect data recovery, many will still imagine that it can never hold its own against direct observation. There can surely be no better alternative than seeing the phenomenon for oneself. We would readily concede that direct observation has many advantages over interviewing, but cognitive interviewing also has advantages that direct observation does not share.

It depends, of course, what is meant by direct observation. The systematic recording of carefully structured observation does allow a considerable measure of control and transparency. However, it has two drawbacks: first, it normally relies on pre-coded observation schedules that assume knowledge of what is important and relevant. Even when this is explicitly theory-driven (as it rarely is in social research), pre-coding entails the risk that of the myriad events occurring during any episode the coding schedule will only be able to identify a few and they may not be those that are genuinely most important. Seeing those events through the eyes of those participating in the situation allows us at least to learn what is important and relevant to *them* (O'Beirne *et al.* 2003). It also, crucially, allows us to appreciate its subjective meaning.

The second drawback is that even the most rigorous direct observation finds it difficult to avoid lapsing into subjective judgement. For instance, in Worden's research on police use of force, the classification of what was 'reasonable' or 'excessive' was left to the observer (Worden 1996). One might ask what qualifications an observer has to arrive at what is essentially a normative judgement. Meaning keeps intruding and perhaps it is better that our methods acknowledge and welcome it. There is no better method for achieving that than to talk to those involved, for through language we access subjectivity and meaning.

Direct observation also embraces more qualitative approaches associated with ethnography. Here the researcher does attempt to grasp the meaning of situations for those involved in them through routine participation. Unfortunately, what is gained in empathetic understanding tends to be sacrificed in the opportunities for unknown bias. Any observer can only observe so much, but whereas systematic structured observation can avail itself of procedures such as time sampling, the participant observer will be haphazardly exposed to some experiences and denied others as they move around the field within which they operate. For instance, an ethnographic observer of routine police practice may be invited to accompany some officers and discouraged from accompanying others for reasons that remain unknown or beyond their control (Brewer 1990). More seriously, *how* the observer compiles their fieldnotes is a process that exists largely, if not wholly, beyond scrutiny. What quality-control procedures can they employ to ensure that their fieldnotes are complete, accurate and lack confabulation?

Cognitive interviewing allows (indeed requires) access to the subjective meaning of events, whilst avoiding unknown observer and recording bias. Of course, selecting one observer of an incident entails as much observer bias as the perspective of a single research observer, but the particularity of their biased observation is at least known. In principle, that bias could be corrected by interviewing several participants, although there are often severe practical obstacles to doing so. Unlike the unknown process through which fieldnotes are constructed, the reconstruction of events through cognitive interviewing relies on techniques validated by theory and empirical evidence.

How this research was conducted

Interviews were conducted with 54 police officers from a single division in the south of England, and 62 social care professionals – 22 in an Accident and Emergency department (A&E) of a large hospital trust; 20 social workers from a single social services department; and 20 mental health staff from three Community Mental Health Trusts adjacent to one another.

These occupations were selected because survey methods had highlighted them as most exposed to workplace violence. The British Crime Survey repeatedly affirms that among the most exposed to violence are the police. Second only to the 'security and protective services' like the police come nurses, 'five per cent of whom experienced some type of violent incident whilst working during a given year' (Budd 1999: 14). Among nurses (and allied medical professions) A&E seems to be one of the most perilous (Gillespie and Melby 2003; National Audit Office 2003b). Another medical specialism that suffers high levels of violence is mental health, which is not restricted to the hospital environment, for 'violence [is] a common feature of community mental health care also' (Coyne 2001: 140). Even the level of violence experienced by nurses is eclipsed by social workers and probation officers when they are distinguished from others in the 'other education and welfare' category, for among them, '9.4% had been assaulted and 9.5% had been threatened' (Budd 1999: 19).

Brady and Dickson (1999b) draw attention to the growth in community-based services that require staff to visit difficult and possibly dangerous people in their own homes. They also point to the irony that these clients and patients 'only come into hospital if they demonstrate that they cannot be managed within the community – in some cases by assaulting a member of staff' (p 167; see also Harvey *et al.* 2002; McLean *et al.* 1999).

It is important to emphasise that because the selection of interviewees was dictated by the expedients of availability and access, our sample was not at all random. No pretensions are made that this sample represents the experience of police officers or caring professionals beyond those who participated. What it does enable us to do, however, is to explore what *some* of those who occupy these positions experienced and how they interpreted it. It thereby complements survey research by adding the experiential dimension.

Police officers were made available for interviews depending on the exigencies of their operational commitments. The process of recruiting interviewees from among social care professionals evolved in almost every case into something akin to 'snowball' sampling. Initially, the interviewer gained access to each site to interview one or a small handful of willing individuals. Those interviewees then acted as ambassadors, prevailing upon others to cooperate and offering reassurance. Also, the scheduling of interviews meant that a block of time was devoted to each profession, with the result that visits were made to the organisation repeatedly over a short duration, which made possible informal opportunities to persuade potential interviewees to cooperate. Like Elston *et al.*'s (2002) study of general practitioners, probation officers and clergy, this sampling strategy is likely to have biased the data in favour of the more serious forms of violence. Certainly, it recruited only those who defined problematic episodes as 'violent'.

Interviewees were asked to recall the most recent occasion when they had experienced 'threats, intimidation, or violence'. It was left to interviewees to determine what qualified as such an experience. However, unlike other research, these interviews concentrated on recovering a highly detailed description of just a single event, rather than probing more general experiences and opinions of violence. Moreover, by asking only about the most recent occasion it was hoped to gain an understanding not of how severe violence might become, but its more routine expression.

Inevitably the approach we have taken is unashamedly interpretative: we seek empathetically to understand the experience of our interviewees. We need also, of course, to convey that experience to the reader. In other research this is commonly achieved through more or less lengthy direct quotes from the interview. However, we have abstained from doing so in this research (except where a turn of phrase describes the quality of the experience with particular force or clarity) for two reasons. The first is general and arises from misgivings about the process of transcription. Researchers who have studied the minutiae of social behaviour have repeatedly discovered that meaning is conveyed not only by words that can appear on a page, but by the way those words are spoken and what accompanies them in the form of non-verbal behaviour. How does one capture only in the words spoken the evident distress of an interviewee recalling an incident? The second reason is that the cognitive interview militates against such quotes, for the process in which the interviewee returns repeatedly to their recollection of the incident produces a series of layers through which the account is progressively elaborated. These layers must then be reduced to a single composite narrative and this is the task of the researcher. The researcher must also edit the narrative for purposes of publication. Of course, so too does any interpretative analysis: passages from interviews are quoted in order to represent a wider reality. However, cognitive interviewing generates enormously rich descriptions of often brief incidents and whilst this detail informs analysis, it exceeds the space available. Therefore, not to obscure the joint roles in the construction of the narrative, we have decided to produce narratives that have been written in the third person.

Conclusion

The purpose of this chapter has been to draw the attention of the social research community to the value of cognitive interviewing as a research tool. We have argued that in contrast to most other methods, cognitive interviewing is based on sound theory and supported by rigorous empirical evaluation. We have *reason to trust* that cognitive interviewing produces complete and accurate recall lacking confabulation. We have shown how this method of interviewing is able to generate testimony that satisfies the rigorous evidential standards of criminal justice. Even in comparison with direct observation it has features that combine the advantages of systematic and ethnographic methods. Perhaps most importantly, cognitive interviewing resides in neither of the methodological camps that currently divide social research. Whilst it makes and underwrites strong claims to reveal objective truths about past events, it also embraces issues of meaning that attach to those events. Whilst it relies on theoretically justified and empirically tested techniques, it retains considerable elements of craft more commonly associated with qualitative approaches.

Undoubtedly it is not the last word in social research methods. At the current stage of its development it is unsuitable for many purposes, but as a method for obtaining detailed recall of discrete incidents or episodes it has considerable advantages. We hope that this exposition and the demonstration that follows in this analysis of violent, threatening and intimidating experiences will convince a wider circle of social researchers to employ this method alongside others.

Chapter 3

Violent actions

Introduction

The connotation of the word 'violence' is of some form of physical assault. 'Workplace violence' might, therefore, be imagined as episodes in which employees are punched, kicked or attacked with weapons. However, what people *experience* as 'violence' is not so narrowly restricted; indeed it covers a broad spectrum of hostile and other encounters that arouse feelings of threat and menace. In this chapter we will begin to explore what the experience of 'violence' actually entailed for the police officers, A&E staff, social workers and mental health professionals who participated in this research. We will begin by examining the most obvious, indeed egregious, examples before exploring some of the wider implications of the term.

Physical violence

Police experience

The most obvious connotation of 'violence' is that of physical assault. As custodians of the state's monopoly of legitimate force over its own population (Waddington 1999), physical contact – referred to euphemistically by many police interviewees as 'laying hands on' someone – was an ever-present possibility. After all, the act of arrest would – if not lawful – amount to an assault. Therefore, it is no surprise to learn that police officers had most experience of physical violence and suffered the most extreme forms of it. Even so, examples of serious violence among our interviewees were rare, indeed one interviewee was unable to participate (despite his willingness to do so) because in the 18 months since joining the police he had experienced no occasions that he considered to have been 'violent' or 'potentially violent'.

At the other end of the spectrum is the example related in Case study 3.1, in which a lone policewoman confronted a man armed with a loaded shotgun that he aimed, but fortunately did not fire, at her. This case has all the elements of the stereotyped violent encounter: the police officer is a woman, unpredictably threatened by a man wielding a deadly weapon, with whom she physically grapples before successfully overpowering him. Annually, the magazine of the Police Federation celebrates (and rightly so) the heroism of ordinary police officers who also confront such life-threatening circumstances. However, it is precisely these features that make this example unique among our sample.

Case Study 3.1: A potentially deadly assault

The interviewee was a woman constable with three years' service. On the night in question she was single-crewed in a patrol car whilst her crewmate was occupied at the police station. Shortly after midnight she was dispatched to a 'violent domestic' between two men, one of whom had been injured and the other had left the scene. As far as the officer was concerned this was a 'typical Friday-night job' – nothing to worry about.

She arrived at the terrace house on a one-way road near the town centre. As she approached the house, a woman rushed out shouting hysterically that the injured man (her husband) had also left. Just then the ambulance arrived. The officer was trying to calm the woman when a male paramedic approached. The officer told him that there was no need for paramedic services and he and his female colleague could leave.

It was then that she noticed a man approaching from what appeared to be far away. The woman also turned towards the approaching figure. The officer then saw that the approaching man was carrying a shotgun on his shoulder. Her initial reaction was that 'this is going to go pear-shaped'. Because the man appeared to be so far away she had time to think. The woman exclaimed,

---

'That's him, that's him'! The officer grabbed the woman and forcefully pushed her back the few feet into the doorway of her house, causing the woman to fall onto her backside. The paramedic looked startled at this turn of events. The officer yelled 'Gun!' and then lost sight of the ambulance crew as she turned towards the approaching gunman. She was now standing on the footpath, her patrol car in the road alongside her and the ambulance parked a few feet behind it with the male paramedic crouched behind the steering wheel and the driver's door slightly ajar.

As the man approached she stepped into the road so that the patrol car separated her from the man, with him at the nearside front corner of the car and the officer diagonally opposite him. Now the man was aiming the shotgun directly at the officer and as she moved, so the man continued to aim the shotgun at her. The man and the officer moved in opposite directions, he remaining on the footpath, whilst she stayed on the far side of the car in the roadway.

The officer screamed at the man, 'Put the gun down. Put the gun down, NOW!' She then opened the microphone on her radio so that it was transmitting and screamed at the man 'This really isn't helping. I don't know who you're upset with, but it isn't me. Put that gun down!' Momentarily the man lowered the gun, but his finger remained on the trigger. The officer ran around the front of the car, approaching the man from his rear. As she explained, 'I just kicked his legs out, literally kicked the back of his legs as hard as I could which sent him onto the floor.' He was now on all fours and the gun, having escaped his grasp, lay beside him. The officer jumped onto his back screaming at him, 'Get on the floor, get on the floor' whilst pushing the gun away with her foot. The man refused to lie on the floor and was constantly trying to get up, saying, 'No, let me get up. I want to explain, I want to explain.'

She now began to hear sirens approaching – 'The loveliest sound in the world.' The man was still struggling to regain his feet. The officer vainly attempted the various techniques learnt during training to overpower him, but the man was much bigger and heavier than she was. So she put all weight on his right shoulder and thus caused him to collapse, allowing her to pull his right arm behind his back and snap on a handcuff. She shouted at the man to put his other hand behind his back so that she could handcuff him; then they could talk. However, the man refused and began struggling again to regain his footing.

As they struggled the handcuffs became entangled in the man's shirt.

The male paramedic then joined the struggle, using his weight to try and force the man to the floor. With the paramedic's assistance the officer now freed the handcuff from the man's clothing but was still unable to cuff the man's other wrist.

The first car to arrive was driven by a sergeant who drove the 'wrong way' up the one-way street. The car mounted the kerb and screeched to a halt immediately behind her. The sergeant jumped from the car, grabbed the man's free arm, snapped on the handcuff, pulled the man to his feet and 'threw him' into the rear of his patrol car. The sergeant then picked up the shotgun and opened the breech exclaiming, 'Fuck me, it was loaded!'

By now another two patrol cars had arrived, the second of which contained two women officers whom the officer knew. The sergeant now 'cancelled' all other patrol cars that were en route to the scene.

After vainly attempting to interview the woman who made the original phone call and was now protesting her husband's innocence, the effects of stress began to make themselves felt and the officer returned to the police station and then went home, taking a few days off sick with stress.

Less heroic, but more common, was the struggle in which an Area Beat Officer found himself whilst accompanying a suspect to the Accident and Emergency department of a local hospital (Case study 3.2). Here the attack was not made by a totally unknown assailant, but by someone with whom the officer had established some familiarity as they sat chatting amiably in the waiting room of the A&E department. After a protracted interlude, the man's behaviour rapidly deteriorated, becoming in turn bizarre and then unpredictably violent.

Case Study 3.2: Struggle in the hospital

The interviewee was an Area Beat Officer whose normal duties involved patrolling a particular district fostering good police–community relations. On the Saturday in question he was assisting a patrol officer and accompanied him to a dispute between an Asian shopkeeper and an African-Caribbean man. The shopkeeper had been injured during the dispute and was taken by ambulance to the hospital A&E. The African-Caribbean man also claimed to have been struck on the head and so (on the advice of the paramedics) the officer took him to the A&E for a check-over. Since the man was calm and compliant, the officer saw no need for his crewmate to remain with him and he also declined assistance offered via the radio by the control room.

After an hour-long wait the man saw a medical doctor and was sent for an X-ray. As the two men waited in the X-ray waiting room they were joined by what appeared to be a mother and her daughter. Coincidentally, the man became more agitated and demanded a cigarette despite hospital rules that forbade smoking to which the officer drew his attention. The man raised his voice and began using obscenities and the officer tried to calm him, drawing attention to the presence of the mother and daughter, but the man seemed not to acknowledge their existence. The officer now formed the impression that the man's odd behaviour must be symptomatic of a mental illness – he concluded that the man was schizophrenic.

The man sprang to his feet and declared that he was 'going out for a fag'. As he strode out of the X-ray waiting room a radiographer accosted him, asking that he have another X-ray taken, but the man brusquely declined. The officer followed the man, hoping that he might 'blow off some steam' and in any case he did not want the mother and daughter exposed to the man's obscenities. The officer followed a few steps behind as the man proceeded haphazardly along corridors and emerged into a quiet area. As they walked through a pair of fire doors, the officer reached out and touched the man's shoulder to attract his attention. Suddenly he found the man behind him (he does not know how this occurred) and the man's arm around his neck. The officer's windpipe was not compressed, but he feared that restricted blood flow would soon render him unconscious. The officer tried striking the man using techniques taught in training, all to no avail. To relieve the pressure on his neck he used both hands to lever the man's arm open. He tried to make an emergency radio transmission, but in the bowels of the hospital his radio could not transmit. As an Area Beat Officer, struggling with an assailant was an uncommon and unwelcome experience. In desperation the officer leant slowly forward from the hip, lifting his assailant off the floor. He then threw himself backwards so that the two men crashed to the floor, with the officer on top, but still the man retained his grip on the officer's neck. Now, the officer felt he was in even greater jeopardy.

As the two men struggled on the floor, a few (he does not

recall how many) nurses arrived at the scene. One of the nurses appeared annoyed and chastised the two men for their unseemly behaviour, but still the assailant's grip remained firmly around the officer's throat. However, a male porter reached down and although the officer could not see what the porter did, it seemed as if suddenly he was able to get some purchase. He was able to roll off the man and use his weight to break the grip. As he did so the assailant seemed to give up the struggle and the officer was able to handcuff him with ease. His colleague, who had been attending to the Asian shopkeeper, arrived and the assailant was escorted to the patrol car and taken to the station where the man received medication to calm him down.

In both these first two examples, officers were *attacked* – that is, the apparent purpose of the assault was to inflict injury or worse on the officer. This is rare, for it is more common for officers to be assaulted as suspects try to escape arrest. Most commonly, violence in such circumstances is restricted to active and forceful resistance: suspects refusing to put their hands behind their backs so that handcuffs can be applied or struggling to break free. This can occasion injury to suspects, police and other involved parties as suspects thrash their arms and legs, striking those around them, or just cause themselves and others to stumble or tumble to the ground. This is exactly what happened in the next case study.

Case Study 3.3: Off-duty arrest

The interviewee was a male police officer in his mid-20s, tall, slim and athletic. He and his future wife had been decorating their house and he visited the local shop to buy a couple of ice lollies. As he pulled his car into the parking bay he noticed three young people – two boys and a girl – all in their mid-teens accompanied by a small unleashed dog. He wondered idly why they were not at school.

As he walked into the shop he passed the young people as they stood in a huddle near the entrance. He took the ice lollies from the freezer and stood in line waiting to pay the cashier. He noticed that the two youths had walked into the shop and gone to where alcoholic drinks were displayed. He contemplated whether they would be allowed to make a purchase because of their age. However, the two youths did not join the line, but walked directly out of the shop. He noticed that one of them was holding a package in such a way as to prevent the cashier seeing it. The officer said to the cashier, 'Have they just taken something?' She replied that she thought they might have done so.

The officer placed the ice lollies and the cash he was holding on the counter and pursued the youths out of the shop. The youths and their female companion had turned left out of the shop and now were turning left again at the end of the small parade of business premises. The officer briskly walked in pursuit and called out, 'Hey, mate!' The trio stopped and turn towards him near a dental surgery with a large shop-front window looking into its reception/waiting room in which some patients were sitting. As he approached, he was aware that he was wearing paint-spattered casual clothes and did not have a warrant card. His intention was to convince the trio to return to the shop and 'sort it out'. The response of the trio was to ask, 'Who the fuck are you?' and to insist that they had bought the drink earlier at a different shop.

At this point the interviewee identified himself as a police officer. Again, he suggested that they should return to the shop, but the trio again refused, asking rhetorically why they should. The girl then said, 'Come on, let's go.' One of the youths handed the package to his male companion. With his left hand the officer then took hold of the youth without the package by his upper right arm and told him that he was being arrested on suspicion of theft and cautioned him.

Immediately, the youth tried to head-butt the officer, but the officer jerked his head aside so that he received a glancing blow to the left cheek. He staggered backwards a couple of steps and as he did so the second youth also attacked him, causing all three of them to tumble to the ground. As they struggled on the ground he was punched and kicked, but retained hold of the youth he had arrested. The officer called out to a middle-aged man standing with a young boy looking at the scene that he was a police officer and asked for help. He does not know how or by whom, but shortly afterwards the second youth was dragged away from him.

He was now struggling with the first youth, who was trying to escape. The two of them regained their feet still struggling violently. The officer now found himself holding the youth in a bear-hug, with the youth facing away from him. The youth pushed backwards and the two of them crashed into the dental surgery window.

The second youth was struggling with the boy who was the companion of the older man. The boy shouted out that he had been bitten by the youth with whom he was struggling. This was followed almost immediately by the youth with whom the officer was struggling biting the officer's right forearm. The officer retained his grasp and immediately the youth threw his head backwards, striking the officer squarely on the nose, which began pouring with blood.

The officer now threw the youth onto the floor and as he did so was joined by another bystander, a man in his mid-20s, who pinned the youth to the floor with his foot and grabbed hold of the youth's arm. The officer meanwhile grabbed the youth's other arm and was able to apply an arm lock whilst half-lying on the youth's back.

Shortly afterwards, police assistance arrived and the three young people were arrested. The officer was invited into the dental surgery for attention to his broken nose and shortly afterwards an ambulance arrived. When his fiancée arrived as he was receiving treatment, she angrily asked, 'What the bloody hell have you done?'

What unites police officers' experience of hostile and violent episodes is that their encounters are invariably initiated by the police, usually the officers who become involved in the violence itself. None of the officers involved in these case studies so far was aware of what they were straying into, but in each case they held the initiative. It is this that sets the police apart from the other three occupational groups.

The experience of caring professionals

Thankfully, the experience of overt physical assault was relatively uncommon among interviewees in the three caring professions: four mental health professionals, five accident and emergency staff, and six social workers reported such incidents. This is roughly in line with survey evidence suggesting that approximately 30 per cent of hostile encounters involving social care professionals consist of physical assaults (Grimwood and La Valle 1993). Between a half and two-thirds of those assaulted sustained some form of injury; however, this was rarely serious (the most serious injury being bruising reported by two interviewees). Physical assaults usually consisted of punching and kicking and, less commonly, the use of (usually improvised) weapons, including an upraised stool, a dog lead (Case study 3.9) and an airgun

(Case study 4.10). However, summary descriptions of this kind conceal an enormous diversity of experience, from incidents that few would doubt were serious to others that arguably do not qualify as a 'physical assault' at all.

Whilst physical assault was relatively uncommon among caring professionals in comparison with police officers, when it did occur it was much more likely to take the form of an *attack*. A&E staff were vulnerable to overwrought and often intoxicated patients and their companions becoming aggressive when they were obliged to wait for lengthy periods for treatment, often at night. The most serious occasion of this kind concerned a man who had accompanied his girlfriend to A&E for treatment to deep lacerations to her forearms. The interviewee formed the impression that the man blamed himself for the argument that had precipitated the injury and was venting his self-recrimination through his attack on the hapless interviewee (Case study 3.4). The lengthy wait made necessary by the orthopaedic team being delayed in surgery further antagonised the man until he launched an unprovoked assault on the nurse.

Case Study 3.4: Assault on a male nurse

The interviewee was a male nurse in his early 40s who had worked in A&E for four and a half years. The incident began at around 3 am on a Sunday morning when the nurse was performing triage – making initial assessments of patients for treatment. A black couple entered the triage room and the male partner immediately impressed the nurse with his powerful physique that was accentuated by the tight-fitting tee-shirt that he wore.

The woman had suffered deep lacerations to her forearm sustained during the course of an argument with her partner when she had punched a pane of glass. The woman accepted the nurse's invitation to sit down, but the man agitatedly strode around the room ignoring the nurse's repeated invitations to be seated. The nurse introduced himself by his first name and explained the triage procedure. He then proceeded to examine the woman's injuries. The nurse feared that the woman had sustained damage to the tendons in her wrist and he advised her that she would need to be examined by an orthopaedic surgeon. He explained that this would entail a prolonged wait because the orthopaedic team were occupied in theatre. Meanwhile, the nurse applied a temporary sterile dressing. As he was doing this a drop of blood fell to the floor and the woman's companion suddenly reached

---

between the patient and the nurse and tore some paper towelling from a holder with an exaggerated movement that caused the nurse to flinch and feel unnerved.

Having dressed the wound the nurse invited the couple to wait in the waiting room. The woman accepted this with equanimity but the man asked rhetorically, 'And who's going to make me?' The nurse was taken aback and replied that he did not understand, he was only asking that they comply with the usual procedures. The man refused to leave. The woman then intervened and pleaded with the man, 'Come on, let's go', but he still refused, alleging that the only reason she was not being treated immediately was because she was black. The nurse was affronted by this allegation and strenuously rebutted it, pointing out that most of those waiting in the waiting room were white people and he was asking this couple to do no more than these other people had been asked to do. Again, the woman pleaded with the man to go to the waiting room and this time prevailed.

During the ensuing wait the nurse several times witnessed the man's aggressive behaviour. He loudly complained to the receptionist about having to wait; was overheard complaining about poor service to others in the waiting room; was seen on the CCTV system pacing around the waiting room in an agitated manner. He approached reception whilst the nurse was present and banged heavily on the security screen and yelled abuse at the receptionist. The nurse stepped forward and pleaded with the man to sit down, only to receive yet more abuse and threats.

Eventually, the woman was examined by a casualty doctor who confirmed the triage assessment and asked her to wait for the orthopaedic team to complete surgery. News was received in A&E that the orthopaedic team would be delayed for an unusually long time because of complications in the surgery they were performing. The nurse went into the waiting room to explain the reason for the lengthy delay, but the man rejected the necessity to wait and demanded immediate treatment.

Just after 5.30 am A&E received news that the orthopaedic team had completed the surgery and would soon be free to attend to casualty patients. The nurse went into the reception area and announced the good news to the woman and her companion. However, the man again reacted aggressively when the nurse was unable to say exactly how much longer they would need to wait. When he remarked that the radiographer would be with them shortly, the man replied, 'Well, he'd fucking better be!' The nurse led the woman and her companion through to the X-ray waiting area before returning to the secure treatment area. Suddenly, the man appeared in this supposedly secure area and asked, 'Where's this fucking bloke who's going to take this fucking X-ray?' The nurse replied, 'He's on his way down from theatre. I'm sorry you've been kept waiting, but he's been busy.' The man retorted that he didn't give a fuck about how busy the radiographer was and demanded immediate treatment for his girlfriend.

A few minutes elapsed before the man returned again to the treatment area. By now the nurse was standing chatting to several female colleagues. He saw the man approach and had the sensation of time appearing to slow down. The man negotiated a path between the female nurses, heading straight for the male nurse. As he bore down on him, the man was yelling abuse at the male nurse accusing him of being racist, an allegation that the nurse rebutted, saying 'anybody who knows me, knows I'm not racist'. The man then said, 'I'm not interested in anybody who knows you' and punched the nurse's right shoulder with his right fist. This impact caused the nurse to swivel to his right. Then the man grabbed the nurse's right wrist and pulled him forwards and down, causing the nurse to fall onto his knees. The nurse saw the security guard grab the man and say, 'Come on brother' and lead him away.

By now the female nurses had scattered and the receptionist hit the panic button that summons an urgent police response. Officers were nearby and quickly rushed through the ambulance entrance and arrested the man, who was being detained by the security guard.

In other circumstances assaults may be attributed to the condition of the assailant, especially when they are suffering some impairment. This is something to which we shall return in the next chapter, but for the present it is worth noting how assaults can appear to be launched unpredictably upon those who routinely deal with vulnerable people. In hospitals one of the most vulnerable categories are elderly patients suffering senile dementia; they are also among the most violence-prone (Winstanley and Whittington 2004). As Case study 3.5 illustrates, even this category of patient can present serious risks of violence to staff. For here an elderly man viciously assaulted a young nurse with his walking stick. The nurse recounting this attack was by the time of the interview working in A&E, an environment that she found far more secure than the sparsely staffed ward in which the assault had taken place.

Case Study 3.5: Elderly senile patient's attack on nurse

The female nurse was in charge of a 24-bed geriatric ward which she found to be 'an uphill struggle'. Among her patients was a demented man in his 80s who had decided that he was going home even though he was dressed only in his pyjamas, slippers and a flat cap. He walked around the ward trying to find the exit, but in his confusion was unable to do so. The nurse considered the situation to be under control until one evening a visitor inadvertently allowed the man to leave the ward and enter a landing where the lifts and stairs were located. The nurse glanced in the direction of the exit and saw the elderly man leaving. She walked smartly out of the ward and intercepted him on the landing where the patient was looking blankly at the lift doors, all of which were closed.

The nurse stood in front of him with the lift doors to her rear and began trying to persuade him to return to the ward; however, he insisted that he was returning to his home. This prolonged and inconclusive conversation was conducted amid the comings and goings of visitors to the various wards in the vicinity of the landing. However, because of his small stature the patient was unable to see beyond the nurse. Eventually, she took the patient by his arm in an attempt to steer him back towards the ward, but the patient shrugged her off. This manoeuvre slightly changed her position relative to that of the patient, so that now he could once again see the lift doors and the three people waiting for a lift to arrive. When a lift arrived and the doors opened, this prompted the patient to move forward towards the lift. The nurse said, 'Oh no, you don't want to do that' and took a step towards the lift intending to ask the people quickly to close the doors. Before she was able to do so the patient suddenly lashed out with his walking stick. The nurse fended off the blow with her forearm and was struck a further five times as she held her arms aloft in a defensive posture.

From the corner of her eye she could see that the lift was so congested that the doors were unable to close. This provoked yet greater anger in the patient as he strove to reach the lift. The nurse yelled to the lift occupants to get the doors closed, but to no avail. Whilst there were people in the lift and in the vicinity of the landing no one came to her aid until another lift arrived and a man in his 40s alighted. He cried, 'Oh my God!', strode over to the patient, 'scooped him up' in his arms and carried him back into the ward where he deposited him on a chair near to the ward entrance. The man's female companion meanwhile consoled the nurse. The man returned to the landing and said how disgusted he was that the patient had attacked the nurse so viciously, but the nurse explained that he was demented and not responsible for his actions. Shortly afterwards two senior nurses arrived, advised the nurse to complete the necessary forms and remarked that such events were to be expected and one simply had to 'get on with it'. The nurse completed her shift and went off duty. She suffered serious bruising to her forearms where the blows had landed.

Dangers such as these are obviously most acute in the care of the mentally ill or handicapped where aberrant behaviour can be transformed into unrestrained violence without warning. This was the fate that befell a social work student who supplemented her income and gained experience by working for an agency that supplied temporary staff to residential care establishments (Case study 3.6). She was unpredictably assaulted by an autistic adolescent whom she had accompanied to the lavatory, and was only rescued from further injury by the intervention of a male member of staff.

Case Study 3.6: Attack by a severely autistic child

The interviewee was a social work student in her late 30s/early 40s who at the time was working part-time at a care home for children with disabilities to gain experience and earn additional income. She admits that she found working in this environment very anxiety-provoking because of the unpredictable and violent behaviour of the children, and also the strict policy of the unit that staff must not use any force against the children whilst failing to provide her with any training in how to deal with violent behaviour. She felt that the policy of focusing exclusively on positive reinforcement meant that severely anti-social behaviour was not only tolerated, but went wholly unacknowledged.

On the day in question she and another colleague were assigned to a group of eight children that included a boy who had not been at the unit very long, but she had already heard of his reputation through tearoom chatter as someone who exhibited very challenging behaviour. She was immediately apprehensive about working with this boy, especially when she first met him, because he was much taller and bigger than she was. Her colleague supervising this group was an experienced male social worker.

The room was large with high ceilings and echoed with the noise made by the children, not the least noisy of whom was the boy of whom she was apprehensive. He stood in one corner of the room, leaping into the air emitting 'whoop, whoop' noises as he did so.

After about an hour of supervising the room, her colleague left, saying that he was assisting in the preparation of lunch. This left her feeling abandoned, because she was utterly inexperienced in dealing with such aberrant behaviour. As she watched the room the boy of whom she was apprehensive became increasingly disturbed and, unprompted, started throwing four tubular chairs around. Although the chairs were not endangering anyone, the interviewee asked the boy to stop, but he continued throwing the chairs and making the 'whooping' noise. He then sat in the corner of the room and piled the chairs around and on top of himself. The interviewee could see the boy beneath the pile of chairs and he was holding his hands over his eyes with his knees up to his chest in almost a foetal position. Concerned for his welfare, she approached him and asked if he was all right, but his reply was to lash out with his foot through the gap in the chairs. As she attempted to move the chairs, he resisted and held them around himself. The boy also lashed out with his fist. She decided to leave the boy alone and returned to where she had been standing across the other side of the room. She felt completely alone and out of her depth, but unable to leave the room and get assistance.

After about half an hour, the boy emerged from his cocoon of chairs and ran from the room. The children were not supposed to leave the room unattended, and so the interviewee followed him, aware that she was leaving the other children unattended but judging that they were not at any immediate risk and the boy was in danger of leaving the building. She followed the boy to the toilet that was up the stairs where she waited alone on the landing for the boy to re-emerge. When he did so he immediately and without warning began punching the interviewee, to which she responded by pulling her folded arms up towards her face and burying her face into her arms. The boy began to 'pummel' the interviewee's arms, starting at the wrists (which were uppermost) and progressively striking her along the length of her forearms whilst emitting screaming noises. The interviewee was against a wall and unable to move and aware that she was forbidden from striking or grabbing her assailant.

Fortunately, a tall man emerged from the drugs room a couple of doors along the corridor about 8 metres away. As he moved towards the boy he called out to him telling him to stop, with the result that the boy ceased the assault. The man stood behind the boy and reaching around him took hold of both his wrists. The man asked if the interviewee was all right and she replied that she was. The man said, 'Why don't you go back into the room and we'll look after him now.' The interviewee was confused: 'I couldn't believe that he'd grabbed him'. As it was nearly lunchtime she took the opportunity to return to her own home to be alone. She decided that she would work at the children's unit no longer and whilst at home wrote a letter of resignation. Upon her return to the unit for the afternoon shift, she placed the letter in the deserted office. After completing her shift, she never returned.

As we noted in Chapter 1, psychiatric hospitals are sites of frequent violence towards staff, but care of psychiatric patients in the community also presents serious hazards. Community psychiatric nurses (CPNs) and social workers operating in the community usually do so alone or, at most, paired with just one colleague. Moreover, the environment in which the professionals work cannot be so carefully controlled as a residential establishment. One social worker in a mental health team found herself dealing with a drunken young woman who had slashed her wrists. As a senior female colleague and a male psychiatrist completed an assessment prior to 'committing' the woman to a 'place of safety' under the Mental Health Act, the patient grabbed the knife with which she had inflicted her wounds and chased all three professionals into the street. The two social workers found sanctuary in the interviewee's car as the woman banged on its roof, smearing blood from her wounds over the windscreen. Eventually, police equipped with riot shields overpowered the woman and she was taken to a psychiatric hospital. A less serious but more injurious incident occurred when a CPN and a social worker were unpredictably attacked by a patient whom they were routinely visiting at her home (Case study 3.7). They managed to physically overpower the woman and subdue her before making their escape.

Case Study 3.7: Violent psychiatric patient

A social worker with a Community Mental Health Team (CMHT) recounted an occasion when she and a CPN paid a home visit to a female patient living in sheltered accommodation and known to be volatile. The social worker was becoming frustrated with the patient, whom she regarded as manipulative. The two professionals knew each other well, but were paired for this visit on an *ad hoc* basis and did not have the shared understandings that came with routine working. They were also obliged to hurry and had little time to prepare. Each drove to the location separately in convoy, which also denied the opportunity to discuss the case en route.

Upon arrival the CPN took the patient into the bedroom to administer an injection. After a few minutes, the two women walked into the living room where the social worker sat waiting in the company of another female guest who sat in the corner. The patient was carrying a mug of hot coffee and as she entered the room looked at the social worker without saying anything (a 'signal' that the social worker felt in retrospect that she had failed to detect). The patient sat on a sofa directly opposite the social worker with a coffee table separating them, and the CPN sat alongside her.

The social worker and patient exchanged a few pleasantries. Without warning the patient threw the mug of hot coffee directly at the social worker, who instinctively ducked to her right. Almost immediately the patient kicked the coffee table, striking the social worker across the shins as she was attempting to rise from the sofa on which she was sitting. Although it caused no injury, the social worker stumbled against the coffee table and sprawled across the room, grabbing the arm of the chair in which the guest was sitting.

As she steadied herself she looked back towards the sofa and saw her colleague and the patient both on their knees struggling in the middle of the room. The CPN had hold of the patient's right arm whilst the patient had hold of the CPN's hair and was repeatedly tugging her head downwards towards the floor. The patient's face was now bright red with anger and exertion.

The social worker launched herself across the room and grabbed the patient's left arm and the woman tumbled backwards. All three came to rest with the patient's upper body on the seat of the sofa and her buttocks on the floor. Each of the professionals retained hold of one of the patient's arms, but were also half lying across her torso. The patient was shouting and swearing at the two professionals, as she had been doing from the moment of the first attack.

There then commenced a repeated process in which the patient appeared to calm down, followed by the two professionals relaxing their grip, whereupon the patient resumed her struggle and tried to break free. Each eruption of anger was accompanied with renewed shouting and swearing, with the patient's face turning red and contorted with rage. These eruptions were interspersed with quieter moments when the patient cried and was apologetic. During these interludes the two professionals tried to calm the patient by talking slowly and gently to her, pointing out that her behaviour was achieving nothing. When she apologised, she was told that the apology was accepted but it wasn't enough: she had behaved like this before and she had to tell them what was going on in her mind.

After an estimated 10–15 minutes the patient began sobbing uncontrollably and appeared to have stopped struggling. The social worker said immediately, 'I'm going now. I don't know what action will be taken. I might go to the police.' The client continued sobbing and repeatedly said 'sorry'. The two professionals released their grip on the patient, stood up and hurried out, leaving the guest (who had remained a passive spectator throughout) consoling the patient. Each went to their respective cars and drove directly back to the office (which had not been the intended schedule). The social worker described how she was trembling, but received the support of her colleagues. Whilst she refused to work with the patient again, she felt that no other action was taken either by her managers or the police.

She learnt after the incident that when the CPN took the patient into the bedroom to administer the injection, the patient had become aggressive. Had she been working with her usual colleague, the social worker feels sure that the CPN would have terminated the visit at that moment.

Caught in the middle

Some of the most serious physical assaults occurred in psychiatric hospitals and units where those suffering the most severe and potentially dangerous symptoms tend to be located. However, this concentration also indicates that colleagues are available to intervene. This is, of course, a double-edged sword, for those who intervene can themselves be attacked, as was a nurse in a psychiatric hospital who rescued a colleague from an office in which a patient was attacking her colleague. In the course of grabbing her colleague and pulling her through the door, the interviewee was also struck by blows from the patient. Equally, professionals working in the community can find themselves caught amid disputes in which they are not directly involved and yet police and caring professionals alike feel a duty to intervene or, at least, protect those who are vulnerable. Moreover, issues of guilt, innocence, responsibility and care often become entangled in these conflicts.

Case Study 3.8: Man with a carpenter's saw

Late one evening, shortly after the interviewee (a police officer still in his probationary period) and a slightly more experienced crewmate had commenced the night shift, they were sent by the control room to a dispute between neighbours who lived on a public housing estate. This dispute concerned abusive and threatening calls being received by a young man on his mobile phone who owed money to neighbours for drugs. Having spoken to the young man, the officers then walked across the street to talk with the neighbours who allegedly were sending the messages. A young woman among the neighbours became very angry at these allegations and began to make inchoate counter-allegations.

This second conversation was interrupted by loud angry knocking on the neighbour's door. The mother of the young man making the allegations was at the door holding a mobile phone and accusing her neighbours of sending further messages there and then. The interviewee's crewmate took the phone and went back into the neighbour's house whilst the interviewee continued talking to the mother near the neighbour's front door. The interviewee was aware that since he and his crewmate had been in the neighbour's house at the time the phone call was made, it was unlikely that it had been made by anyone in that house. The mother of the complainant turned and walked away from the neighbour's house. The officer pursued her and called out to her so that they could talk further. The mother was cooperative and they now stood on a wide semi-circular verge in front of the neighbour's house.

As he and the mother stood talking, the interviewee saw a young man approaching. As the young man passed a street light, the officer saw that he was carrying a metal object that he later identified as a carpenter's saw. The man was shouting towards the neighbour's house. Further away, the officer could see eight other people (including a number of young men and one young woman) emerge from the house of the original complainant. He saw the complainant's father go to the rear of a white van and retrieve a metal object that the officer was unable to identify.

The interviewee radioed for back-up (the first time he had been obliged to do so in his short career). He felt scared and focused on the youth with the carpenter's saw, which he was now waving in an aggressive manner. The interviewee reported feeling very aware of his surroundings and what was occurring. He shouted at the youth to stop and put the saw down. As he did so, he unclipped the restraining strap on his baton, but did not draw it – something he was in the habit of doing in confrontational situations.

At this point the mother to whom the interviewee had been speaking intervened, taking hold of her son's arm and leading him back towards her house.

Two patrol cars arrived, followed by an unmarked car with CID officers in it and a personnel carrier that pulled up some distance away. However, by now the people who had emerged from the house had returned from whence they had come. Meanwhile, the interviewee's crewmate remained in the other house oblivious of what had been occurring outside. The interviewee and one of the responding officers joined the interviewee's crewmate in the accused's house, whilst three other officers went to the complainant's house. The interviewee and his two companions then retired to the driveway of the house to discuss how to proceed. Whilst they were standing there a further call was made to the phone that the mother of the complainant had earlier handed to the interviewee's crewmate. The female caller was abusive to the officer and the three officers concluded that it was obviously made by someone privy to the dispute who knew that the officer was in possession of the phone.

Now that the situation had calmed down the backup officers departed and the interviewee and his crewmate returned to the house of the original complainant. They warned the occupants that if there was any recurrence of the aggression they had earlier shown they would be arrested. The young man who had originally made the allegations apologised and his mother appeared to calm down. After a protracted discussion the young man and his family agreed that they did not wish to make a formal complaint and the officers departed.

Mental health professionals could also find themselves entangled in similar circumstances, as Case study 3.9 illustrates. A CPN visiting a mother whose son suffered Asperger's syndrome found herself in the midst of a violent attack by the son on his mother. Having rescued the mother, the CPN then had to restrain the mother who pursued her son into his bedroom and began attacking him.

Case Study 3.9: Mother and disabled son attack each other

The interviewee was a CPN in her mid-30s with seven years' experience. The incident occurred whilst the interviewee was visiting the mother of a boy who suffered Asperger's syndrome and was suffering depression because of the intense demands that her son's condition was making upon her.

On the day in question the CPN had been in the house between five and ten minutes before the boy joined her and his mother. When she saw him she felt that he appeared odd – 'out of it' – but attributed this to his strong medication. As he entered the sitting room he immediately accused the two women of trying to get rid of him, but this was not unusual. Nor was it unusual when he began pestering his mother; however, this did prompt his mother to scold him, telling him to return to his room.

The son left the two women, but returned almost immediately. He was standing in the doorway. He was a very big child for his age, and had the physique of a youth aged 16–17, but was quite infantile in his behaviour. He began yelling at his mother, swearing violently at her, and his complexion was very pale. He approached his mother, shouting and screaming abuse and obscenities into her face. Then he stood and stared at the two women in turn before going to the hallway from where he took a dog lead from a hook and strode quickly and deliberately across the sitting room, 'launching himself' at his mother, striking her with the chain part of the lead. His mother's reaction was initially to bring her arms and leg up in a defensive posture as the dog lead struck her across the arm and back. Immediately she was hit, she seemed to momentarily lose all muscle tone and sank into the chair. The boy, apparently realising what he had done, stood looking at his mother. He then turned and ran out of the room. By now his mother had recovered and with a speed that left the

CPN amazed, she leapt from the chair and raced after her son. This jolted the shocked CPN into a reaction and she followed hot on the heels of the mother.

The three of them ran upstairs where the door to the boy's bedroom was directly facing them at the head of the stairs. The boy dashed into the room and slammed the door behind him, leaning his weight against it. His mother tussled with the door whilst the CPN stood to her left-hand side. Fearing that the boy would begin smashing up his room, the CPN joined the mother in forcing the door open and pushing the boy back. As soon as they entered the room, the mother pushed her son down on the bed and was on top of him crying and screaming at him that she was going to kill him. The CPN really thought that the mother was going to seriously harm her son and so she grabbed the woman from behind and pulled her off him. The mother ended up sitting on the end of the bed whilst the boy had sprung to his feet. The CPN grabbed him and pushed him against the wall immediately to the left of the bed, shouting at him initially to calm down. She felt him relax and so she relaxed her hold. She suggested that he should go for a walk and get some fresh air to relax. He indicated a willingness to do so and the CPN released her grip and allowed him to walk through the door. She followed him down the stairs and was followed, in turn, by the mother. As soon as the boy walked through the door the CPN double-locked it to prevent the boy returning.

She then turned to the mother and asked if she wanted a cup of tea. The mother thanked her and accepted the offer, before returning to the sitting room and sitting in the chair she had previously occupied. Whilst the kettle was boiling, the CPN announced (she didn't ask) that she was phoning the police. She went to the phone in the sitting room and dialled 999. She told the control room that she was a CPN; that she needed assistance urgently; that the boy was known to the police; and that he'd attacked his mother. The police arrived shortly afterwards and arrested the boy for assault.

Even when caring professionals feel unable to quell the disturbance, they feel obliged to protect vulnerable parties. On one occasion, two social workers visited a young couple because of fears expressed by neighbours regarding the welfare of the couple's two infant children. Whilst visiting, the social workers witnessed an assault upon the children's father by drug-dealers demanding payment. Each social worker grabbed one of the children and escaped with the mother through the flailing fists and kicks of the attackers. Nurses too sometimes found themselves trying to intervene in fights that erupted in the waiting room between parties to earlier disputes that had resulted in injuries requiring treatment. What is common to the experience of all four professions is that their role involves routinely working with people living disorganised lives who might make ready recourse to violence in which professionals might be embroiled.

Passive obstruction

All the cases considered so far have involved either the use or unambiguous threat of physical violence. However, most incidents are not nearly so straightforward; for instance, in Case study 3.10 a social worker found herself virtually held captive by a much heavier woman client who used her bulk physically to prevent the social worker leaving, but neither offered nor threatened physical violence as such. This account is related in some detail since it graphically illustrates how, despite the absence of any significant physical violence, the fear instilled in the social worker is quite serious and easily understood by the reader.

Case Study 3.10: Social worker held captive by client

The interviewee was an experienced middle-aged social worker employed by a CMHT. She had been visiting the client concerned in this incident for many years. The client was a physically large, heavy woman who could be threatening if she had been drinking. For this reason the social worker had negotiated an agreement that if she found the client had been drinking she would not enter the client's house and would terminate the meeting immediately – it was a 'boundary' designed to regulate the two women's relationship.

The social worker visited the client mid-morning and found her sweaty and red in the face – signs that she had been drinking – but she wasn't obviously drunk. The client began talking and the social worker concluded that the client had indeed been drinking. So the social worker said to the client, 'Look, I can see that you've been drinking and so there's no point in my staying.' She reminded the client of their agreement that the social worker would not stay if the client had been drinking. She told the client that she would return the following week. The social worker rose to leave and turned towards the door, but the client moved towards her and shouted, 'No, you're not going. I need to speak to you. You're not going.' The two women were now facing each other and standing close together so that the social worker could smell the drink on the client's breath. The client was staring in an intimidating way into the social worker's face and getting sweatier with every moment. The client continued to shout, 'You're not bloody going. You're not fucking leaving this house.' The social worker was beginning to feel anxious and intimidated at this point, but she tried to retain a calm demeanour.

The social worker tried to reason with the client: 'Look, I'm going now. This is the agreement we've had. If you've been drinking when I arrive, I'm going to leave. It's pointless trying to talk to you because you're too drunk.' She said all this in a deliberately calm and slow manner. The client repeated, 'You're not fucking leaving this house. You're not bloody leaving.' As the social worker moved towards the door, the client physically stood in the way and barred access to the door. The social worker said calmly, 'Look, this is silly. Just let me go. This is the agreement. We've talked about this before. There's no point my being here because you've been drinking. We can't discuss things because you don't remember afterwards. So it's a waste of your time and my time. I will be back next week. Let me go.' Deliberately avoiding any physical contact, the social worker moved to the side in order to get past the client. However, the client moved to block her path and then pushed the social worker quite aggressively away from the door, saying 'You're not fucking leaving this house. If you do, I know you're not coming back.'

The social worker then sat down again on the sofa, hoping to take some heat out of the situation, and was now quite alarmed and could feel her pulse racing. She was thinking to herself, 'Christ! What do I do? How do I deal with this? Do I physically push her out of the way because she won't attack me, or do I keep talking to her?' She kept repeating to the client, 'Look, this is pointless. This is our agreement. I'm not going to stay here because you're drunk. Let's deal with this sensibly. You've been drinking.' The client remained blocking the exit. Again, she said, 'This is silly. I don't want to get into a fight with you. I don't want it to be like this. I just want to go now. I'm not staying. I will come back, I promise. That's our agreement. But I'm leaving now.' With that the social worker stood up. The client repeated, 'You're not leaving. You're not fucking going out of my house.' By now the social worker was frightened, for although she still believed that the client would not harm her physically, she had never thought that she would act as she was now acting. She started to wonder how she might escape. She had a mobile phone and considered running up the stairs, shutting herself in a bedroom and calling for help. The social worker knew that when the client was drunk she could become aggressive and attack people like the police. She felt, however, that if she ran it would only make the situation worse. So she continued to maintain a calm demeanour and repeated that she was leaving, that it was silly, that she would return the following week, and so on. She moved towards the door again saying, 'Look, I'm going now. You're frightening me.' The client replied, 'You're not fucking going. You know I wouldn't hurt you. But you're not leaving here.'

The social worker was losing patience and said, 'If you won't let me go I'm going to phone the police and ask them to come because you won't let me go.' The client replied, 'Phone the fucking police.' The social worker moved towards the kitchen, where the household phone was hanging, with the client a few steps behind her. The social worker was able to use the phone, but the client stood very close to her, breathing very heavily and sweating profusely. The social worker dialled 999. She was very anxious by now, because she did not know what the client was going to do next. Was she likely to become more violent and aggressive, or what? She explained the situation to the police, but worried that she might be thought to be over-reacting and wasting their time. As she put the phone down she realised that she'd given the wrong house number. She wondered what to do: should she phone 999 again and admit that she'd given the wrong number? She decided that the police would think she was completely stupid. The client was continuing to stand extremely close to the social worker and she could smell the alcohol on her breath.

She then appealed to the woman, saying again that it was silly and she should let her go. The social worker describes this as 'rational, social work, calm stuff', but she wasn't feeling calm. She was contemplating what she would do once the police arrived. The front of the house had no windows, but there were two front doors, one of which contained a pane of glass. However, this door was no longer used and a sofa was positioned directly in front of it preventing it from being opened. There was no means of escape through the back of the house. She tried to move towards the door but the client became increasingly aggressive and pushed her away with increasing force. She now felt frightened but continued calmly to appeal to the client. At some stage the client left her unattended in the kitchen, which enabled the social worker to grab the client's house keys and go into the room with the unused door in it and unlock the door. However, the client returned and pushed her away from the door and back into the kitchen, but the door remained unlocked.

Then the police arrived and the social worker could see the personnel carrier and the officers rushing from it and heading to the house next door. There was also a police car in attendance. The social worker thought to herself, 'Oh shit!' So, she rushed for the door (now abandoning any calculation as to what might antagonise the client), jumped on the sofa and began knocking on the window shouting 'I'm here! I'm here!' to attract the attention of the police officers. The police officers saw her and tried to gain entrance through the door. The client grabbed the social worker and pulled her away from the door. The client then collapsed onto the sofa and lay sobbing 'like a beached whale' and shouting 'You're not fucking leaving here. You're not fucking leaving my house. You'll not bloody come back!'

With the police in the vicinity, the social worker's anxiety level dropped markedly and she began to worry lest the police damaged the door in gaining entry. So, the social worker pulled at the sofa with the client still lying on top of it. She managed to pull it sufficiently far from the door for the police to squeeze through the gap. The client remained lying on the sofa. The social worker felt embarrassed that she'd had to call the police, but at least the client hadn't meekly opened the door. The police now came into the house and the social worker went outside with a woman officer and two male officers. The social worker apologised to the police, but the woman officer said not to be silly and that she had done the right thing by calling them. The woman officer asked what the social worker wanted the police to do now. She replied that she did not want the client charged with any offences.

Damage to property

Attacks were not only directed against people; they could also be directed at property. When these occurred they tended to be expressions of frustration: for instance, a drunken man with an injured foot responded to being told that he would have a lengthy wait in A&E by throwing chairs around the waiting room. A psychiatric patient who received unwelcome news about her treatment wrecked the waiting room of a CMHT office.

Perhaps the most bizarre and yet terrifying incident occurred when a female police officer attended a call to a large house that had been converted into apartments. One of the tenants had become involved in a dispute with his landlord and in rage had utterly wrecked the apartment in which he lived with his girlfriend. When the police arrived they discovered that the man now lay injured amid the destruction that he had wrought (Case study 3.11).

Case Study 3.11: Destruction of apartment

The interviewee was one of four officers in two cars that responded to a 'violent domestic' at around 9 pm. On arrival the female occupant of a first-floor apartment in a large Victorian house explained that her male partner had become enraged as a result of a quarrel with the landlord and had completely wrecked the apartment. When the officers looked into the stairwell leading to the apartment all they could see was a pile of central-heating radiators, white goods (cooker, refrigerator and the like) and sundry other items. From the first floor the officers could hear the voice of a man crying for help apparently because he had hurt his ankle and was now unable to move. Because of her relatively diminutive stature, the interviewee agreed to climb through the pile of precariously perched household items and attend to the man. She was somewhat apprehensive about the possibility that the pile might collapse and cause her injury, but also because, according to his partner, the man had a visceral dislike of the police. There remained the possibility that she was entering a trap. She used a small torch to light her way up the stairs because in his rage the tenant had fused the electricity supply.

At the top of the stairs she saw the man lying on his back along the landing, his feet stretching towards her. Resting on his elbows he repeatedly cried, 'My fucking ankle's broken!' Although he was physically a big man, he looked pathetic and the officer no longer felt afraid. However, he remained volatile – periodically erupting into vituperation against the landlord, interrupted by demands for medical attention – and he was clearly very drunk. Although she now considered him harmless, she avoided saying anything

---

that might spark antagonism, such as asking why he had caused such damage. She began to appreciate the scale of the destruction: the landing banister had been completely smashed, leaving a line of spikes of wood pointing upwards. A tyre iron that the man had evidently used as his instrument of destruction lay beside him, so she tossed it aside with the casual remark, 'You won't be needing this, will you?' She checked the man's injuries and saw that apart from the ankle they were slight.

By now she had been joined by one of the male officers from the other car to attend and together they began exploring the devastation. She explained that the two officers did not want any 'nasty surprises' such as further dangers or a dead body in the utterly darkened apartment. As they explored, the officer called down to colleagues below, reassuring them. As they passed where the man lay, she took time to inquire how he was and to reassure him, for she was worried at the obvious ferocity of the destruction.

However, when the two officers returned to the landing the interviewee found to her horror that the man was no longer where they had left him lying. Then she smelt burning and this led her into a bedroom. She saw the man lying in front of an open coal fire pulling hot coals onto the carpet that was beginning to smoulder. She shouted to her colleague to join her. Together they pulled the man away and began stamping on the flames. She radioed for the Fire Service to attend immediately, but her colleague had by now managed to extinguish the flames.

Eventually the Fire Service did arrive and helped remove the man, who was taken to hospital.

In only one instance was violence used in an overtly calculating manner, but it was among the most serious, even if it did not result in direct physical assault (Case study 3.12). It concerned two young men who had earlier brought a young woman into A&E and when denied access to her they began hurling themselves at the security doors that divided the treatment area from the waiting room.

Case Study 3.12: Youths trying to force entry

The interviewee was the Sister in charge of the A&E department during her shift. She was a woman in her late 30s/early 40s with 20 years' experience of nursing, 13 of them in A&E. On the night in question the four nurses and one doctor on duty were all female. Apart from a couple of porters and the security staff there were no men in the department.

At around 2 am a young white woman in a semi-collapsed condition was brought in by two black youths who said that she had 'gone funny in the car'. The girl was admitted and her companions waited in the waiting room. Staff came to suspect that the woman had been drugged and possibly raped. The Sister described the young woman as early-20s, well dressed, well spoken, 'not cheap', 'a stereotypical "nice girl"'.

The young men demanded to speak to the woman and so the Sister went to the reception desk to talk to them. One professed to be the woman's 'boyfriend' but the woman later rejected this description. He was the more prominent of the two and was around six foot tall, wearing a short tee-shirt that revealed a developed musculature. His companion was not so prominent nor so 'up front' aggressive in appearance as the other youth. After consulting the patient, the Sister explained that the young woman did not want to speak to them. The more prominent man accused the Sister of being racist and denied that she had any 'fucking authority' to deny him access to his 'girlfriend'. The Sister returned to the young woman several times to check what she wanted and she steadfastly refused to see the men, becoming more anxious as time passed. The staff also felt frightened: they were standing in the nurses' area watching the CCTV monitors. No patients were being admitted from the waiting room because of the threat posed by the young men.

On one of her repeated visits to the reception desk to confirm that the young woman did not want to see them, the men were extremely abusive to the Sister, calling her a 'fucking white cunt' and 'fucking white bitch'. This was her most vivid recollection and the most disagreeable. At the same time the one youth was banging on the perspex screen with his fist and the Sister was aware that it was not an impregnable barrier. She felt humiliated and belittled in front of a crowded waiting room because she felt unable to retaliate in any way. She felt that her obvious fear encouraged the 'boyfriend' to escalate his abusive and violent behaviour. It was also her impression that they would not listen to anything she said because she was female – 'a bitch'. Throughout this confrontation the Sister said that she raised her voice, but never acted 'unprofessionally' or responded in kind to the taunts and abuse of the youths.

The Sister then told the youths to leave the waiting room,

59

but they refused and continued to be abusive. She said that she would call the police and the prominent black youth challenged her to do so. She picked up the phone and called the police. The youths continued to shout abuse whilst she was on the phone, so that the police could hear them and said they would respond immediately. When she did so, the more prominent of the two men decided that each of them should target one of the access doors to the treatment area. He began shoulder-charging the triage door in an attempt to break it down whilst his companion did likewise to the main treatment door, interspersing each charge with abuse directed at the nurses through the doors. The Sister was personally very frightened because she feared that they 'were going to get me', 'they were gunning for me'.

During the time whilst they awaited the arrival of the police, the Sister arranged for all the patients to be moved to cubicles away from the doors connecting the treatment area and waiting room. Because she and the other nurses were so frightened, they were doing this frantically. She also was aware that there were sick patients awaiting assessment and treatment in the waiting room itself. However, ambulances continued to arrive and patients were admitted through the ambulance doors and staff were anxious that the two youths would realise this and gain access through these doors. Throughout this period the youths were continuing to shout abuse and threats that clearly be could heard throughout the department and were adding to the stress that the Sister and her nurses felt.

Eventually the police arrived and this was greeted with immense relief by the Sister and her colleagues. Four male police officers came into the waiting room whilst the youths were continuing to attack the doors. There was a 'big fight' in the waiting room, the youths were handcuffed and removed.

The whole incident lasted about three hours.

Verbal aggression and threats

The incident in A&E also illustrates the importance of threats, for whilst the young men did not succeed in breaking into the treatment area, the Nursing Sister was apprehensive about her own safety and that of the staff had the men done so. Equally, whilst the social worker passively held captive by the drunken client was not physically harmed, she too was apprehensive about what the woman might do next. Threat is troubling because it indicates willingness on the part of the aggressor to, at the very least, contemplate violence and a disposition to employ violent means. Of course, not all threats eventuate in violent acts and some violence is perpetrated without threats, but it is difficult experientially to divorce the threat of violence and its consummation.

It was commonplace for police officers to find themselves confronting people who were threatening in their demeanour and appearance. On one occasion two officers stopped a vehicle to check driving documents. Their suspicions were aroused and they decided to arrest the driver. The man was physically big and powerfully built, and he immediately adopted an aggressive posture. The officers summoned help and once it arrived prevailed upon the man's companions to persuade him to 'go quietly', which he eventually did.

Whereas police officers tended to take such displays in their stride, caring professionals were seriously disturbed by displays of anger even when they were not consummated in any physical attack. Antagonists who clenched their fists and teeth, whose faces became florid with rage, who adopted a posture of 'squaring up' to them, caused intense intimidation even if the situation developed no further. Over three-quarters of all cases entailed displays of anger, often accompanied by obscenities and less often the making of explicit threats. Many interviewees displayed considerable distaste at recalling the obscenities that had been used and made recourse to euphemisms rather than repeat the actual words used. It was evident that this was experienced as just as distressing as the threat or even actuality of physical assaults.

However, not all threats indicated the prospect of physical assault. Some of the most serious threats related to the professional self through the use and abuse of complaints procedures. One incident that is particularly telling in this regard is Case study 3.13 in which a social worker was present at a case conference at which the mother of a young boy sought to convince the professionals that her son was autistic. Thwarted in this endeavour, the boy's mother flew into a rage and physically attacked the interviewee. Interestingly, what discomfited and distressed the interviewee much more than the physical attack was the woman's threats to destroy the social worker's career by making official complaints. In the view of the social worker, this was a credible threat because the woman 'knew her way around the system'.

Case Study 3.13: Attacking the professional self

This case involved a disagreement about the nature of a mental condition suffered by a young boy. The boy's mother insisted that he was autistic, but according to the interviewee (a social worker) many professionals involved in the case felt that he was the victim of his mother's condition of Munchausen's Syndrome by Proxy, which led her to disable the child by preventing him realising his potential. However, because the mother was 'well connected in the disability world' and 'knew her way around the system', she proved very effective at 'keeping the professionals at bay'. She had obtained, it was alleged by the interviewee, a private diagnosis from a psychiatrist in London that confirmed the boy's autism, even though this diagnosis was reached without consultation with any of the professionals involved with him locally. The interviewee also believed that the mother's general practitioner was 'colluding' with her demand to have the boy enrolled in a special school, which the interviewee feared would impede his intellectual development.

It was at the mother's initiative that a case conference was convened to decide upon whether or not the boy should attend the school. Prior to the meeting the mother had 'lobbied' various participants including the interviewee. It was the interviewee's opinion that once the mother realised that the weight of opinion was against her she called for the meeting to be cancelled. However, the meeting went ahead and both the parents attended despite threats from the mother to boycott it. During the meeting the mother made several allegations concerning the care that the boy was currently receiving but again was unable to persuade others present of the force of her argument.

Suddenly the mother stood up, screaming hysterically and picking up papers that she had brought to the meeting apparently with the intention of leaving abruptly. The social worker had a premonition that she was about to be assaulted but tried not to escalate the situation and so sat with her hands in her lap looking down at the table – 'meekly, like a lamb to the slaughter'. The expected assault was launched by the mother, but was swiftly terminated by the boy's father who grabbed his wife and led her 'screaming out of the building'.

Whilst the interviewee suffered shock following this assault, it was the subsequent events that she found most disturbing. An independent person present at the case conference was asked for a report by the interviewee's employer, but claimed not to have witnessed any incident. This led to the interviewee writing to this person expressing her 'disgust' and this prompted a formal complaint against her. Meanwhile the mother had also made a series of official complaints against the interviewee among others, and the interviewee feels that this has undermined her confidence. At the time of the interview she was still awaiting the outcome of these various procedures. She feared the mother because of the latter's connections, knowledge and fluency, but she did not discount the possibility of some kind of physical attack on her or her property (such as her car).

In other cases, CPNs reported how concerned they had become by the efforts of vengeful psychiatric patients to pursue false allegations against them. These interviewees displayed some of the strongest adverse reactions of anyone to recalling the events: one of them described the assault on her professional propriety and competence as like 'being violated'. This graphically illustrates the lack of any simple correlation between the overt nature of an attack and its severity for the victim. Many police officers also mentioned *inter alia* the risk of being complained about; for instance, when the officer threatened with a loaded shotgun (Case study 3.1) was asked why she had not used either CS spray or her baton, she dismissed the suggestion saying that it 'might have got me into trouble' – as if being threatened with a loaded gun wasn't trouble enough!

Conclusion

The experiences of interviewees related in this chapter demonstrate that 'violence' is a concept that embraces an enormous range of experience. It is not restricted to physical assault, nor even to the threat of such, but also to less direct threats against other aspects of the self and even the environment. When the policewoman was clambering through the pile of household equipment thrown into the stairwell by the enraged tenant (Case study 3.11), what was going through her mind was imagining what she might encounter at the top of the stairs. Someone who was capable of such destruction might be capable of much else besides.

What this chapter also illustrates is the very different qualitative experience of violence among police officers compared with caring professionals. For the police violence is 'part of the job': they employ it as well as suffer from it. For caring professionals it is an alien intrusion quite separate from their role. Whereas police tended to be phlegmatic about violence and threats, caring professionals were deeply disturbed. This is something to which we will return in the penultimate chapter.

Chapter 4

Violent people

Introduction

The obvious conclusion from the previous chapter is that violent episodes are not experienced solely in terms of the ostensible actions of aggressors, for the range of what constitutes 'violence' is much too broad for that. Equally important is *who* the aggressor is. A shaven-headed thug threatening physical attack is clearly a very different matter to a small child doing the same. The thug appears to have the motivation and capacities to make good his threat, whereas a small child has few capacities whatever his or her motive. However, we are reminded of the joke, 'What do you call a toddler with a machine gun?': 'Sir!' Apart from the capacity to inflict harm is the willingness or motivation to do so and this might arise from an array of sources: anger, intoxication, mental illness, and so on. Being intimidated by a threat implies that there has been some threat assessment – however brief and rudimentary – that grants the threat credibility.

In this chapter we will explore how those who participated in this research assessed the threats that they faced. What did they take into account? How did they reach their assessment? As in the previous chapter we will begin by considering the most obvious examples before proceeding to more challenging cases.

Men behaving badly

There are gender variations in patterns of occupational violence. Over all industry sectors, there is a tendency for women workers to experience higher levels of verbal abuse, while men tend to receive more threats and physical assaults. This variation can be partially explained by the gender division of labour, with women being concentrated in 'caring' jobs that involve greater face-to-face contact between workers and their customers/clients. (Mayhew and Chappell 2003: 6)

It is with some considerable hesitation that we reproduce Table 4.1 since it might be taken to imply that our data are more quantitatively robust than is in fact the case. It simply summarises what this non-randomly selected sample of people recounted. More importantly, it cannot be judged against any baseline. We simply do not know what the sex balance was in each of these professional groups at the time (it proved too administratively inconvenient for the data to be produced) and, as importantly, we do not know the sex distribution of all contacts between these various professionals and their respective clientele. So any generalisations must be made with the utmost care.

Nevertheless it is striking that confrontations between police officers and members of the public are overwhelmingly male-to-male encounters. By contrast, the experience of the caring professions is far more mixed. It is hardly surprising that more women reported violent and hostile encounters given that these professions attract a higher proportion of women. However, there is clearly a distinction to be drawn between social workers and mental health professionals on the one hand, and A&E staff on the other. A&E staff seem far more exposed to male violence and hostility than do the other two caring

Table 4.1 Gendered violence

		Police		Social Work		Mental Health		A&E		Total
		Male	Female	Male	Female	Male	Female	Male	Female	
Adversary	Male	41	6	5	7	4	5	5	12	85
	Female	2	0	1	7	0	9	0	2	21
Total		43	6	6	14	4	14	5	14	106

professions. It is likely (but cannot be confirmed from this research) that this reflects the sex balance between professionals and clientele in these respective spheres of work.

There are qualitative aspects of this pattern that need highlighting. First is the different quality of male–male compared with male–female confrontations. The majority of male police officers recalled violent encounters in a phlegmatic manner. These experiences may not have been recalled as being enjoyable, but as challenges to be overcome, and success in doing so produces some satisfaction. Even the off-duty officer whose nose was broken when he tried to arrest three youthful shoplifters (Case study 3.3) appeared to take satisfaction from the fact that despite the violence of the struggle and the injuries that he suffered, he succeeded in arresting the youths. He described his future wife's reaction as a humorous finale.

Deviations from this pattern are instructive. For a male police officer what is far more problematic are those rare occasions when they become involved in a violent encounter with a woman. Such was the fate of a detective who answered a call for assistance from a local school for children excluded from mainstream education where one of the pupils was apparently damaging a classroom (Case study 4.1). When he arrived, and much to his surprise, he found himself confronting a highly volatile, young, physically powerful, adolescent girl determined to escape. Despite the fact that he succeeded in containing the young woman and eventually arresting her, as a man he found the experience deeply unsatisfactory because of the physical nature of the contact. He gave repeated emphasis to the need to have other adults in attendance so as to protect him from unfounded allegations.

Case Study 4.1: Adolescent female

The interviewee was a detective constable in his middle/late 20s. Although not tall, he has a stocky physique. He recalled that on the occasion in question he was alone, in plain clothes, driving an unmarked police car and apart from a radio and handcuffs he was in possession of no other equipment. He answered a radio call for assistance at a nearby school for children excluded from mainstream education because of behavioural problems. The radio transmission mentioned a 'violent 13-year-old'. He expected 'kids' stuff'!

On arrival at the school the headmistress, whom he found to be sympathetic to the police and eager to help, told him that a girl had 'smashed up a classroom' and had been threatening staff.

She explained that the girl had a turbulent home life and there had been similar difficulties with her in the past, adding that on this occasion the school would be prepared to 'press charges', although he insisted that this did not have much impact upon him.

The classroom was a temporary building, with windows on every side. As he approached the classroom he expected minor criminal damage, which it was – she had caused damage but mostly to disposable items. She had not damaged the building itself or its fixtures. He expected that he would sort the situation out fairly quickly and satisfactorily.

The girl was 13 years old, of mixed race, who the interviewee described as fat and about 5'6" tall. She was wearing black jeans and a large black 'puffer' jacket. The other pupils were in attendance and she was sitting on a table being very 'nonchalant' and aggressive to teachers who were present. The headmistress entered the room with the officer and tried to talk to the girl, but was told to 'fuck off you black bitch' and she left.

The officer formed the view that much of her behaviour was 'for show' to the other pupils and thought their presence was aggravating the situation. So, he instructed the teacher to clear the classroom in order to deprive her of an audience. The male teacher remained after the pupils left, for which the officer was grateful. The teacher did not intervene in any way, simply standing and observing, but his presence offered protection from any allegations of impropriety. This was a serious consideration at the forefront of his mind throughout and he repeatedly referred to it.

He identified himself as a police officer, to which the girl responded by telling him to 'fuck off' and used other unspecified obscenities. He recalled asking her why she was behaving like this and again she responded by telling him to 'fuck off'. He was trying to find some reason for her behaviour so that he could suggest that they sort out the problem away from the classroom and avoid him arresting her. He remembered saying, 'Look, I don't want to have to arrest you.' Each repeated overture was rebuffed invariably with obscenities.

It became obvious to the officer that he had no alternative but to arrest the girl. He called for back-up after only a couple of minutes of the encounter beginning. He radioed to say that the girl was unlikely to come quietly and so he asked for another unit, because he was going to have go '311' (make an arrest). He backed off a little in order to radio the control room, but says that the girl was paying no attention to what he was doing. He deliberately avoided giving the impression that there was any kind of panic. She challenged him to 'try' to arrest her, which he considered the cut-off point and he said, 'Look, you're liable to arrest now. You're not leaving me any option.' He said that he was trying to get her to see that this was one extreme, but if she calmed down it would be unnecessary and could be resolved another way.

Throughout this, she continued to shout at him that it was none of his business and that he should 'fuck off'. He'd formed the view that the girl would not come quietly, but he felt he had to continue to try to persuade her to do so. He felt that he could not use restraint techniques on a 13-year-old without another officer present, because although young she was big and heavy and the only equipment he had was his handcuffs. So he decided not to take the risk. He was conscious throughout that whilst he was bigger and stronger than her, she was a juvenile female and he wanted someone to back him up: (a) in the event of a complaint being made (despite the presence of a male teacher throughout), and (b) to prevent either the girl or himself being injured. To achieve this he felt two officers were obviously better than one.

There then commenced what he described as a 'game of cat and mouse': as the girl moved towards one of the windows or the door he blocked her path, but they did not come into contact. This went on for what seemed like ten minutes until back-up arrived. She continued being abusive and began pushing tables at the officer. He describes the girl as 'posturing and threatening'. She went to the windows to shout at the kids who were watching from outside, 'making as much of it as she could'.

Eventually she made a 'bolt' for the door. She shoved a table towards the officer and headed for the corner where the door to the classroom was. He was standing in the middle of the room. He pushed the table out of the way and moved towards the corner still trying to calm her down. Then she 'just legged it for the door' and he cut her off before she got there. He expected her to stop and back off, but instead she ran straight into him and he forced her against the wall, holding on to one of her arms. He tried handcuffing her, but was unable to do so because she was kicking and spitting. So he decided to push her to the ground using his superior physical strength. There was a violent struggle with the girl kicking, spitting and screaming abuse, during which his radio went skidding across the room. The male teacher still did not intervene, apart from handing the officer the police radio. Her puffer jacket made it difficult to retain hold of her arm because the fabric was so slippery. Once he'd pinned her to the floor, he managed to get one cuff on. Just then his colleague arrived and the latter took hold of the girl's free arm and helped cuff that wrist. The struggle probably lasted no more than 5–10 seconds, but seemed longer. His most vivid recollection of the incident was the girl's strength, despite her age.

Once handcuffed she continued to scream abuse and threatened to complain. She said, 'You can't treat me like this you fucking bastards.' He and his colleague replied that she should calm down and then she could stand up and be walked out without further embarrassment. Her retort was, 'I'm not doing that you fucking bastard.' So the two officers lifted her up onto her feet and walked her out backwards, thereby preventing her from spitting at them or biting. As she was led the 60 yards to the police car she was screaming at the headteacher, 'You fucking black bitch' and 'You fucking bastard', which the officer found rather shocking. The journey through the school was difficult, because many of the onlooking kids had been in trouble with the police. They were abusing her and she was screaming abuse back at them, which escalated the situation.

Once in the car she stopped struggling and calmed down a little, but even so, throughout the journey to the station she continued to be abusive, saying that the officers were racist 'fucking bastards'.

At the police station she seemed not to care at all. Since the school did not want to press charges, she was released into the care of her aunt who was looking after her.

This illuminates the gendered nature of violence and hostility: men behaving violently towards each other accords with gender stereotypes, but men behaving violently towards women offends those stereotypes (even if sadly it is all too common in the domestic sphere).

Perhaps because of this gendered nature of violent and hostile encounters some male social workers reported that they were selected to deal with more volatile situations, a practice that McLean (2000) suggests is not uncommon. One social worker recounted how he and another male colleague were selected to interview a woman because her husband had recently been released from prison and was known to be violent. As the two colleagues sat alone in the interview room reviewing the exchanges they had had with the woman, her husband strode in. There was then an orally aggressive exchange with him before he strode out. But such was the interviewee's apprehension that he was fingering the attack alarm that he had placed in his pocket as a precaution. An even more serious example was when a junior male colleague was asked to accompany a colleague – 'riding shotgun', as he called it. This was to interview at his home a man with a reputation for violence, resulting in the two social workers being threatened and abused, and an attempt by the man to strike the interviewee as he left the house (Case study 4.2).

Case Study 4.2: 'Riding shotgun'

The interviewee was asked to accompany a colleague to visit the home of a client, the mother of two young children. The client's ex-husband had returned to the family home after serving a term of imprisonment for serious sexual offences involving children, and Social Services were anxious over the welfare of the couple's own children. The purpose of the visit was to persuade the man to leave the house and no longer live there with his ex-wife and sons.

The prospect of a visit had been discussed with senior staff who had expressed concerns that the interviewee's colleague, although physically a big man, should not go alone to see the client because he might not be able to deal with the situation. The client's ex-husband had previously threatened other social workers and his housing officer and had a criminal record for assault and affray. There were ample grounds for believing that he might become physically aggressive and abusive. The interviewee felt that he was selected to accompany his colleague because he was a man rather than a woman. 'So basically I was there to "ride shotgun"' albeit that he described himself as 'Eleven stone wringing wet. I'm not a muscle man at all.' Despite the ex-husband's reputation the interviewee had anticipated that when he and his colleague actually made the visit they would be greeted with abuse and threats, but none of it credible – 'a lot of hot air, but no actual physical threat'.

The man's ex-wife answered the door but she declined to invite the social workers into the house. The interviewee's colleague explained that it was necessary for them to enter the house to check on the welfare of the children and to speak with the ex-husband about him being at home. Reluctantly the mother allowed the two social workers into the house.

The social workers walked into the living room where the curtains were drawn even though it was a 'scalding hot day' and this gave the room a 'cave-like appearance'. The house generally was in a state of squalor – 'you wiped your feet on the way out'. There were signs that the man was engaged in redecorating the room: torn paper littered the floor, a bucket of wallpaper paste stood on the floor and a pasting table stood in the middle of the room. The room had the appearance of clutter and mess. There were two men present: the ex-husband was crouched down with his back to the social workers as they entered. The interviewee described this man as dressed in a tee-shirt and jeans, 'very sweaty' and displaying a number of 'old tattoos' on his arms. His reddish hair was 'long, lank and thinning'. He was unshaven, dirty and smelly. 'If you saw the guy in the street you'd say "dodgy character", y'know.' The interviewee's colleague tried to engage the ex-husband in conversation, but received little or no response. The interviewee felt immediately intimidated because, not being able to see the man's face, he found it impossible to anticipate what the man might do next. On what appeared to the interviewee to be the pretext of continuing with the redecoration, the man busied himself in a very agitated fashion in pulling wallpaper from the wall and re-arranging things 'from one bundle of rubbish to another bundle of rubbish'. He spoke to himself, to his friend and to his ex-wife, but not to the social workers. The interviewee described the man's behaviour as a 'state of frenzy'. This refusal by the man to reply to the social workers' questions unsettled both social workers and the interviewee felt that this probably communicated a sense of nervousness to the two men present in the room. The interviewee felt that from the outset he and his colleague were 'one-nil down; on the back foot really' and from there on they were unable to 're-assert any sort of equilibrium at all'.

The other man who was present also failed to acknowledge the social workers. Instead he remained extremely calm and just 'eyeballed us' and 'coolly appraised us', which the interviewee found 'hugely intimidating'. Both men were smoking and that made the atmosphere more oppressive.

Realising that they were getting nowhere with the man, the interviewee's colleague said that they would allow the man a little time to calm down and instead would have a few words with the children. The ex-wife looked towards her ex-husband, who did not respond. She replied, 'Yes, I'll see if they're around.'

The two social workers left the living room and stepped into the kitchen. The interviewee felt that this was 'bad news' because there was no means of escape. The kitchen was piled high with rubbish and this prevented access to the exterior door. It was 'as if they hadn't emptied the bins for weeks'. The kitchen itself was dirty and grimy – 'shit rubbed into the wall to be honest'. The kettle and pots and pans were all dirty and grimy. Saucepans contained the remains of food and were left stacked on the stove. Work surfaces were dirty and cluttered. And it stank of 'that sour smell of unwashed clothes' and the smell of pets. It was 'flyblown and dark'.

The social workers stood in the doorway to the kitchen from the hallway. At first the ex-wife refused to speak to the social workers; instead she sent the children through to the kitchen. The couple had three children, the oldest of whom was 17 and although he suffered 'profound learning difficulties', he was not a matter of concern to the social workers. The social workers engaged this lad in 'small talk' whilst awaiting the other two children. The two younger boys (8–9 year olds) then arrived and the social workers spoke to them. They were the only two aspects of normality in the house, because they were two '"cheeky chappies" really'.

As the social workers chatted with the children, they could hear the man talking to his ex-wife in the sitting room and inferred that he was becoming progressively agitated. The noise level from the next room was escalating and the interviewee felt that the man was 'pumping himself up' with anger in order to confront the two social workers. The interviewee looked towards his colleague and inferred that the latter was as anxious as he was. All the while, the two social workers were trying to maintain a 'veneer of professionalism' by talking to the children in measured tones.

The ex-wife came through to the kitchen and said that her ex-husband was very unhappy about the social workers visiting and asked why they had come. So the interviewee's colleague explained the concerns that there were about the offences her ex-husband had committed and his history of violence and the implications that this had for the children. The ex-wife concluded this conversation by saying that she needed to go and get her ex-husband. During this conversation the two younger children left the kitchen.

She returned shortly afterwards in the company of her ex-husband. The social workers could clearly hear him approach down the corridor. Before he had entered the kitchen the man had begun to speak. The interviewee's colleague began by trying to explain why they had visited and the interviewee believed that for the first minute or so the man was listening and taking in what his colleague was saying. He also believed that the presence of two male social workers was seen by the man as a threat. However, the interviewee rapidly could see the man's comprehension and understanding deserting him to be replaced by anger. He then launched into 'a rant', saying 'how dare [the social workers] come into his house' and telling them to leave; all this punctuated by the frequent use of obscenities and the wagging of his finger. This prompted the interviewee to take a step backwards and as he did so was aware that he didn't want to be seen to be intimidated, but had he not stepped back he would have been 'well within range' of a punch.

Shortly afterwards, the man's finger wagging gave way to more expansive gestures of the hand. The interviewee can remember thinking 'somebody's going to get whacked here' and predicting that 'whoever talks the most or asks the most intrusive question is going to be the one who gets it'. The man kept telling the social workers to leave, but the only way to leave was to squeeze past him. 'The more we tried to get him to calm down, the more angry [the man] got.' The interviewee's colleague drew the man's attention to the fact of his conviction for a sexual assault on his niece. The man reacted by denying his guilt and asking the social workers if they were 'calling him a nonce' because he wasn't interested in little boys. The interviewee heard his colleague saying, 'If you'll just listen' and that, he thought, was 'really the wrong thing to say'. The man immediately replied, 'I'll not fucking listening to you, you won't listen to me.'

The interviewee admitted, 'All I wanted to do was to get out of the bloody house.' He felt trapped in what he described as a 'stinking house with crap everywhere'. The interviewee felt that he and his colleague were faltering: their questions were tailing off and being left unanswered. 'If anyone was being listened to it was [the ex-husband] not us.' As the man's 'tirade' continued so he appeared to the interviewee to grow physically and to fill the doorway. Behind the man the interviewee could see his ex-wife who appeared to be 'quite panicked by his behaviour' and the children were sitting on the stairs peering through the banister rails and appearing to shrink from the hostility of the situation in front of them. The interviewee began to think, 'We're never going to get out of here.' Then his colleague said, 'Look, we're going to go and see our manager.'

This seemed to have the desired effect and the man retreated a couple of steps into the hallway. The two social workers moved out of the kitchen and into the hallway, with the interviewee leading. Although only a few metres in length, the hallway was 'an assault course' with bundles of clothing lying around, the man, his ex-wife and children obstructing their path to the door. As the two social workers made their way along the hallway, the interviewee had 'one last obstacle', the man himself, to pass. As he attempted to do so the man the man suddenly stretched out his arm so that his hand rested on the opposite wall, thus blocking the interviewee's progress. This came as quite a shock to the interviewee who thought he was nearly free. The man and the interviewee were so close at this point that the interviewee could see and smell the sweat running down the man's arm and smell his tobacco-impregnated breath. The man thrust his face into that of the interviewee and said, 'Don't you fucking come here. I don't want to see you here again.' The interviewee replied, 'OK, OK, we're leaving now' and felt 'completely disempowered' because the social workers were leaving 'completely on his terms' and had achieved nothing. The man then withdrew his arm and allowed the interviewee to pass, following him to the front door.

Upon reaching the front door the interviewee opened it and stepped aside to allow his colleague to walk through. As he followed his colleague out of the house he was obliged to descend a couple of steps onto the path. As he did so he stumbled slightly in his haste to leave and simultaneously he felt a 'whooosh' from immediately behind his head. At first he did not realise what had happened, but now realises that the ex-husband had swung a fist at the back of his head and had just failed to connect because the interviewee had stumbled. Upon reaching the bottom of the steps, his colleague grabbed him and said, 'We've got to go; we've got to go.' As the two social workers walked along the front path the man dropped to his knees in the doorway and yelled after them, 'If you come back again I'll kill the children. I'll slit my throat on the doorstep. I'm not having you here again.' The interviewee said that as he walked along the front path, instead of walking with his back to the man, he walked backwards as if hypnotised by him. He remembered feeling with incredulity that the man might indeed actually harm himself as he had threatened.

The other side of the coin is more common, especially in A&E, where men are aggressive towards women. Clearly for many of the staff, the fact that it was men whom they faced added significantly to the threat potential of the incident. Reference was made in the previous chapter to the occasion when two young men tried to batter their way into the treatment area to gain access to a young female patient whom staff suspected these young men might have drugged (Case study 3.12). The nursing sister who recounted this episode made it clear that what added immeasurably to her anxiety was the fact that not only were these two apparently strong and fit young men, but also that all the staff on duty were female. Had the two young men succeeded in their attempt to break into the treatment area, she feared that there was little that the female staff could have done to protect their patient or themselves.

Because of the additional threat potential of men in confrontations with women, their words and behaviour carry much more significance. This is illustrated by the experience of a nursing sister who late one night stepped out into the waiting room to try to calm a group of young men, one of whom had sustained an injury to his scalp during a fight. They had been making a nuisance of themselves, demanding to know how much longer they would be obliged to wait. They had begun venting their frustration by beating on the reception security screen. The nursing sister hoped to be able to explain the situation calmly and reassure them that their friend would shortly receive treatment. However, once the group advanced towards her in what she perceived to be a menacing fashion, she fled into the sanctuary of the treatment area and summoned security guards. Young men, especially in a group, need not *do* very much for their actions to be seen as threatening.

Looking the part

This leads on to the wider issue of the role of appearance in inducing fear. For those who 'look the part' are able to instil fear whilst doing little. If they shout obscenities, utter threats of physical violence, and their faces become florid with rage, whilst their fists and teeth are clenched, then they are able to convey a much greater sense of menace than someone who does not 'look the part'. Indeed, they need hardly *do* anything at all in order to induce fear. This capacity to instil fear through appearance is illustrated in Case study 4.3. This concerned a man receiving community psychiatric treatment who affected an intimidating appearance. When his CPN visited to convey the news that he was moving to another job, all the man needed to do was abruptly stand up and begin denouncing the treatment that he had received from the local CMHT for the CPN to flee in near panic.

Case Study 4.3: Shaven-headed thug

The interviewee was a male Community Psychiatric Nurse in his late 30s who related an incident that occurred at a previous CMHT when he had taken over the caseload of another CPN who was temporarily absent. The incident occurred during a home visit, the purpose of which was to inform the patient that the CPN was moving to another job and to explain arrangements for his care and treatment during the change-over.

The patient lived in the community under no restriction despite a long history of violence and including several terms of imprisonment for violent crime. He was deemed to be suffering from paranoid schizophrenia, a diagnosis that the CPN disputed – he thought the man was psychopathic. He had no conscience about hurting or harming people and no remorse when he did. He had had a very disturbed childhood and had begun his criminal career at a young age. The patient also had a large, aggressive German Shepherd dog.

The CPN from whom the interviewee had inherited this patient had expressed great anxieties about visiting this patient. He had said that the patient was very unpredictable and so this CPN advised his successor to always sit near the door in order to make an escape if needed. The interviewee came to the view that the man was deeply disturbed, unpredictable and aggressive, which made it difficult to become involved in any therapeutic work with him. The CPN came to regard his role as simply monitoring the patient in the community. The man 'oozed anger' and had a very aggressive demeanour. He was paranoid and had got into fights because he interpreted other people as hostile.

The CPN arrived at the patient's house at around 9.30 am. The man lived on a private housing estate with narrow winding roads that made it difficult to park and so he did not leave his car directly outside the house. He had assumed that the meeting would be pretty routine.

He went to the door where usually he was met by the man's wife, but on this occasion there was no sign of her. The wife was very effective at defusing the man's anger. The man opened the door and invited the CPN into the kitchen. In the centre of the kitchen was a white-topped round table and four chairs. The CPN sat in the chair nearest to the door with the patient sitting immediately opposite and the dog lying down to the CPN's right. The dog watched the CPN intently and was quickly aroused by any rapid movement. The man was about the same age as the CPN but looked older. He was smaller than the CPN with very muscular, highly tattooed arms. He was wearing a tight tee-shirt that accentuated his muscular appearance. He had closely cropped hair and wore an earring in his right ear. 'He looked what he was – a thug!' said the CPN.

After some preliminaries about how the patient was feeling and whether he was taking his medication, the CPN said, 'Well, I have to tell you that I'll soon be leaving and you'll have someone else coming to visit you.' The man sprang to his feet and angrily said that the CPN had let him down by leaving now and that the CPN was useless and no good anyway. The man's voice was raised, but not shouting. The dog also sprang to its feet and was barking at the CPN. The CPN was quite frightened by this sudden explosion of anger and felt that the man could easily assault him physically, but he was self-consciously trying to give the appearance of remaining calm. He tried to explain why he was leaving and what alternative arrangements would be made, but the man's aggression was unrelenting. So (remembering the advice of his predecessor), he slowly stood up (so as not to provoke the dog in any way) and said that he did not think it was very useful continuing the conversation so he would arrange for someone to contact the patient about the new arrangements, turned away from the dog and slowly walked the short distance to the door and left. As he did so, the man continued to abuse him, telling him to get out. The CPN was surprised that the man had reacted in this way because hitherto he had given the appearance of not particularly wanting the CPN to visit – 'You can if you want. It's up to you.'

The interviewee walked directly, but not hurriedly, to his car, locked himself in and sat collecting his thoughts for a moment. He then realised that the man might attack the car, so he drove a short distance, parked and gathered himself before continuing to the office where he immediately wrote up his case notes on the incident. He felt very relieved at having got out of the house.

Men who sport shaven heads, aggressive tattoos professing allegiance to far-right political groups, develop muscular torsos that they display through tight-fitting garments, might legitimately be thought to be cultivating a 'tough' or even 'violent' persona. In so doing they presumably *seek* to intimidate others by their mere presence. However, in some cases a person's appearance may not be contrived and the reaction they have upon others may not be desired. This possibility is illustrated by a homeless drug addict suffering from jaundice whose annoyance with the treatment he had previously received at A&E acquired additional menace because of his squalid appearance (Case study 4.4).

Case study 4.4: Angry jaundiced patient

The interviewee was performing triage during a busy, but otherwise unexceptional, morning. She stood in the open doorway into the waiting room to summon the next patient. A man in his mid-20s responded and walked towards her: tall and 'skinny', with ginger/blonde hair cut in a crew cut, he wore an earring and he was unshaven, with stubble around his chin. He was dressed in a dirty bomber jacket and jeans. His appearance was unkempt, with yellow teeth, and he suffered body odour. He had scabs and abrasions over his exposed skin (including his face) and kept scratching his arms. The nurse detected signs of the man being an IV drug user. He also looked as though he had been in a fight, because his eyes were bruised. She felt immediately intimidated as soon as she saw the man because his general demeanour indicated that he was very angry. He was very tense and walked quickly past her and into the triage room. At first he refused to sit down, and strode around with his fists clenched. The nurse remained standing herself, unwilling to sit down before the man did. As she stood there she put on a pair of gloves. After a little while he yielded to the nurse's insistence that he sit down, but he did not sit comfortably; instead he remained on the edge of his seat with his fists clenched and unable to keep still, staring at the nurse who also sat down.

During this initial phase, the man had persistently shouted that he had been to A&E before and they had done nothing for him; that they did not care about him because he was a homeless drug-user. She asked what the problem was and his reaction was that, 'You can see what my bloody problem is can't you?' The man was jaundiced and his skin was correspondingly yellow. The nurse asked him to explain what was wrong. He replied, 'Well look at the colour of me – I'm yellow! Every time I wee it's bright yellow and it's not right is it?' The nurse asked when the problem had started. The man replied, 'You damn well know when it started. I've been here three times already and you lot do nothing about it.' As he said this he moved his chair closer to the nurse so that they were now sitting very close together. She asked when he had been to the A&E before and the man replied that it had been two days previously. The nurse asked what had been done then and the man shouting very loudly in reply, 'Nothing!' He continued in a loud voice, 'You didn't do anything; no one told me anything; no one wants to know. They know I use drugs and no one cares about me because they know I haven't got a place to live. And you know I use drugs and you think I'm a waster and don't care.' The nurse said, 'OK, but can you just tell me what they actually did?' The man then began striking his forehead with the heel of his right hand and saying, 'I don't fucking believe what I'm hearing. I'm going to smash your head in in a minute.' As he said this the man half rose from his chair, but then resumed his seated position. This threat made the nurse 'cross' that he was speaking to her like this. She didn't think that the man would really hit her. The nurse was 'firm' with him at this point and said that he was not to speak to her like that and that if he did so she would get security to eject him from the department. The nurse then said, 'OK, just calm down. All I want to know is what the problem is; what we did for you last time; and what you think we can do for you this time. I can't do anything for you without the facts. I need the facts. You say we've not helped you. I want to help you, but to do that I need the facts.' The man apologised and acknowledged that his previous treatment was not the nurse's responsibility. Having apologised, the man immediately returned to being abusive. The man repeated himself.

The Sister opened the door that the patients use to enter triage and behind the man's back mouthed, 'Are you all right? Shall I get Security?' The nurse replied that she was fine and there was no need for Security. Thereafter, the nurse was aware that the Sister was 'hanging around' in the vicinity, which gave her reassurance and confidence in dealing with the man. So the nurse tried to explain what the system was, what they could and couldn't do for him. She was able to ascertain from the man that on his last visit he had given a blood sample for analysis and that he had been advised to attend the sexually transmitted disease clinic. She asked when he had been scheduled to visit the clinic and the man replied 'Today'. So she asked why he wasn't there now. The man replied that he had been to the clinic, but they had said that they did not want to see him 'because they don't care about me either'. He accused the A&E staff of sending him to the clinic as a ruse to get rid of him. She was unable to ascertain why the clinic had not seen him, but suspected that it was because he had been aggressive there also.

Thereafter the nurse tried repeatedly to calm the man, but his mood continued to oscillate between apologetic quiescence and boisterous anger. Finally, he was taken to a cubicle because he was too agitated to return to the waiting room. Eventually, the man was seen by a doctor and admitted because he was actually quite ill. As soon as he knew that he was being admitted he was fine.

In the previous case study one might argue that the reaction of the nurse resulted from the patient's lifestyle for which he must accept some responsibility. However, Case study 4.5 puts these issues into particularly acute relief, for the fact that this patient, apart from being difficult and demanding, also had the appearance of a *black* drug-dealer suggests that racism might play a part in what people find threatening. We will return to issues of racism in the final chapter; suffice to say here that this interviewee was by no means alone in drawing attention (unbidden) to the race of the person with whom she was in conflict. For instance, the Sister who described how two young men tried to break in to the treatment area to gain access to a female patient (Case study 3.12) drew explicit attention to their race.

Case Study 4.5: Bejewelled black youth

During a busy night shift, about 3 am, two young men were admitted to A&E with injuries sustained in a fight with each other. One was seriously injured and lying in 'Resus' receiving treatment for a life-threatening stab wound, and the other was in a cubicle awaiting treatment for a head wound. The staff had been mindful of the need to keep the two opponents apart. There were about six police officers present in A&E because there had been a serious traffic accident in addition to the stabbing and their high-visibility jackets made them conspicuous. However, the nursing staff on duty were exclusively female and so was the duty doctor.

The nurse returned from an errand to find the second man standing outside the cubicle to which he had been assigned;

instead of remaining in the cubicle he was wandering around looking at the computers. The interviewee described the man as being African-Caribbean, of average height, slim with short hair. He was wearing a leather jacket and considerable amount of gold jewellery (which she laughingly described as 'sounding very stereotypical, doesn't it'). He was about 19–20 years old. She thought he looked 'dodgy', but that was nothing unusual on a Saturday night. She wasn't frightened by him, but she was wary of him.

In accord with normal practice she approached the man and asked, 'Would you mind remaining in your cubicle and wait your turn to see the doctor? We have lots of people coming through, ambulances coming through, people on trolleys, so if you wouldn't mind...?' She also feared that the man was checking out where the police were and might have been planning to resume his fight with his opponent. The man agreed to return to his cubicle. She understood from colleagues that others had asked him to remain in his cubicle previously.

A few minutes later she had occasion to go down that side of the department and again the man was outside his cubicle, walking around. She caught his eye as she approached and the man returned to his cubicle without either the nurse or the man saying anything.

About an hour later, she was standing doing some administrative task at the nursing station and she heard raised voices. She looked down the corridor to see this same man and the female doctor on duty standing in the middle of the corridor. In a raised voice the man was demanding to be treated immediately so that he could go home. The doctor was calmly explaining to the man that they could not stitch over a possible fracture site and an X-ray was needed before further treatment was given. The man was towering over the doctor, standing very close to her and was quite intimidating. The doctor was retreating as the man repeatedly invaded her personal space. The man was saying, 'I don't want an X-ray. I don't need it. I don't want anything. Just let me go.' Because she was now the only other staff member in the vicinity the nurse felt it particularly important to show solidarity with the doctor, whom she described as a woman of only small stature. So the nurse walked down the corridor towards the pair of them to give the doctor moral support and addressing the man by his first name asked, on her arrival, 'What's the problem?' The doctor repeated what she had told the patient and the nurse supported her. She found that the man now 'backed off' in her presence. She said to the man that he had obviously suffered a serious blow to the head that caused him to come to hospital. They would not be happy to let him go until they were satisfied that he was fit to do so and that there was someone at home to look after him. The man's response was that he wanted to go. So, the nurse said it was his choice. He could leave if he wanted to do so. He could self-discharge, refuse treatment and leave. All he needed to do was to sign the form. The man insisted on being stitched before he left, but the nurse and doctor explained that they would not stitch over the site of a suspected fracture. She described his demeanour at this stage as being 'very staring' and standing very close in an intimidating way. He seemed very angry and agitated, probably as a consequence of the fight in which he had been involved. She felt quite scared, but also felt that one cannot allow people to 'walk all over you'. So, again, she told him that he could discharge himself if he insisted. The man replied, 'Fine', but didn't wait and walked directly out into the waiting room through the nearby door.

The man and his companions, who were waiting in the waiting room, remained in the hospital for some considerable time. Eventually they became involved in an altercation with an associate of the man who had been stabbed and the police were called. The man left in a taxi before the police arrived.

Signs of trouble

A person's appearance is an obvious sign of impending threat, but many of those interviewed were attentive to other indications that the person they were dealing with might prove troublesome. This was particularly true of police officers and A&E staff, both of whose working environments were populated by other people whom they did not know and about whom they had only the most meagre information (see Table 4.2). The signs of trouble to which they were particularly attentive were: mental illness, emotional disturbance, drunkenness and drug use; delinquency; and the presence of others.

Mental illness

All four occupations routinely have contact with people suffering mental illnesses that might lead to unpredictable, volatile and potentially dangerous behaviour. Attention has already been drawn to some of

Table 4.2 Knowledge of antagonists

	Known	Unknown
Mental health	16	4
Social work	13	7
Accident and Emergency	3	19
Police	3	46*

*In a further five cases it was unclear whether the officer had any knowledge of the person they were dealing with, but at most it was very limited knowledge

the problems that might arise: the boy suffering Asperger's syndrome who attacked his mother with a dog lead; the autistic child in the residential home who launched an unprovoked physical assault on the supervising social worker. The impression that those suffering mental illness represent a threat is supported by wider research.

Despite continued assertions to the contrary, individuals experiencing almost all forms of mental illness appear, in many studies, to show an increased predisposition to violence. The degree of risk shows considerable variation by diagnosis. Those experiencing severe mental illness, particularly schizophrenia, are significantly more likely to commit acts of serious violence, including homicide, than individuals who are not mentally ill, even when other variables are controlled for. (Paterson and Stark 2001)

Even if the person poses no apparent and immediate threat, bizarre behaviour can itself prove very discomfiting. This is illustrated by Case study 4.6, in which a young man of Far Eastern origin behaved in a bizarre and unpredictable manner whilst undergoing triage in A&E.

Case Study 4.6: Bizarre Kung-Fu display

The interviewee, a middle-aged woman, was in triage when a young (early 20s), tall, slim, smartly dressed man of Far Eastern appearance came for assessment accompanied by another man of similar appearance who announced himself to be the younger man's employer. The young man did not speak English and the employer had come to explain and translate.

The two men sat down facing the nurse. The patient sat before her very erect, smart, smiling and tranquil. The employer then explained that he was worried about the young man's behaviour, for he was acting rather bizarrely at times. The nurse was busily writing down her notes of what was being said in the small space allocated on the form. At this stage everything seemed routine. Then the young man started speaking in a foreign language and gently stroking the nurse's arm. The nurse turned to the employer and asked what the young man was saying. The employer replied that the young man was addressing the nurse as 'mother'. She then appreciated that perhaps the patient did have behavioural-psychiatric problems and her inclination was to award a high priority to prevent him becoming distressed by waiting in the waiting room. However, she did not feel at all alarmed by his behaviour and she allowed him to stroke her arm.

Abruptly, the young man stood up and began kicking the air in a Kung-Fu style to accompanying shouts and screams in what sounded like Chinese to the nurse. The nurse was greatly alarmed by this sudden eruption. Since she was sitting very close to the man, she used the castors on the swivel chair to push herself away towards the door into the nurses' area. Very soon the other door to the triage room was opened by one of the nurse's colleagues, who asked if everything was all right. By this time, the nurse had come to appreciate that the man's actions were not directed at her and they had, at least momentarily, ceased. So she replied that everything was fine.

She then asked if 'cubicle 11 is free' and suggested that this might be a suitable place to go to. Cubicle 11 is a small room that was used for the purpose, among others, of keeping psychiatric patients reasonably secure and private. So, the nurse stood up and said, 'I think we'd better just go down the corridor and let one of the doctors examine you.' She and her colleague escorted the two men down the treatment corridor to cubicle 11. The two men walked meekly between the two nurses and there was no problem. Upon arriving at cubicle 11 the nurse showed them in but did not enter the room with the men. She understood that the man was later admitted as a psychiatric in-patient.

Whilst the nurse accepted that this man presented no harm, other A&E staff recalled occasions when mentally ill patients had presented an aggressive or deeply offensive manner (see Case study 6.3).

Police also routinely come into contact with psychiatrically disturbed people, occasionally in the strangest circumstances. Case study 4.7 shows how an initially humorous encounter unpredictably degenerated into a violent struggle.

Case Study 4.7: Girl wanting to be arrested

The interviewee and his colleague were conveying a suspect to the police station and their patrol car was stationary on a narrow ramp leading to the cells. The interviewee became aware of a car squeezing its way alongside their own down the ramp. At its steering wheel was an attractive young woman. Through the passenger window he asked what she wanted, her reply was, 'I'm pissed, do you want to arrest me?' His initial reaction was that this was a wind-up and he said 'No'. He squeezed out of the patrol car and was very apprehensive about the situation he was in, effectively trapped between the two cars. He bent down as best he could and as he did so smelt alcohol on the woman's breath and he now realised that her speech was slurred. She repeated 'I'm pissed' and the interviewee reached into the car and removed the ignition key. Then she got out of the car. She was laughing very loudly. She said that she had been drinking and needed a place to stay for the night.

The interviewee described the young woman as white, about 5' 6" tall, of average build with dark brown hair cropped to about 2 millimetres long so that her scalp was visible. She had an earring in one ear and a pair of designer-label sunglasses perched on the top of her head and a set of headphones stuck in her ears with tape machine in her pocket. She wore a tee-shirt, combat trousers and training shoes.

Once the young woman was out of the car, his colleague drove the patrol car into the custody block whilst the interviewee escorted the young woman to the custody door. As they walked she started screaming at the top of her voice about 'fucking police,' 'never trust the police' and 'you can never get a policeman when you want one'. The interviewee recognised by this time that it was not just the alcohol talking and that there was something wrong with this girl.

As they entered the custody suite the female gaoler greeted the young woman by name. *Sotto voce* the gaoler explained to the interviewee that the young woman was well known to the police because she was periodically committed under the Mental Health Act.

Whilst the gaoler was trying to get her name, address and other relevant details the young woman was walking around the charge room chanting, 'never trust the police, you can never find the fucking pigs when you want them'. Whilst this was going on she interspersed it with replies to the gaoler punctuated with swearing. The custody sergeant allowed her to walk around shouting so long as she was not causing problems and they got all the information they needed. She said that if she was put in a cell she would kick, scream and head butt anything to keep the police 'bastards' awake. So she was allowed to sit in the custody suite where the officers on duty kept an eye on her. She made abusive comments to people who came in to the custody suite but she tended to make them laugh.

Eventually she was taken to give a specimen of breath. She said 'Oh good I like this bit it makes me feel rude' and she cooperatively blew into the machine and was tested 'positive'. This now meant that she would be placed in a cell rather than left in the custody suite.

Once she had been searched she sat back down on the bench and the custody sergeant directed that she should be placed in the female cell. The interviewee, assisted by a female colleague, told the young woman to go with him to the cell but she refused. It was then that she became resistant. The interviewee explained to her that she would have to go in the cell even if it was just for a little while because she could not remain in the custody suite. He took hold of one of her arms. She did not resist but just sat there, so he had to stand her up. The woman officer then assisted by directing the young woman towards the cell. As they reached the cell they stopped and the young woman said that she was not going into the cell. The interviewee turned the lights on but it did not make any difference to the girl. The interviewee said that he and his colleague pressed her arms to her sides so that she could get through the door and walked her into the cell. Once in the cell the young woman sat down on the bench without resistance.

She announced that the officers were not taking her shoes. The officers insisted that her shoes must be removed. She refused. The interviewee felt it was almost as if she was challenging them to get her shoes off her. The interviewee grabbed her legs and the woman officer grabbed her arms. The young woman kicked the interviewee and he told her to calm down, but she replied that as soon as the officers tried to walk out she was going to try to get out of the door. The woman officer grabbed one of her arms and threw her onto the floor so that she was on her stomach face down on the floor and she then began to struggle. The woman officer sat on her but her legs were flailing, so the interviewee held her legs and had his knees either side of her legs. He clamped her legs together and pulled her shoes off and held her ankles together. She was screaming that they were beating her up. The interviewee tried to put her legs in a figure of four but her legs were really strong and he could not bend one of her legs up. The interviewee jumped out of the way but she did manage to kick him, but she did not have any shoes on. The two police officers tried to get out of the door but she got there first and just stood in their way in the doorway with her hands gripping the doorjamb. The interviewee said that they ended up pulling both hands off the inside of the doorjamb by her fingers and then he pushed her and she fell to the floor, landing on her bum. The officers just shut the door and looked at each other and almost laughed.

Emotion

Apart from the kind of continuing psychiatric condition exhibited by the young woman in Case study 4.7, some situations can provoke more or less intense emotional disturbance in those who do not suffer mental illness. For instance, the parents of a small child who had been brought to A&E with a minor head injury became irate when, having completed the X-ray, they were kept waiting for an hour before the doctor was able to see them again and discharge the little girl. The doctor readily conceded that it was unfortunate that they had waited so long and acknowledged that the delay may have provoked some alarm at the possibility that the injury was more serious than it appeared. She imagined that when she was eventually able to return to the little girl only to discharge her and give advice about head injury, this may have appeared anticlimactic or even dismissive, thereby inadvertently causing irritation to parents already suffering some stress. A&E staff are familiar with such problems that arise from the sometimes lengthy and unpredictable delays in treatment, especially late at night when people are drunk.

Social workers dealing with child protection issues have the additional problem that they are sometimes conveyors of bad news, for instance that children are to be taken into care. This is the focus of Case study 4.8 in which an otherwise placid woman suddenly and unpredictably lashed out at the news, breaking a glass-fronted display cabinet to the alarm of those present.

Case Study 4.8: Smashed glass door

The family had been known to Social Services for a long while because of a history of criminality in which the children were used as accomplices and the use of the family home by local youngsters for smoking dope; inappropriate sexual behaviour by adults in the presence of the children; and general neglect. Being both a depressive and an alcoholic the mother was unable to respond to many of the suggestions and initiatives of her social worker. Now it had been decided to remove the children into care.

The interviewee and her supervisor arrived at the house at about 5 pm after a tiring day making arrangements. On the way to the house, it was agreed that the supervisor would lead the conversation because she was more familiar with the mother than the interviewee. The interviewee would take the children to the placement and get the parents to sign the relevant paperwork. There was no expectation that the mother would be aggressive. However, the supervisor had insisted that she should accompany the interviewee because it was an unpleasant task to perform. Although the interviewee was a little discomfited finding herself in such a difficult situation so early in her career, she also had confidence in her supervisor as someone who knew the ropes and could handle the situation.

Although the house looked quite 'respectable' from the outside, it was 'chaos'. There was a gaggle of young people around the front of the house. The social workers pushed their way through the milling throng, which left her feeling rather apprehensive because she wondered how these youngsters might react to the removal of the children.

The social workers walked into the sitting room where the mother was sitting in the corner of the room. Next to the mother sat her sister-in-law on a sofa with her own child. The interviewee was taken aback because earlier in the day she had been speaking to the mother's sister-in-law, who had been expressing concern for the mother and her mental health. Yet it was now evident to the interviewee that the sister-in-law had spent the day shoplifting with the mother. Moreover, the interviewee inferred that the two women had taken their children with them whilst they were shoplifting. The interviewee sat on this sofa and her supervisor sat in a chair a little nearer to the mother.

Then the father of children – who was now estranged from the mother – arrived and stood in the doorway. He was very tall and filled the door frame. He appeared 'miserable and fed up, but not angry'. He hadn't been drinking, but looked as though he had. He had eyes that looked as though 'he wanted to get away from life', he looked tired. He didn't look aggressive. The interviewee was surprised that the father looked so attractive. However, the interviewee thought that his position in the doorway had a slightly menacing element because it 'was blocking us all in'.

The interviewee describes the mother as appearing very passive. She wasn't happy, but this did not prevent her from laughing if she found something funny. She often laughed immediately after saying something herself.

The supervisor began to engage the mother in conversation and to explain why the social workers were there. The mother interrupted to say that she knew why the social workers had come. She alleged that another member of the family had prevented the mother from collecting her children from school at the instigation of the social workers. The supervisor reassured her that this was not so and that they would not have told someone else before they had spoken to the mother.

The father remained standing in the doorway, looking at the mother with a demeanour that suggested that he was pretty fed up. He interjected that he had foretold that this would happen but the mother replied, telling him to shut up and that it was nothing to do with him. She followed this by telling the father to get out but he refused, telling the mother that she had to face up to the situation. The mother began to get progressively more excited and began shouting at the father, telling him to 'fuck off, fuck off' very loudly. The father was replying by saying, 'For goodness sake, for goodness sake, shut up, shut up'. The mother was progressively wound up until she was 'screaming her head off at him'. The father was repeatedly telling his ex-partner to calm down and edging forward towards her as he did so. The mother was replying by telling the father to get out or she would kill him.

The interviewee became increasingly anxious because she did not know what might happen. She feared that the mother might physically attack her or her supervisor. She felt no threat from the father. On the other hand, the mother might calm down of her own accord. She just didn't know what to expect. Having familiarised herself with the case history, the interviewee felt reasonably reassured that she and her colleague would be safe, because there was no evidence of previous violence on the part of the mother. Yet, since this was the first time that the mother had had her children taken into care she was conscious that the mother might do anything.

The mother threatened that if the father didn't desist she would hit something. Then the mother flung her fist to her left and hit a glass-fronted display cabinet, causing the glass to shatter. The father responded by saying something like, 'Don't start that. Don't be ridiculous.' The supervisor said to the mother, 'Look, you've ruined your cabinet now' and then turned to the father and suggested that it would be best if he was to leave them. The supervisor turned to the interviewee and asked rhetorically if she wanted to have a chat with the father outside whilst she remained with the mother. So the interviewee rose and walked over to the father, inviting him to step out of the house. She and the father then went into the garden where they chatted amicably for a few minutes and were joined by the eldest daughter.

A doctor was called and gave the mother some medication to help calm her down. The social workers were then able to remove the children without there being any further aggression or disorder.

Drunkenness

Drunkenness played a part in the events depicted in Case study 4.8 and was a common feature in many of the violent or hostile encounters that interviewees recalled. Needless to say, dealing with drunken people has been a staple of police work since the inception of professional policing in 1829. It is equally clear that the growth of 'binge drinking' among young people has done nothing to reduce confrontations between police and drunken young people, nor to mollify their volatile nature (Hobbs *et al.* 2003). Case study 4.9 is an unexceptional example of such routine encounters for police officers that nonetheless highlights how drunkenness elevates an otherwise routine encounter into a volatile situation needing careful management.

Case Study 4.9: Drunken dispute

The interviewee was the only sergeant on duty when he heard two calls broadcast by the control room asking for officers to attend separate fights in different locations. The sergeant decided to attend the nearest fight, on the forecourt of the railway station.

On arrival at the scene the interviewee could see a PC surrounded by five youths aged about 18 years old. One, wearing a white top, had clearly been injured and had blood over his face and clothing. According to the interviewee the youths were 'the worse for wear through drink'. They were casually but smartly dressed. A short distance away another officer was trying to contain the occupants of a 17-seater minibus. (He quickly learnt that the bus and passengers had been detained by station security who had apparently come across the fight and had tried to break it up and then prevented the bus from leaving.)

Simultaneous with the sergeant's arrival another police car arrived containing two officers, one of whom was a particularly new probationer.

The interviewee joined the PC who had been talking to the five lads to find out what had happened. The youths surrounding the PC were angry that one of them had been assaulted and wanted the police to arrest the people on the bus. The PC explained to the interviewee what he had been able to glean so far: both groups had been drinking in a nearby pub and two of the people from the bus had assaulted the victim, breaking his nose. The altercation happened because the group from the bus thought one of the youths had been selling drugs and had tried to 'chat up' their girlfriends. The interviewee directed the officer and another PC present to search the youth accused of selling drugs but no drugs were found.

The interviewee then went to the bus, which contained a mixture of men and women aged about 20–25 years, none of whom had been injured. They were from a pub in a nearby village (including the pub's landlord) and had been celebrating a stag party. In the interviewee's opinion the landlord was 'fairly responsible': he was older than the others and apparently respected by them. The interviewee commented that had it not been for the landlord they 'would have had major problems'. The interviewee acted as liaison between the two police units and took responsibility to keep the station updated with the situation. He also asked for the CCTV to be trained onto the scene but the operators were off duty.

The interviewee returned to the group of five youths, none of whom could identify the assailants. Moreover, the victim did not want to make a statement or make a decision whether he was prepared to go to court until he had spoken to his father. He said that his father was a solicitor but was unavailable at that time as he was abroad, although due to return the following day. They had been drinking and were upset that one of them had been assaulted and wanted those responsible arrested. The interviewee did not want to arrest anyone until he was satisfied that the assailants had been properly identified and that the victim would subsequently attend court and give evidence. The youths found this approach difficult to accept and were aggressive and confrontational with the police. The interviewee described how one youth with blond hair was shouting and swearing and then began to poke him. He commented that he was prepared to tolerate shouting and being sworn at but not physical contact. He told the youth that if he poked him again he would be arrested. This warning caused the youth to stop and seemed to quell the aggression of his companions.

Then another of the PCs present introduced the interviewee to a man whom the PC knew personally and who had seen the assault and could identify the assailants. However, this witness was reluctant to get involved as he was living in the bail hostel and was in breach of his curfew. The interviewee contacted the control room and directed them to contact the bail hostel to inform them that the witness was helping police with their enquiries. On hearing this, the witness was reassured and agreed to identify the suspects. The offenders were sitting side by side in the bus and the witness was able to simply point them out to the interviewee.

The interviewee returned to the victim and told him that he now knew who the suspects were and that he was prepared to arrest them there and then. However, first he needed the victim to make a decision as to whether or not he was prepared to go to court, although he could make a statement later. The victim was still unable to decide without first speaking with his father. The interviewee considered the possibility of contacting his solicitor by telephone but the victim declined to say who he was. After consulting the two PCs who had been first on the scene, it was decided to give the victim one of the PC's business cards and ask him to make contact in the morning when he had made up his mind.

The interviewee then returned to the bus where he again spoke to the landlord, telling him that two passengers had been identified as being responsible for carrying out the assault and that he wanted to speak to them and obtain their details before allowing them all to leave. The interviewee persuaded the two suspects to leave the bus. One was 6ft. tall and about 18 stone, the other was about 5ft. 10 inches tall, well built and a bricklayer. Whilst checks were being carried out on the details supplied by the suspects, two women got off the bus. They were drunk and verbally aggressive, wanting to know why the youth accused of drug-dealing had not been arrested. He went on to describe them as being quite well dressed but wearing a lot of make-up and looking like a 'couple of tarts'. The interviewee explained to the women that the youth accused of drug-dealing had been searched and no drugs had been found. The two suspects told the women to get back on the bus and their friends returned them to the bus. The interviewee said that he explained to both suspects what was going to happen and that they were compliant and cooperative; he deduced that their conduct showed that they had committed the offence and that they believed they were 'on a sticky wicket'. He also said that he thought that the landlord must have told them that they were not going to be arrested or charged and that knowing what was going to happen had influenced their behaviour.

Shortly afterwards the minibus was allowed to leave and an ambulance arrived to take the injured man to hospital.

Delinquency

Where people have a history of delinquency any threat they pose is increased by the credibility that comes from having committed similar acts in the past. Clearly the threat potential of even a young adolescent can rise significantly when that child has a history of delinquency and unruliness, for this adds credibility to his or her actions, as Case study 4.10 demonstrates.

Case Study 4.10: Delinquent with a gun

The incident occurred in the home of a client with whom the interviewee had been working for some time. The client's son had recently been released from a 'secure foster placement' and returned home. The interviewee understood that the son had

had a tumultuous relationship with his step-father and had a long history of committing minor criminal offences, mostly theft, and had run away from home on several occasions. He also hung around with a group of 'older lads'. The son also had a reputation of being intimidating, aggressive and abusive towards other people generally. He had been placed in a 'secure foster placement' for several weeks because, although his offences were minor, he repeatedly refused to attend court. Whilst the son was in this secure setting he had received some intense therapeutic intervention. Nevertheless, he did commit a number of offences whilst he was there. The interviewee's role was to support the mother and look after the welfare of her son and help them develop some guidelines about appropriate behaviour. The aim was to get the mother into a support network on a one-to-one basis.

On the day in question the interviewee arrived at the house of the client at about 9.30 am. She felt 'a little bit anxious' because she had had two previous encounters with the son, both of which had been in a 'meeting format' and she had experienced him as 'moody and verbal'. In the first of these meetings he had been 'really abusive: he just swore his head off'. He had been 'really angry because he had been given an 8 o'clock curfew, so he was really angry'. So, the interviewee 'knew that he was aggressive, unreasonable and difficult to talk to'. On the second occasion that the interviewee had met the boy it was the day after he had received a supervision order from the court. The meeting was with the Youth Offending Team and again the son had been aggressive and unreasonable.

At the same time the interviewee was interested in meeting him in the domestic context and on a one-to-one basis. The interviewee knew something of the history of the family and realised that the son had been 'scapegoated from pillar to post' by his step-father. The family consisted of two older children, including the son, by the mother's first partner, and three younger ones by the step-father. She felt that this encouraged the marginalisation and isolation of the older children. The mother was, in the judgement of the interviewee, 'ineffectual'. The interviewee had worked with children in similar circumstances before and was hopeful that she could develop a good relationship with this boy. So it was with distinctly mixed feelings that she approached the visit.

The mother opened the door whilst simultaneously speaking on the telephone that hung just inside the front door. The mother waved the interviewee into the house, but when the interviewee approached the sitting room the mother stopped her and explained that her son was in that room asleep with his friend. This unsettled the interviewee, for she started to wonder who the 'mate' was. She also wondered whether the son would be angered by the fact that she had arrived early whilst he was still in bed.

The interviewee continued along the hallway and into the kitchen. It was quite noisy and busy, with the washing machine going. In the kitchen there were three children with whom the interviewee made amicable and polite conversation. The interviewee described this encounter with the children as 'quite fun' and laughed as she recounted it.

The children left the interviewee and mother alone and the two of them began talking, the interviewee sitting on a folding chair in the middle of the kitchen. The mother busied herself around the kitchen whilst talking to the interviewee. Meanwhile, the children in the family were going in and out of the sitting room where the son had been sleeping with 'his mate' and from the snatches of conversation that she could hear, the interviewee deduced from shouted obscenities that the son knew that the interviewee had arrived.

After a little while the son stood in the doorway of the kitchen. The interviewee described him as 13 years old; shorter than her [about 5 foot] with short medium-brown hair and freckles. He was 'skinny' and was wearing tracksuit bottoms and a dark top. What was most noticeable was the angry expression on his face. The interviewee could not see the sitting room door from where she was sitting and found it unnerving, especially when the son appeared in the doorway a couple of metres away from where the interviewee was sitting (within reaching distance). The interviewee was drinking a cup of tea and had just taken a sip. She had to swivel around to her right in order to see him.

Addressing the interviewee, who remained seated, he began to reel off all the obligations he had not fulfilled [e.g. to see his Probation Officer] and challengingly declared that there was nothing that the interviewee could do about it – 'You think you can tell me what to do, but you can't. I haven't been to my meetings...' She described the content of what the son said as being 'childish' and betraying the image of toughness that he was trying to convey. Again, this was accompanied by obscenities, but it was delivered at medium volume rather than shouted. He accompanied this with more or less aggressive hand gestures and moved around in an agitated fashion. This prompted some anxiety in the interviewee and she was conscious of how she was presenting herself and intent on showing that she was not unnerved by what he was saying. She was deliberately seeking ways of avoiding been dragged into a squabble with the boy at his childish level. She wanted to 'get rid of him' so that she and mother could continue their conversation. The interviewee replied 'That's OK, that's not my role here. If you've got a problem ... talk to your Probation Officer ... I'm not here for that; I'm here to see your mum.' The son responded by saying, 'How ridiculous. What the fucking hell are you doing here at 9 o'clock in the morning? What do ya think you're playing at? And how pathetic is that?' The interviewee answered, 'Well actually, this was a planned arrangement with your mum, a couple of weeks ago. So don't worry about it, I'm here to talk to your mum, not you. So let's just drop it.'

The son then returned to the sitting room in an obviously disgruntled mood. The interviewee explained her strategy as one of trying to deflect the son's anger away from herself – what she called a 'defence mechanism'. She hoped that the son would think, 'There's no point in being angry with that person because she hasn't got authority over me.' Once the boy left, the interviewee thought to herself 'That's it.' However, the encounter left the interviewee feeling a little more nervous: 'Oh dear, he's not in a good mood and he doesn't like the idea that I'm here'. She also realised, with regret, that there was little prospect of being able to spend a little time with the son that day to try to establish some measure of rapport.

During this exchange between the interviewee and the son, his mother had simply stood and watched without comment. The interviewee thought to herself, 'You [the mother] aren't taking this seriously are you? Why aren't you freaked out? Why aren't you worried?' After the son had left, but still in hushed tones, the mother referred to her son's behaviour and advised the interviewee to take no notice of it and at first tried to make out that everything was OK. However, she then admitted that things had been difficult since her son had returned from care. She said that her son had been out until 3 am and had been stealing things. She mentioned a 'bin load of CDs' that her son had stolen. The interviewee said that she had made application for one-to-one support and the mother eagerly welcomed the news. Previously the mother had opposed the idea of participating in group work.

As they were talking, the mother's younger son (aged 4) walked into the kitchen and asked if he could show his older brother's [i.e. 'the son'] friend his gun. The interviewee sat on the stool and thought to herself, 'Please don't say that this is a real gun.' The mother replied to her son, 'No, no, you can't. Leave the gun alone.' The 4-year-old said, 'No, no, I want to' and as he spoke he went behind where the interviewee was sitting to where various items were jumbled up and pulled out an air rifle. The interviewee thought to herself, 'Right, this is brilliant' and anticipated what was going to happen, namely that the son would return with the gun and threaten her. She was aware that the son had previously intimidated a neighbour with an air rifle. Nevertheless, the interviewee was determined not to walk out and remained seated. Her motive was to avoid the son believing that 'he had got one over on me'. She said that although it was a 'stupid thing to think', she felt 'No, I'm not having a 13-year-old thinking they can control me.' In her judgement that was a major source of the son's problems: he tried to control everyone by intimidation. The interviewee was experienced in youth work on a voluntary basis and had seen it happen before with other children.

The interviewee asked the mother whether the gun was loaded and the mother reassured her that it was not: 'It's definitely not loaded.' Thoughts raced through her mind. She thought, 'Well, he might shoot me…shoot me in the leg to prove a point. OK I'm not going to die.' The interviewee said, 'I was petrified to be honest…really shaking…really shaking. And taking deep breaths…And praying as well!!! Yes, I was very scared.'

The 4-year-old staggered off down the hallway carrying the air rifle that was nearly as big as himself. He then went into the sitting room where most of the children were now gathered. The interviewee could hear snatches of the conversation from the sitting room which seemed to consist of various children saying, 'No, you do it', 'No, you do it'. She formed the view that this referred to some proposed action against herself.

Shortly afterwards, the 13-year-old son emerged from the sitting room and again stood in the doorway to the kitchen. Again, he stood within reaching distance of the interviewee, to her right-hand side and behind her. He was carrying the air rifle with his right hand on or near the trigger and his left hand on the stock. Because the son wasn't very big, the rifle looked much larger in comparison to him. As the son walked into the room he was swinging the gun through an arc, but when he halted the air rifle was pointing towards the floor. He said to the interviewee, 'OK, time to leave' – it was, said the interviewee, like a parody of 'Time gentleman please' but he wasn't joking and certainly no one was laughing. The interviewee sat on the stool and studiously ignored him. The son then said, 'Come on, you've got to get out.' The interviewee replied in as matter-of-fact manner as she could, 'I haven't finished yet. I'm just talking to your mum.' The interviewee aimed to communicate that the gun was no big deal and she wasn't intimidated by it or the son. The son then launched into a tirade of abuse, 'You don't know what you're talking about. You're an idiot. Nobody can stop me doing nothing.' All this was freely laced with obscenities. He then said, 'I'll do to you what I did to [and named someone].' The interviewee knew nothing of the named person, but she felt 'Flipping heck what was that then?!' He then discharged the air rifle with the muzzle pointing towards the floor very near to where the interviewee was sitting. It contained no ammunition, but the discharge startled the interviewee. Although this caused the interviewee some distress – 'By then I was scared, I was shaking' – she strove to maintain the appearance of composure.

There was a brief pause during which the interviewee thought that the son was appraising her reaction to the discharge. The interviewee strove hard to retain her composure. The son then said, 'Oh, I remember where I put the pellets' and he turned and went back along the hallway. The interviewee thought that this was probably a bluff and then the mother added, 'Oh, don't worry about it. He hasn't got any pellets.' The mother had made no intervention during the incident, which annoyed the interviewee. The interviewee replied, 'Well, actually, I'd prefer it if you went and took that air rifle off him. I don't fancy sitting here to see if he finds some or not. So could you do that?' The mother replied that she would and she walked along the hallway and into the sitting room. The interviewee could here the son's mother saying 'Give me that air rifle. Don't be so fucking pathetic. Stop showing off in front of your mates.' This prompted the son to 'hit the roof, because she [his mother] had embarrassed him in front of his mates'. The son angrily denied that he was showing off. His mother told him to grow up. The boy retorted, 'I'm not fucking showing off.' He added, 'You tell her that I'm going to get a knife and stab her. I'm going to get her outside and I'm going to cut her heart open and cut it into small pieces. The fucking slag.' There was much more of this in similar vein that the interviewee could not recall in detail. The interviewee could hear the mother telling her son to shut up and stop being pathetic. Eventually, the mother left the sitting room and returned to the kitchen without the rifle. This left the interviewee feeling anxious that the son was genuinely going to attack her as she left the house and/or vandalise her car.

These events had left the interviewee 'shaking like a leaf' and she 'felt like running out in tears to be honest', but she deliberately remained and planned to finish her cup of tea and then leave in her own time. She was determined not to show that she had been intimidated. When the interviewee had drained her cup, she said to the mother that she had to be on her way. She made no attempt to make another appointment because 'there was no way I was going back there'. However, she undertook to phone and arrange to meet somewhere else. As the interviewee walked along the hallway she decided to go into the sitting room and say goodbye, because she didn't want to conclude the encounter with him angry with her and she being scared of him. 'I just didn't want him to feel that he'd intimidated me.' The interviewee noticed that the sitting room door was closed, so she knocked on it and opened it, stepping half inside. She said, 'You'll be glad to know that I'm leaving now.' The interviewee was anxious to 'leave on a positive note and to let him see that I'm not intimidated and that I care about him'. The son was sitting in a chair wrapped in a blanket and just replied, 'Yeh, right, OK'. 'He wasn't angry, he was just sitting there as if it was an everyday occurrence, what he'd done', said the interviewee. The interviewee turned towards the son's friend and said 'All right' and then left. The interviewee was left with an image of the son as being just a little boy, rather than the fearful presence that he'd tried to present.

The interviewee returned to the office by car. She felt enormously relieved to be out of the house.

In this case, whilst the social worker was unnerved by the boy's threats, she felt confident enough to refuse to be intimidated. However, another social worker was presented with a markedly more fearsome prospect. For even a casual threatening remark when uttered by a person with a known propensity for extreme violence acquires almost overwhelming force, as Case study 4.11 demonstrates.

Case Study 4.11: The murderous boyfriend

The interviewee, a social worker in child protection, was supervising a child in care whose mother had begun cohabiting with a man recently released from prison. The mother and her boyfriend were allowed supervised visits to her child at a family centre. One day the interviewee received a message from the family centre asking him to contact the mother. When the interviewee phoned the family centre it was the boyfriend who came to the phone. The boyfriend complained, 'Look, they're not letting us take [the baby] out of the building. They're saying you've got to agree it.' The interviewee replied, 'Well, where are you going to go? It's contact and restricted to the building.' The boyfriend invidiously compared the restrictions imposed by the interviewee with the more flexible approach of another social worker. The boyfriend was clearly unhappy and handed the phone to the child's mother, to whom the interviewee explained the arrangements for visiting the child.

Shortly afterwards the interviewee was told by his manager that the boyfriend had phoned the office threatening to 'torch' the interviewee's car and claiming to know where he lived and the number of his car and he had said he was going to kill him. The manager said that the boyfriend had been 'ranting and raving' at the family centre, 'mouthing off'. The interviewee was taken aback: he realised that the boyfriend was unhappy about his decision regarding the child, but had no idea that he felt so strongly. However, he was rather disturbed by these threats and decided to change the arrangement he had made to meet the mother and boyfriend the following day so that it took place at the office rather than at the mother's home. He was obliged to leave this message on an answering machine at the mother's flat. In the event neither the mother nor the boyfriend showed up for the meeting.

The interviewee then encountered the boyfriend a couple of days afterwards at the family centre in a formal meeting designed to clarify the terms of the contact. The boyfriend was very apologetic, saying that he had lost his rag and said things he should not have said and didn't mean them.

The following day, the interviewee went around to the mother's flat to discuss the future care of the child. The flat was in a four-storey block with abandoned cars littering the forecourt. There was no one around. He made his way into a warren of corridors and passageways through which he had to find his way. The mother's flat was in an isolated corner. The interviewee recalled that as he stood on the doorstep he thought to himself, 'This is bloody crazy. I know this guy's absolutely bonkers.'

He recalled that the first time the interviewee had met the boyfriend the latter had been telling him of the violence in which he'd been involved in the past. Waiting for the door to be answered, he thought to himself, 'This could get a bit tasty.' He wondered whether the stories the boyfriend had told were fantasy or exaggerations. He felt that the boyfriend was capable of serious violence; on the other hand, he thought that he could 'sus' the boyfriend. He also felt that the boyfriend would do nothing to jeopardise his relationship with the mother.

The mother opened the door and led the interviewee along a corridor into the sitting room. The room was very untidy with tobacco and cigarette papers littering the scene. There were items of drug-taking equipment lying around and an empty Jack Daniels bottle on the sideboard. The TV was turned on. The atmosphere was heavy with cigarette smoke. The curtains were drawn, which made it dark save for the light from the TV. He was invited to sit down in a vacant chair at the far side of the room well away from the door whilst the boyfriend sat by the door. The interviewee realised that this was not a good position to be in. He was offered a cup of tea and a cigarette, both of which he declined. They then began talking about the contact with the child, the court process and various related matters. The boyfriend almost immediately apologised for making threats towards the interviewee. The boyfriend was sweating heavily and suffered from a speech impediment. The interviewee describes him as a 'big, stocky guy', not tall (only 5' 8") but well built (apparently he had 'got into weight training' whilst in prison) with a developed musculature and tattooed arms. He wore a long leather jacket that the interviewee associated with criminals, and lots of jewellery.

In the course of this conversation the boyfriend began elaborating upon his past criminal career, describing his attempt to kill a drug-dealer in Manchester in revenge for the murder of his nephew and for which he'd just completed a term of imprisonment; how he'd been a part of a gang of armed robbers who had turned 'Queen's Evidence' and thus escaped a long sentence; and of the other acts of violence he had committed during the Strangeways prison riot. He mentioned that he considered that he had one last act of serious criminality 'left in him' for which he expected to spend a considerable time in gaol. The interviewee could see that the mother, who sat apart from the man thus forming a triangle, was becoming alarmed at these revelations. The interviewee turned to the girlfriend and said, 'Did you know any of this?' The girlfriend replied that she knew nothing about it. The boyfriend then turned to the mother and assured her that she need not worry, he would do nothing violent towards her. He then matter-of-factly and in an unemotional dead-pan voice, said 'But I'd not bat an eyelid in sticking a knife in him over there', referring to the interviewee. The interviewee regarded this as a very credible threat because of the man's previous convictions for violence. The interviewee reacted with fear and shock to this remark and just wanted to leave the flat as soon as possible. The interviewee tried to laugh off the remark, 'Don't worry [mother's name]. You see it's not *you* he's going to kill. It's *me*!' The conversation returned to the arrangements for the welfare of the child. On reflection the interviewee was confident that the man had uttered his threat as a way of intimidating the interviewee and gaining control. The conversation then became 'very jolly', focusing on setting up the next contact with the child. The interviewee nevertheless felt thankful when he eventually emerged from the flat.

Signs misread

Reading signs of trouble in contact with strangers means relying on stereotypes, such as those of drug-dealers upon which the nurse relied when confronting the bejewelled youth who refused to wait for a cranial X-ray and demanded that his head wound be stitched (Case study 4.5). As cognitive psychologists have been at pains to point out, the reliance on such devices is not only inevitable, it is also essential for conducting social behaviour. Unless one has some basis upon which to predict how others will act it is impossible to calculate how they are likely to react to one's own actions.

However, predicting others' actions and reactions is fraught with the possibility of error and in Case study 4.12 we see an example of how easily a police officer could misread the signs of trouble and take action he later regretted.

Interestingly, this incident was recalled not as either a violent or potentially violent encounter, but as the most recent occasion on which the interviewee had made an arrest.

Case Study 4:12: Confrontation in police station reception

The interviewee had been on light duties for some weeks because of a broken finger and was taking a routine statement at the police station from a victim of a robbery during the middle of the afternoon. The interviewee explained that whilst taking the statement he could hear banging noises and shouting coming from the reception area. At first he thought nothing of it and carried on taking the statement but the noise began to get louder and he began to feel concerned. As the shouting became louder the interviewee was able to hear abusive language. The noise reached such a pitch that the interviewee excused himself and stepped out into the reception area to see what was happening.

In the reception area he saw a man at the far end of the counter from where the noise was emanating. The man was facing an officer behind the desk whom the interviewee knew well as a colleague. In the reception area there were three adults and two children (one was about 7 years old and an older one about 10 or 11 years old) waiting quietly. The interviewee thought about asking them to leave, for the kids' sake, but decided against doing so.

The interviewee then turned his attention to the man, who he described as approximately 45–50 years old with greyish thin hair and scruffy appearance. The man was standing with both feet on the floor, leaning on the counter. The man then started to kick the front of the counter three or four times and was abusive to the officer behind it. The interviewee realised then that the banging noise he had heard earlier had been the man kicking the counter. The interviewee remained near the door and just stood and waited to see if the man would notice him and calm down, but he didn't. The man continued to shout abuse at officer behind the counter who remained calm and explained to the man that there was nothing the police could do for him and that he would have to go back to Social Services (regarding what, the interviewee did not know at this stage). The interviewee recalled the man saying, 'Fucking help me, you don't fucking do anything for me.' The interviewee commented that it was not conversation, just abuse, and he took exception mainly because of the children who were in the reception area and the fact that the man was kicking the counter. The interviewee said that he could see that the man was not steady on his feet, which led him to believe that the man was drunk.

After standing at the door for a minute or so the interviewee said he was not going to tolerate the behaviour any more and he wanted to get closer to the man to become conspicuous and to place himself in a position to arrest the man if it became necessary. So he moved over to the man's right-hand side where the counter forms a right angle, and stood about 2 metres from the man (out of touching distance). The man continued to shout abuse towards the officer behind the counter and appeared not to notice the arrival of the interviewee. The interviewee could now see the man's face clearly and formed the impression that the man was very angry with the police. The interviewee was not quite sure what the problem was. The man mentioned that his benefit book had been 'stolen' but then said he had 'lost' it. The officer behind the counter repeated that the police could not help the man and that he would have to go back to Social Services. However, the man was not considering what the officer was saying and kept interrupting and swearing. The exchange continued repetitiously until it seemed that the man had reluctantly decided to leave the police station.

The man stepped back from the counter but instead of leaving the reception area he took out his cigarettes, matches and some documents from his pockets and threw them on the floor muttering like a spoilt child. The interviewee felt that the situation 'was going nowhere' and something had to be done. He said to the man, 'Don't do that.'

The man turned to walk towards the main door and the interviewee could see that he was walking with a slight limp and had some sort of facial injury; there was no scarring but it was as if the man's face was deformed. The man had only taken about two steps when the interviewee stretched out his right foot and kicked the cigarette packet across the floor towards the man and said, 'Take your rubbish with you while you're leaving.' The interviewee acknowledged that his attitude probably upset the man; he explained that he was thinking, 'hang on a minute, don't come in here throwing your litter around – we will respect you if you give us a bit of respect'. Looking back he realised he should not have done that and felt that maybe his action had incited the man. Perhaps he should have adopted the same approach as his colleague behind the counter.

The man then stopped, turned towards the interviewee and squared up to him with his face about 4–5 inches from his own face. The interviewee doubted whether the man even realised at that stage that the interviewee was a police officer. At this point the interviewee could smell alcohol on the man's breath, which reinforced his belief that he was under the influence of alcohol. The man's expression was quite unpleasant and the interviewee felt that he needed to protect himself and pushed him away and stepped back, but did not want to push him to the ground in case he hurt himself. However, the man came towards him again, frothing at the mouth, and said words to the effect of, 'What did you say? What's your problem?' The interviewee repeated to the man that he should take his stuff with him, but the man stood right up to him as if he was going to 'have a go'. The man then started shouting abuse and the interviewee told him he was not having this swearing and being drunk and took hold of the man by the arm and slowly brought him down to the ground, the man did not fight him and it was quite easy. He thought then of what had happened to him when he had injured his finger, 'I was thinking safety all the time.'

As he arrested the man, his colleague bounded over the counter to assist. Two other officers, one in uniform and the other in plain clothes, came through the security door and grabbed hold of the man. The man was handcuffed and then the three officers escorted the man down to the custody suite where he was booked in. The interviewee explained that whilst he was the arresting officer, a colleague took over the booking-in procedure, allowing him to return to continue taking the interrupted statement.

Later on the interviewee said he got in touch with the custody sergeant who informed him that the man had come into the police station because he had had his social security book stolen and he wanted to report the theft. When he came in originally he said he had lost it, which is why the officer on the counter had quite rightly told him to go back to the Social Services and tell them he had lost it. But now he was saying it was stolen. It was only during this conversation that the interviewee learnt that the man was disabled: a year previously he had been hit by a bus and was paralysed down one side, which accounted for the deformity in his face. The interviewee also said that from the way the man smelt and by his speech that he would have thought he had drunk more than five pints, whereas in fact he had drunk only two pints. For the man, with his mental disability, the effect was as if a normal person had had six or seven pints. The custody sergeant also told the interviewee that the man suffered from short-term memory loss and could not recollect anything that happened in the reception area.

Notwithstanding the man's condition the interviewee thought it appropriate to charge him with being drunk and disorderly. However, the officer who had been behind the reception counter queried the need for this and persuaded him not to take any further action. In retrospect the interviewee regretted the action he had taken and recognised that he had misunderstood the situation because he was unaware of the man's mental handicap.

Knowledge and predictability

The previous case study illustrates how the fleeting relationship that police have with angry and distraught people can lead to erroneous stereotyping and misunderstanding. By contrast, social workers and mental health professionals normally enjoy more lasting relationships with their clientele that enable them to build a solid foundation of knowledge upon which to base their actions in possibly fraught circumstances. The utility to which such knowledge can be put is vividly illustrated by Case study 4.12, in which a social worker found himself in the midst of a heated and drunken argument between a couple with whom he had being working for some time.

Case Study 4.13: Drunken couple

The interviewee was informed that the police had attended the home of a family with whom he had been working for some time. The woman had been found intoxicated, but her male partner was sober and the police felt that the children were safe. Nevertheless, it was felt prudent for the interviewee to pay a visit at some point during the day. The woman had a history of 'bizarre behaviour' and violence when drunk. His familiarity with the family meant that the prospect of the encounter did not discomfit the interviewee at all.

The interviewee phoned the house and the call was answered by the male partner [who will be referred to throughout as the 'husband' to avoid confusion, even though the couple were not married] and it was immediately clear that the latter was slurring his speech, indicating that he too was now drunk. This was unusual: the husband had developed a pattern in which he avoided drinking when his wife was on a binge. This led the interviewee to feel concern for the safety of the children. The interviewee said to the husband that he would have to come and visit. The husband replied that was fine with him, but repeatedly said 'just don't judge us, don't judge us'. The interviewee asked what he meant, and the husband simply repeated the phrase. The interviewee knew the husband well and felt he could be honest with him. So he said, 'I don't think I ever have judged you, but when [the mother] is drinking and you're drinking there usually is a problem between you two.' He added that he wanted to come around to the house to ensure that the children were safe.

On arrival at the house all appeared quiet. The husband opened the door quite quickly. The interviewee described him as a 'small, slightly built bloke – fairly placid' who smokes a lot of cannabis. He was wearing a tee-shirt and jeans. It was immediately obvious to the interviewee that the husband had been drinking. The husband said, 'You'll need to come in and talk to her.' For the first time the interviewee saw that the husband was angry. He had long known that the husband had a capacity for violence when drunk: he had been arrested several times by the police and an 'out of hours social worker' had been chased by the husband 'down the street with a frying pan'. So, he knew that when the husband had been drinking he could be 'quite dangerous'. Also present was an alcoholic male friend of the couple with whom the interviewee was also familiar – a 'placid bloke,' 'always quite polite and respectful'. The interviewee described him as 5' 8/9", quite 'solidly built', with shoulder-length dyed-black hair. The interviewee was familiar with this family friend both in connection with the couple, but also as a client of Social Services in his own right. He understood that he and the couple had become friends through their drinking. The mother had disclosed to the interviewee that she had had sex with this friend on several occasions.

The interviewee went into the sitting room where he found the mother – an alcoholic who was clearly intoxicated. The interviewee described her as 22/23 years old, average height but 'heavily built' with a 'fattish face' and spectacles, 'fairly unkempt most of the time', short hair in poor condition; a 'very disturbed and manipulative' woman with a history of enduring child abuse herself. She suffered from a 'hysterical personality disorder' and was an inveterate liar. She and the husband had met when they were both on the street as alcoholics. Social Services became involved when the couple were found in a squat with the mother heavily pregnant.

When the interviewee first saw the mother she was lying on the couch telling him how drunk and depressed she was, and how she'd thought about committing suicide. She was going over issues that had been discussed often enough in the past. She had been attending counselling, but she complained that this caused her to have nightmares. During this conversation her small son came into the room. The boy was crawling, unable yet to walk and very chubby. The boy was followed shortly afterwards by the husband who asked, 'Have you talked to her yet? Have you got to the bottom of it?' The husband's appearance led to the mother becoming very aggressive towards him. So the husband again withdrew into the garden. In the interviewee's estimation the mother was 'looking for a fight' with her husband. She was goading him and he was getting angry. Whilst he was the father of the older twins, he was not the father of the small boy who was crawling around in the sitting room and when she was drunk she had used this fact as a weapon against her husband in the past.

As the husband was leaving the room, his wife picked up a beer glass and began threatening that she would smash it and use the glass to slash her wrists. Just then the family friend entered the room. The interviewee grappled with the mother and was able to wrest the glass from her grasp. The mother then picked up a small table mirror, but knocked it across the room, causing the glass to shatter. A shard of glass just missed the small child still crawling around on the floor. Thinking that things were getting out of hand, the interviewee picked up the child and took him outside to where the husband was standing with the older twins.

The interviewee was standing near the rear door with the husband and the children, whilst the mother and the family friend remained indoors. The husband was beginning to get agitated and angry. Although he was not directing any of his anger at the interviewee, he was complaining about Social Services 'coming into his house and interfering'. The husband then said that the mother had begun telling him things that she claimed to have previously shared with the interviewee in confidence. The interviewee tried to reassure the husband that he didn't allow the mother to say things to him that she wouldn't tell the husband. If she tried, the interviewee insisted, he stopped her because he knew that it had been a source of conflict in the past.

Then the mother appeared from the side of the house carrying a long stick. The interviewee formed the impression that she was acting in a 'calculated way' and 'certainly she wasn't out of control' although she was 'displaying anger'. The interviewee found himself positioned between the mother and husband as the mother began again to goad the husband. The interviewee continued to try to calm things down, pointing out to the mother that she was goading the husband, whilst encouraging the husband not to react. Again the husband raised the issue of the mother sharing information with the interviewee that the interviewee did not pass on to the husband. Again the interviewee sought to reassure the husband that this was not so. This did not prevent the husband becoming increasingly angry. After a short time the husband said, 'Take the fucking kids. I don't want any more to do with Social Services.' With that the husband went into the kitchen and shut the door.

This left the mother outside with the interviewee and the three children. Then the mother began smashing windows with the stick. The mother and husband were hurling insults and abuse at each other. The interviewee couldn't hear what was being said, but he could tell that the husband was getting progressively angry. The interviewee was becoming increasingly anxious about the safety of the children, especially with glass flying about. He felt unable to prevent further escalation, so he called the police on his mobile phone and said that he considered the children to be at risk. However, the children themselves seemed oblivious to what was happening, showing no signs of distress, probably because (in the interviewee's view) 'they had seen it all before'. The family friend had by now left the house via the front door and came around to the rear and was standing with the interviewee. He wasn't drunk and said that he would look after the children in the garden and make sure they remained safe whilst their parents fought in the house.

Before the police arrived the interviewee left because he felt confident that the children were safe and that his presence was exacerbating the situation. There was, he felt, a lot of anger indirectly aimed at him because of his quite intense relationship with the family. The interviewee believed that the husband was quite jealous of him because the mother talked to him. Normally, this didn't surface, but it did on this occasion because the husband was drunk.

The husband was arrested for a public order offence. After consulting with the interviewee on the phone, the police took the children around to the family friend's house for the night.

In this case the social worker was able to detect various signs of trouble: that the husband was drunk at the same time as his partner; that the woman was goading her husband about the paternity of one of the children; that she used her relationship with the social worker as a weapon against her husband; and that the conflict had reached a point where his own presence was escalating the situation. Thus he was able to phone the police and withdraw, having made arrangements for the safety of the children. 'Survival guides' for caring professionals (for example, Brady 1993) emphasise the value of such knowledge in enabling the professional to predict and prepare for any encounter, as well as making informed interpretations of the person's conduct during the course of any meeting with them.

Unfortunately, the predictability that knowledge provides does not always produce reassurance; indeed in some circumstances it can add to the threat. As the example of the boy with the airgun (Case study 4.10) demonstrates, *because* the social worker knew a considerable amount about the boy's delinquent history as well as the general circumstances of the family, this knowledge not only conferred credibility upon the threats of the boy but also helped to condition her response to his taunts, for instance her refusal to give the appearance of being intimidated by his behaviour. In Case study 4.14 a mental health professional acquired knowledge that allowed her to take elaborate precautions against a potentially life-threatening assault by a patient, but at considerable emotional cost.

Case Study 4.14: Taking precautions against a homicidal threat

The interviewee was an experienced CPN who had met the patient on six or seven previous occasions without incident. The CPN thought that she enjoyed a good working relationship with the patient. The patient suffered from hallucinations and he feared that he was schizophrenic, but the CPN did not agree. She felt that the patient was perpetually trying to compensate for his small stature by adopting an expansive persona, a pretence that he found stressful. During their most recent meetings the CPN had begun to challenge the patient's self-diagnosis and felt that they were making headway.

The CPN made a routine phone call to the Occupational Health Nurse (OHN) at the patient's workplace. Her reason for making contact was that the patient had expressed fantasies about harming someone at his workplace whom he disliked. During the course of their conversation it came as an 'absolute shock' when the OHN disclosed that the patient had also admitted to having fantasies about harming the CPN. He had graphically described to the OHN how he fantasised that when next he came for an appointment he would wait until the CPN turned to lead the way to a consulting room, whereupon he would stab her in the top of her back. He described where he would secrete the knife and how he would perform the act. The OHN was extremely scared by this, but didn't want to tell the CPN about the details; the CPN virtually had to drag it out of her. The fact that the OHN was reticent about going into details caused the CPN anxiety, since it suggested to her that the fantasies must be 'pretty gruesome'. At the conclusion of the conversation she turned to two colleagues seated at her cluster of desks and said, 'Would you believe that someone has thoughts about harming me?' One asked, 'Oh, what are you going to do?' The other added, 'Oh, you're not going to see him on your own, are you? Make sure you take someone with you.'

Her initial reaction was one of fear and then she began to feel angry. 'How dare he express these feelings about me?' She had thought that her relationship with this patient was such that he would be open and honest with her. This revelation seemed to invalidate this image she had of their relationship (almost a betrayal). She began to wonder whether she had brought the situation about herself: perhaps she had challenged him too freely. On the one hand, she felt that the fact that the patient had spoken in this way suggested that he might actually be convincing himself to attack her. On the other hand, she didn't think that he would be so silly as to actually do anything. She wondered whether the patient had done this deliberately, knowing that it would get back to her and thus scare her, thereby establishing power over her. She was preoccupied with thoughts about the patient and what he might do. She found herself visualising what the patient intended to do to her and the consequences for herself. She could imagine herself lying on the floor; she worried about whether anyone would contact her husband; she wondered whether she would survive and be able to resume her work. Her imagination was 'working overtime'.

She thought about the situation and considered whether to cancel the next meeting; whether to continue seeing the patient; whether to change the time of the next appointment. She discussed it with the patient's psychiatrist and a senior colleague and it was agreed that she would see him at the time and day arranged, but in a room that was the safest available and she would be accompanied by a senior colleague whom she regarded highly. Whilst she found this reassuring, she also found that it enhanced her fears since the psychiatrist and colleagues were taking this as a credible threat. The reception staff were forewarned when this patient would be arriving.

As the time for the appointment approached she and her senior colleague made elaborate plans for how they would conduct themselves; arranging the furniture in the room so that they would sit nearest the exit and removing anything that could be used as a weapon.

At the appointed time reception notified her that the patient had arrived. She and her colleague went into reception and looked through the one-way mirrored glass and could see the patient sitting with the hood of his fleece over his head and his hands deep in his pockets. The CPN and her colleague were delayed by making preparations and she anticipated that the patient might get a little edgy, but the receptionist said that the patient had sat quite calmly whilst he waited. As she and her colleague walked to the door, they debated who would open it. After some hesitation she said that it would be 'silly' for her colleague to do so. She pulled the door open and the patient rose from his seat without bidding. She considered whether he might be holding a knife in his pocket. She had hoped that as he rose from his seat he would take his hands out of his pockets, but he didn't. He came towards her still with his hands thrust deep into the pockets across the front of the fleece. Her heart was 'pounding away like mad'. She detected surprise on the patient's part when she invited him in, because he could see her colleague standing in the background. She thought he was doubtless expecting that she would be alone as usual. She was hot and distinctly uncomfortable with the situation. As the patient reached the door the CPN introduced him to her colleague; the senior colleague then turned and led the way with the patient following her and the CPN bringing up the rear.

In the event the interview was conducted without incident although suffused with anxiety on the part of the CPN. She confronted the patient with what the OHN had told her. The patient replied by apologising and said that he did not like having those thoughts. The interview then 'turned into a confession' as the patient told her about his thoughts and apologised repeatedly. It lasted for two hours as the three of them explored why the patient had these fantasies and why he had told the OHN about them but not the CPN.

The patient failed to turn up for any further appointments. The CPN felt this denied her the opportunity to be alone with the patient and have a positive experience.

As this case study illustrates, prior knowledge has both advantages and disadvantages. The advantages of being able to take precautions are obvious, but it comes at the price of the stress of knowing that someone intends harm. Even when, as in this case, the professional is experienced and has worked in circumstances where violence was common (a psychiatric hospital), the threat of physical harm is hard to bear. Moreover, recalling these circumstances caused the interviewee obvious distress. In other words, knowledge of a potential threat is itself a cause of heightened fear and vulnerability. Information received about the specific intentions of clients and patients can both forewarn and intimidate. The CPN's experience was far from unique: when a social worker was informed by her supervisor that one of her female clients had expressed threats to kill her, this caused the social worker to fear not only for her own safety, but also for that of her children. It caused her to be watchful as she went about her domestic chores because she lived in the same area of the town as the client and feared an unplanned meeting.

Prior knowledge of the idiosyncrasies and personality of a client or patient gained through lengthy casework can alleviate or elevate anxiety. Whilst the social worker's familiarity with the drunken couple provided him with a rich context in which to assess any potential threat, for others prior knowledge of just how disturbed, violent or vindictive a patient or client has been in the past enhanced the credibility of their threats. For instance, a lengthy exchange of correspondence and phone calls between a CPN and a patient complaining about his treatment owed much of its traumatic impact to the nurse's knowledge about the vindictiveness of the patient and his success in causing problems for medical staff in the past. Much of this interview focused not upon the specifics of what the patient had said and written, but on what the nurse knew about his background. This inevitably led her to attribute far more significance to his every action than might otherwise have been the case.

Equally disconcerting can be false assumptions founded upon inadequate knowledge. Attention has already been drawn to one such example, when a woman forcibly confined her social worker in her apartment by blocking the exit. The social worker in this case imagined that she and the woman had agreed upon clear 'boundaries' that the woman would respect. It was not until the social worker was confined inside the woman's apartment that she realised that the woman did not feel as committed to these boundaries as she was.

For police officers, knowledge of whom they are dealing with is a rare commodity, but not always a welcome one, as Case study 4.15 confirms.

Case Study 4.15: On one's knees amongst the hooligans

The interviewee was a PC deployed to patrol the town centre one evening following a home soccer match earlier in the day. It had been predicted that violence was likely to occur after the match. Apart from the interviewee, the personnel carrier in which the officer was a passenger contained a driver and radio operator in the front, and a female Special Constable with him in the back. At around midnight the radio had reported that CCTV operators could see a man lying injured on the pavement outside a town centre shopping mall and that members of a local soccer hooligan gang were in the vicinity.

On arrival at the scene the interviewee found the victim lying face up on the ground with his head towards the kerb amid a scene of general disorder. The injured man had a serious wound to the back of his head and blood was running across the footpath and into the gutter. Whilst the interviewee's two male colleagues chased after the alleged offenders, the interviewee ran directly to the victim to administer first aid. He shouted to the female Special Constable to remain in the vicinity and he kept her in view. The interviewee went down on his knees and took hold of the victim's head, cupping it in his hands and squeezing the edges of wound together to staunch the flow of blood.

The officer immediately recognised the victim as a member of a soccer hooligan gang – a 'nominal'. 'He kept saying to me, "Get off you fucking pig. Get off you fucking pig" even though I was trying to help him.' It was the fact that he was continuing to be abusive that indicated that he was conscious. The interviewee said that the most amusing moment was when he asked the victim if he wanted to make a crime complaint, which earned the riposte 'Fuck off, of course I don't!'

At first he had been unaware of the presence of others, but then became aware of a group standing around him. These were other members of the same hooligan gang who were all very drunk. He describes them as ranging in age from 17 to 35, predominantly white (there was a single black member of the group), and all well dressed. They were known to the officer and he had had previous contact with them and had no problems, unlike some of his colleagues. Five stood to the right-hand side and three to the other side. They were standing very close 'in a very tight huddle', which the interviewee found 'very claustrophobic'. They were being 'extremely aggressive' and 'since I'm a police officer, they took an instant dislike to me'. The assault had allegedly been made by a fan from the opposing team. The surrounding group were uttering repeated threats that 'there's going to be a fucking riot tonight'. They were anxious to get hold of the assailant and 'rip him to bits'. The interviewee felt that they would do the same to anyone (including himself) who got in their way.

Several of the surrounding group were drinking bottled beer and it would have been easy for them to have struck the officer, who was wearing no headgear – not even a cap. He knew that the incident was being monitored by CCTV, but that could not protect him in such a vulnerable position. Through his earpiece he could hear the radio transmissions from the CCTV that there was an officer on the floor dealing with the injured party and surrounded by others. He also heard a female sergeant transmit that she was hastily en route to the incident. He felt confident that other units were on the way and would arrive shortly. He was also concerned for the Special Constable and kept looking up to see whether she was OK, but he found it difficult to monitor where exactly she was.

The interviewee began to form a bond with the group by deliberately trying to reason with them and calm them down. He told them that the police had caught the offender even though he knew this to be untrue (at least when he said it). He kept asking for descriptions of those opposing fans involved in the attack. He thought this would take their mind off attacking someone else (in fact, the assailant was captured some time afterwards). Just before back-up arrived he felt that the tension had gone out of the situation because he'd managed to gain rapport with the group that 'saved me a kicking basically'. The trigger for this change of mood was when members of the group began referring to him as 'mate' rather than 'pig'.

The ambulance arrived and the officer assisted the crew in loading the victim onto a stretcher. The interviewee was thanked by the victim who declared, 'You're not bad for a pig. Thanks mate.' Some of the victim's friends also thanked the officer.

Knowing that he was surrounded by members of a local hooligan gang did little to assist the officer in dealing with the situation, for he literally had his hands full holding the victim's wounded head. It did serve to increase his anxiety about his predicament.

Knowledge and predictability are, then, a mixed blessing. Whereas A&E staff and police officers are usually obliged often to deal with people wholly unknown to them, mental health professionals and social workers have often acquired a depth of knowledge upon which they can draw. However, this knowledge can serve to add credibility to any threatening behaviour that the person exhibits, thereby increasing their menace. Knowledge can enable staff to take precautions, but on the other hand taking precautions can itself be stressful.

Conclusion

What is common to all four professions is that they routinely deal with difficult, challenging and demanding people who have the potential for violent and hostile actions. This is obviously true of mental health professionals who apart from the examples given in the case studies above also reported incidents involving violent schizophrenics and others suffering serious mental illness as well as personality disorders. Likewise, social workers (especially those represented here whose responsibility lay mainly in the area of 'child protection') are particularly exposed to people with temporary emotional disturbance.

What distinguishes social work and mental health from A&E and police is that the former normally have some long-term relationship with those whom they encounter. People who present themselves at A&E or come to the attention of the police are usually unknown to those who must deal with them. Therefore, A&E staff and police officers need to be particularly alert to signs of trouble. On the other hand, knowledge of the potential for violence and hostility on the part of adversaries can prove a double-edged sword. Whilst it enables staff to take appropriate precautions, it also lends credibility to the threat potential posed by people they cannot easily avoid.

Chapter 5

Violent contexts

Introduction

The previous chapters have shown that interviewees regarded 'violence' as spanning a broad array of actions (and inactions) and that some of this variance was explicable in terms of the characteristics of adversaries. If people (usually men) 'looked the part' or had an appropriate reputation, then they did not need to *do* very much in order to frighten those with whom they were in conflict. A hostile glare from a forbidding individual might have more impact than an overtly violent act from someone whose appearance or reputation did not inspire dread.

We now turn to the wider context within which these encounters took place. Common sense teaches us that an encounter in a reasonably crowded high street in the middle of the day is likely to prove less menacing than a similar encounter in a lonely alleyway in the middle of the night. The 'workplace' in which these four professions operated were quite different and within each profession there were also significant contextual differences that influenced the interviewees' appraisal of others' behaviour. In this chapter we will explore the influence that location has upon the impact of an encounter; how isolation exacerbates fear; the significance of timing; the role of ambient noise and hostility; and the impact of organisation policy.

'Location, location, location'

The four professions represented by our interviewees worked in a variety of locations. Clearly, casualty staff were confined to that department of the local general hospital (albeit that two interviewees referred to incidents elsewhere). Hence it comes as no surprise that almost all incidents occurred either in the treatment area or waiting room. Social workers and mental health staff experienced confrontations in a much wider array of locations – offices, waiting rooms and institutional settings – but what distinguishes these professions from accident and emergency is that the primary site in which conflict occurred is the home of the client/patient (where 24 of the 40 incidents occurred). Police found themselves in the widest range of locations, from police cells to the streets. For the purposes of this exploration we will consider confrontations occurring on the professionals' own territory, in public places, and in private space such as other people's homes.

Own territory

A&E

We have already seen how the workplace of A&E staff confers significant advantages. Firstly, this territory is physically secured: the public has access to a waiting room but their contact with A&E staff is through security screens that surround the reception desk and via locked doors that control access to the treatment area. The staff have the benefit of CCTV surveillance of public areas, security guards, 'panic buttons' with which to summon assistance, and a 'hot line' to the local police control room. Secondly, staff have colleagues readily available to intervene if necessary. All this stands in some contrast to the waiting room, which is regarded as unsecured territory.

We have seen how the attempt by two young men to batter their way into the treatment area (Case study 3.12) was experienced as a frightening breach of the security that staff normally felt within the secured treatment area. What remains to be explained about that incident is that the Sister who recalled it explained that once the young men began battering the doors into the treatment area, she instructed the staff to 'lock down' (albeit that the police arrived before her instruction could be fully implemented). Apparently at this A&E there was a procedure to deal with such incidents that involved keeping all access locked, refusing further admissions by ambulance, moving less seriously injured patients away from the treatment area nearest the waiting room, and summoning an emergency response by the police. Whilst the need for such a procedure may evoke concern that it should be considered necessary, it also testifies to the security that is afforded by working in one's own territory – it is possible, if necessary, to 'lock down'.

We have also become aware of another aspect of working in one's territory that we might imagine will enhance a feeling of security, which is the power to expel those who fail or refuse to comply with the rules. The bejewelled black man who refused to wait for a cranial X-ray before receiving stitches to his head wound was invited to discharge himself without treatment of any kind (Case study 4.5). In effect A&E staff had the power to insist that patients accept the terms upon which treatment was given or not to receive treatment at all. As we will see later in this chapter, it is not always as clear-cut as this, but ejection from the building remained an option and effectively a sanction.

Residential institutions

Others who work in their own territory are those involved in institutional care and they share many of the same advantages. However, these may be offset by working amidst the concentration of people who suffer a variety of psychiatric and emotional problems that result in them being volatile (Health Services Advisory Committee 1987; Nolan *et al.* 1999). Case study 3.6 illustrated the dangers that lurk for staff in such institutions. It also illustrated how the availability of staff offers some protection, for a male colleague was on hand to restrain the severely autistic child. The downside of this kind of intervention is that it exposes those who intervene to the risk of injury.

Police stations

Police stations share with residential institutions a capacity to elicit compliance from those who are taken into them by the police (Choongh 1997, 1998; Irving and Hilgendorf 1980). However, they too work with a clientele that can often be volatile, as the incident with the drunken young woman (Case study 4.7) testifies.

Offices

It is noteworthy that when social work clients or the patients of CPNs behave unacceptably, one of the sanctions that is applied is the removal of 'home visits', which means that any future meeting must be held in the offices of Social Services or the CMHT, possibly in an interview room reserved for the purpose. The enhanced security that this provides has also been previously illustrated in Case study 4.14, which showed how the CPNs were able to arrange the physical environment to protect their own safety against a man who entertained homicidal fantasies towards one of them.

Public places

Public places afford few of the enhancements of security that are available in one's own occupational territory. It might be imagined that this – the street – is the normal working environment of the police whereas, in fact, few interviewees referred to confrontations in public places other than large-scale public-order incidents. Nevertheless, those cases that were mentioned highlighted the problem of retaining control of the situation in a public setting. We have already seen (Case study 4.9) how keeping participants in a dispute apart can be difficult in such an uncontrolled setting. But the problems of maintaining control extend beyond those most directly involved, for a continuing preoccupation of officers dealing with confrontations in public settings is the potential for other people to become involved and escalate hostility and violence. The following case studies illustrate these problems: the first concerns the involvement of third parties who are affiliated to one of the disputants.

Case Study 5.1: Dispute between neighbours

In the early evening of a dismal winter's day the interviewee and his crewmate were dispatched to an incident at which an 'IC3 male' was reported to have been rushing in and out of flats in an apartment block 'threatening people with a kitchen knife'. Given the description of the problem, the officers pulled up their car just around the corner from the apartment block and put on their 'stab-proof' body armour as a precaution.

Arriving at the building, they found a large number (about 20–30) of Asian people (men, women and children) gathered outside in a rather agitated mood. The interviewee said that both he and his colleague tried to calm everyone down and get the story from them. It became apparent that these were the complainants and they were accusing a black male resident in a first-floor flat of having threatened them with a knife. As the officers entered the flats other residents appeared in the hallway and stairs area.

The officers went to the first floor where an African-Caribbean man lived with his girlfriend. Here the occupants counter-alleged that one of those among the gathering of Asian people outside had thrown a brick through their window, narrowly missing their child. A brick was lying on the floor of the flat amidst the shards of glass from the broken window. According to the couple, this incident was the pinnacle of continuing friction between this

---

couple and their Asian neighbours. Other neighbours volunteered evidence that supported the African-Caribbean man's version of events including his denial that he threatened anyone with a knife. The occupants of the flat identified a man among the crowd outside as having thrown the brick.

Because the circumstances were so obviously tense, the officers called for assistance; however, they felt unable to await the arrival of other units for fear that the suspect would escape. When the officers went outside, members of the crowd began pushing and pulling at the officers, asking why they had not arrested the alleged 'knife wielder'. Because they were outnumbered, the intention of the officer was to lead the man suspected of throwing the brick away from the main group so that they could talk to him. As they approached the suspect, the interviewee said something like, 'Can we have a chat?' and tried to lead him away. He added that the 'last thing' he wanted was to go 'straight in and lay hands on him'. However, the suspect resisted and the officer told him he was being arrested for criminal damage, at which the suspect began struggling. The interviewee took hold of the suspect and so did his colleague who had been standing to the interviewee's right-hand side. They led the man up the grassy bank to the top of the steps, either side of which is a wire mesh fence. The officers began handcuffing the suspect using the interviewee's cuffs. Nevertheless, after the first cuff was applied the man began to struggle very violently – 'He really started to go for it'. He repeatedly tried to pull his arms away, but he did not throw any punches. At the conclusion of the cuffing, the arrested man was pinned against a fence and it was here that the crowd surrounded them, preventing them returning to their car which was approximately a 'couple of hundred yards' away.

Members of the crowd were angrily asking why the police were arresting this man. The interviewee's most vivid recollection of the incident was of a woman hanging on his back pulling his hair, which is short. He turned his head and saw that the woman, who was small, was completely off the ground, hanging on to him by his hair. People were screaming at the officers, calling them 'scum', 'pigs' and 'that sort of thing' – 'the usual stuff you get really'. He remembered being accused of racism. His main concern was keeping hold of the suspect – 'there was no way I was letting go of [him]'. The interviewee felt members of the crowd 'grabbing at my kit' and he responded by knocking their hands away and fending them off. Although the prisoner was now handcuffed he

> feared that he might escape and be spirited away by friends and relatives. So, both he and his colleague had hold of the suspect with both hands.
>
> It was during this stage of the incident that the interviewee radioed for 'urgent assistance'. Other officers arrived within a few minutes, but not before the interviewee's colleague found it necessary to arrest another member of the crowd. After a skirmish in which police drew their batons, the arrested men were taken away in a police van.

Public places can be a frightening location for caring professionals too, as Case study 5.2 makes plain. Here a social worker attempted to protect a client from the unwanted attentions of an abusive spouse in a crowded street populated by bystanders unwilling to become involved.

Case Study 5.2: Street confrontation

This incident occurred when the interviewee (a middle-aged female social worker) accompanied the wife of an abusive husband to the County Court to obtain an injunction preventing her husband from returning to the family home. The husband had a history of violence towards his wife and had served a term of imprisonment for violence. 'So I knew that things could be a bit hairy', said the interviewee. The husband had refused to appear before the court, but had interrupted the proceedings and denounced the interviewee as a liar before being ejected. The injunction was granted in the husband's absence.

Knowing that the husband was in the vicinity of the court aroused anxiety in the interviewee and she obtained an assurance from the wife's solicitor that the husband had left the court building, but beyond that no one was sure where the husband had gone. After a delay of 'a few minutes' the two women left the court building en route for Social Services via a café where they might have a cup of tea. The two women anxiously ventured out onto the main shopping street.

They had not gone far before the husband suddenly appeared, having run from behind and caught them up. The husband was described by the interviewee as being much taller than either of the women; 'a skinhead' in his early 20s with a broken nose, several facial scars and a big scar on his scalp. His appearance was very intimidating.

The husband grabbed the interviewee's right arm from behind and pulled her away from his wife, but his wife continued to cling on to the interviewee. The husband was shouting that the interviewee was a 'fucking bitch' and asked rhetorically how the interviewee could do this to him and his family. The husband was yelling that the interviewee should leave his wife alone so that he could speak to her, because his wife couldn't possibly agree with what was happening. He was protesting that the accusation that he was a violent man was a lie. He alleged that there were no problems between the couple until the interviewee had become involved. The break-up of his marriage was all the interviewee's fault. During this diatribe the husband's face was contorted with rage. His wife appeared stunned by the suddenness of the onslaught and continued clinging on to the interviewee as if for protection. The interviewee was shocked too, but part of her shock lay in the fact that she was in a shopping street during a lunch period with many people in the vicinity and no one came to the women's assistance. People turned or stood and watched as the husband continued his tirade.

The interviewee's strategy was to continue walking, hanging on to the wife whilst the husband continued trying to prise the interviewee away from his wife. The interviewee said, 'I have never walked so far so fast in all my life!' The interviewee now threatened to call the police if the husband did not let her go. The husband replied that the police didn't frighten him and she could call them if she wished. The interviewee was carrying the office mobile phone and so she dialled 999 by holding the phone in her coat pocket and feeling for the keys. Continuing to walk along the shopping street, the interviewee told the police operator, 'Social worker under duress. Please assist.' The operator asked where she was. The interviewee named the shopping street. She was then put through to what she thought was the local police control room and the operator asked the interviewee to make her way to the Civic Centre where the police would meet her. The interviewee was astounded because the Civic Centre was several hundred yards away.

During the phone conversation the husband managed to prise the wife out of the grasp of the interviewee amid much shouting and crying. As soon as the phone call was completed, the interviewee 'grabbed her [the wife] back'. There being no alternative, she walked with the wife as fast as possible towards the Civic Centre, being pursued by the husband who continued

> to shout obscenities, allegations and threats. The interviewee was thinking, 'Bloody hell! Let's get to the Civic Centre as quick as we can!' Apart from that she cannot recall thinking or feeling anything else.
>
> At the Civic Centre the two women were met by four police officers and the husband was arrested.
>
> The interviewee continued to have contact with the wife (and occasionally with the husband). The husband remained in the family home and the interviewee was left feeling that the stress of this incident had been to no avail.

Private space

For social workers, mental health professionals and police officers the most common working environment is the home of those with whom they are dealing.

> Importance should be credited to the psychological value attached to the territorial location of the client at the time of the assault. [Social workers] are more often required to enter the primary territory of the client, not infrequently against the client's wishes, and attempt to persuade the client to comply with a requirement, expectation or demand. (Rowett 1986: 128)

This poses a number of practical and socio-cultural challenges that are not present when the professional is operating on their own territory. The major practical problem is the sheer unfamiliarity with the environment. This is illustrated by the incident in which the 13-year-old boy intimidated the social worker with an air gun (Case study 4.10). Here a sense of vulnerability and anxiety was exacerbated by not knowing who else was in the sitting room with the boy, whether the gun was loaded, and to what other weapons the boy might have access. Of course, houses may be full of unknown hazards, not least of which is the arsenal of weaponry that is located in most kitchens. Police officers often mentioned how they were attentive to whether those with whom they were in confrontation were in or near a kitchen.

Needless to say, there is little opportunity to configure the physical environment for one's own protection, as the two social workers who visited the home of the recently released child abuser discovered to their consternation. The garbage-strewn kitchen into which they were ushered offered no means of escape (Case study 4.2). Manuals of guidance on self-protection advise social workers and other professionals to avoid finding themselves in situations where they cannot escape, but this advice is predicated on the assumption that the social worker can take sufficient control of the circumstances to determine where they and others sit. However, to do so is to violate the normal rules of social behaviour, for upon entering another person's home one becomes a 'guest' and is expected to comply with appropriate norms of conduct. For instance, whereas a social worker could legitimately usher a visitor to their own office to a chair carefully located in a defensible position, in someone's home it would be impolite to insist on sitting in a particular chair and bid the householders to sit where the social worker determined. Thus, even the social worker who feared that he was walking into a threatening situation with the client's boyfriend who had recently served a term of imprisonment for manslaughter felt unable to do other than sit, as bidden, in a chair far away from the door to which his path was blocked by the boyfriend (Case study 4.11). To do otherwise may have precipitated the very confrontation that the interviewee feared.

It has long been recognised by academics that police officers find intruding into private space problematic (Reiss 1987; Stinchcombe 1963). It is perhaps predictable that many confrontations with householders take place on the threshold of the premises where police are denied entry. For in these circumstances the authority of the police comes most directly into conflict with the proprietory rights of the householder. Case study 5.3 describes one such confrontation that illustrates how the police capacity to use legitimate force is used as the ultimate 'trump card'.

Case Study 5.3: Doorstep confrontation

The interviewee and his crewmate were dispatched to a 'domestic incident' about which little was known because the call was originally received by another force and then relayed to the local control room. There was also no previous history of 'domestics' at the address. On arrival the officers had difficulty attracting the attention of the occupants, but he could hear shouting and the commotion from within.

Eventually the door was opened by a black woman in her 30s. The interviewee could see she was distressed for she had obviously been crying. The interviewee asked the woman what had been going on and whether everyone was OK. The woman replied that she and her husband were just having an argument. However, he could now clearly hear people inside the house shouting and screaming.

The officers became aware of a man standing behind the woman. The interviewee described the man as short and thin with long hair and a beard, and felt that he did not pose any threat to himself. The man launched into a torrent of abuse that was initially directed at the interviewee but very quickly seemed redirected onto the interviewee's crewmate, whom he called 'a four-eyed cunt', threatening to 'have him first'. The man demanded to know why the police were there and told them that they were not wanted and referred to them as white trash. The interviewee felt that the man was trying to goad him and his crewmate into a reaction and concluded that the man was under the influence of alcohol. The woman told the man to go back indoors and that she would deal with the police. The woman assured the interviewee that there was no problem and that she and the man were having an argument about some issue of marital fidelity.

The woman refused the officers' offer of assistance, whilst the man continued being abusive and obscene. In the course of the conversation the officers managed to establish the man's name and date of birth from the woman and the interviewee's colleague carried out a check on him. The check revealed that the man was known to but not wanted by the police and there were no warnings that he might prove violent.

As the encounter progressed, the interviewee was able to detect the presence of young children in the house. This convinced the interviewee that he could not just abandon the situation and needed to ensure that at least he left the man in a calmer state of mind.

Talking to the woman on the doorstep, the interviewee gleaned that a short time before the police arrived the boyfriend had had a fight with the woman's ex-boyfriend that resulted in the man injuring his leg, possibly breaking his ankle. She had made it clear that she had not been assaulted and the interviewee surmised that she did not want the police there. The interviewee wondered whether he and his crewmate should now just back off.

The man then reappeared and the interviewee's crewmate warned him that the man had a knife. The man said to his crewmate, 'I will have you fucking first you four-eyed cunt.' The interviewee took his CS spray canister from its holster but realised immediately that the woman was directly in front of him and the children were in the vicinity. He felt unable to use it in the circumstances and returned it to its holster. However, he was aware that his colleague had drawn his baton.

The interviewee said that the situation had escalated and that the presence of the police seemed to be infuriating the man and so he stepped backwards. The interviewee recalled telling the man not to be stupid and asking him what he was doing with the knife and at that point the woman shut the door, leaving the officers outside. The interviewee was not sure what action to take but did feel that something had to be done. He radioed requesting the attendance of a sergeant who arrived shortly afterwards accompanied by a shield entry team.

On arrival, the sergeant was briefed by the interviewee. The interviewee explained that the situation was an 'unknown quantity', the man had armed himself with a knife and there were a female and five children in the property. He and the sergeant agreed that the man needed to be arrested. The sergeant instructed all the officers present to wear their protective vests.

The sergeant, the interviewee and his crewmate approached the door whilst two other officers remained by the gate. The sergeant knocked on the door, which this time was immediately opened by the woman. The situation was very similar to the previous occasion with the man coming to the door and being abusive, but on this occasion he was not in possession of a weapon. The man again saw the interviewee's colleague and once again directed obscenities at him. The sergeant tried to reason with the man but this had no effect. The sergeant who was on the right-hand side of the interviewee suddenly pulled the man from the doorway. The interviewee joined in and grabbed the man's right arm and assisted the sergeant to get him from the doorway of the house onto the garden path. The man banged his head as he fell forwards, grazing it slightly; the interviewee and sergeant were joined by the interviewee's crewmate and the two officers who had remained at the gate.

At that stage the female was joined by the children at the doorway all wanting to know why the man had been arrested and saying that he had done nothing wrong. The female started to cry and they all refused to go back into the house. The man was taken away as quickly as possible in the van, leaving the interviewee and his crewmate to deal with the woman and the children. Eventually the woman calmed down and the officers left the scene.

Here we see how a 'private matter' becomes a police matter when the man brandishes a knife, defies police officers, and there are children present. The sergeant had no hesitation in grabbing the man and pulling him across the threshold.

Once inside private premises the authority with which police are invested also enables them to 'take charge' and direct people to act in ways that officers find acceptable. Not only do officers use oral commands to direct how those present should behave, but they typically deploy themselves physically to dominate space. Repeatedly, officers described matter-of-factly how they would stand apart from each other so that a person would find it difficult to keep them both in view. Again, if people overtly resisted this authority they were vulnerable to arrest. Moreover, once the police have gained access to the domestic sphere, there open up additional possibilities for coercive intervention. Case study 5.4 illustrates not only how police authoritatively conduct themselves once inside premises but also how they can pursue their own agenda irrespective of the original reason for their intervention.

Case Study 5.4: Police property

The interviewee and his crewmate were dispatched to a 'domestic' in an apartment block that was the frequent source of such calls. The control room informed the officers that a woman had made a 999 call regarding problems with her boyfriend but that the call was interrupted and terminated. This indicated that the woman concerned might be in danger and there was a potential for violence.

Upon arrival the officers could hear no sounds of turmoil from within the flat. The officers' knock was answered by a white woman in her early 20s. The woman seemed calm and her voice betrayed no emotion. She obviously knew why the officers were there and did not ask; she simply insisted that 'everything's OK now'. However, the officers had been trained to assure themselves that the man had not forced the woman to give false reassurance. So, the officers insisted on entering the flat to check the situation.

The door opened directly into a combined bedroom/sitting room. Inside the flat, they found a man in his mid-20s sitting on a bed. He was speaking on the telephone. He was white, about 5' 8" and of slim build, but was fit and strong. He was wearing a tee-shirt, jeans and trainers. Behind him, asleep on the bed, lay an 18-month-old baby. With the door open behind them the officers felt comfortable and were able to keep both the man and woman easily in full view. The interviewee's crewmate repeatedly asked the man to finish his phone call as soon as possible so that they could have a word with him. He studiously refused to pay any attention to what the officer said and continued his phone call which seemed to be of a social nature, making arrangements to meet the caller. The woman, by contrast, seemed 'quite happy' and sat down on the sofa indicating that she was expecting to talk to the officers. She was suffering from no apparent visible injuries and there appeared to be no damage. The officers remained standing.

The woman encouraged the man to finish his call, which he did, but his attitude to the officers continued to be hostile, asking what they thought they were doing coming into his flat. Ideally, the interviewee explained, the officers would have wanted to separate the couple so that the woman did not feel intimidated into saying that everything was OK; however, the layout of the flat did not allow this. The officers explained that they had been called to the flat and that the call had been terminated. The man confirmed that he had pulled the phone plug from the socket. The officers then asked routine questions about what had happened and whether either party wanted the police to take action. Both the occupants were calm – not 'having a go at one another'. The man continued to maintain his challenging stance, saying that he had not called the police. The woman did most of the talking, expressing the view that the man had got a little angry and overbearing and she was concerned especially with the young child in the room, but everything was fine now. She said that there had been no physical assault, just an argument. The officers regarded this as unproblematic and expected to complete the paperwork and leave it at that.

The man then stood up, picked up his keys and jacket and declared that he was going to leave. The officers who were standing side by side moved slightly apart to make it clear that they were blocking his exit from the flat. The interviewee explained to the man that they needed to take a few details and would then leave the couple to their own devices. He addressed the man directly, making it clear that he was talking to him and conveying the impression that the man would not be allowed to leave by his own and his crewmate's general demeanour. Thus delayed, the man began wandering around the flat busying himself and the woman gave minimal details of the incident, leaving the officer 'happy' that the woman was uninjured, and that the dispute had been non-violent.

As a matter of course, the officers conducted by radio a check on both parties and the control room replied that the man was wanted for unpaid fines. This reply could not be heard by the couple because the officers were both wearing ear-pieces. Again the officers refused to allow the man to leave. At this point the man became more assertive and stood up and started being confrontational both verbally and in his mannerisms. Legally, it was necessary for the warrant to be brought to the location before the man could be arrested. The interviewee said that had the man attempted to leave the flat they would not have prevented him because 'there would be another day', but it was right that he should pay his fines which had been outstanding for a couple of months. So, the officer told the man that there was a warrant for his arrest in respect of unpaid fines and the man replied that the matter had been dealt with at court – a response with which officers were familiar when dealing with unpaid fines.

The man now became less confrontational and started talking reasonably. The man produced a wad of legal paperwork from beside the sofa and the officers were able to consume time by going through it in a painstaking fashion and asking him to explain what had happened at court. As they checked it became apparent that one of the warrants had been dealt with, but another remained outstanding. The man then wanted to make a phone call to his solicitor, which the officers allowed him to do. The man explained to his solicitor that the police were in the flat and were proposing to arrest him for non-payment of fines. Although unable to hear the solicitor's remarks, the officer gained the impression that the solicitor's view was that the police were perfectly within their rights. The man concluded the conversation with his solicitor abruptly and seemed angry with the reply he had received. Throughout this period the interviewee's colleague was talking to the control room intermittently about the progress of finding and transporting the warrant to the location.

At this juncture the woman started to become antipathetic to the police and in view of her size and physique the officers considered her a potential threat. She began demanding that the police leave the flat, denying that the officers had any right to be there and opposing her boyfriend's arrest. It was the view of the officers that if the officers left the flat, waited for the warrant and then knocked on the door, the occupants would refuse them entry and the police would have no power to enter forcibly. So, the officers sought to remain in the flat.

The woman made another 999 call complaining that the police were in her flat and unwanted, and that they proposed arresting her boyfriend. She said that when she had originally called she had been in danger, but she was no longer in danger and wanted the police to leave. She replaced the receiver and became abusive towards the two officers.

Eventually, a third officer arrived with the warrant. The interviewee stepped outside and spoke to him in the stairwell, explaining the situation inside the flat. He made sure that the warrant was still in force and referred to the man in the flat. He told the newly-arrived officer that the man was likely to resist arrest and that the woman might well seek to intervene. The two of them then returned to the flat; the interviewee and his crewmate went straight up to the man, warrant in hand, showed it to him and asked the man if he was able to pay the outstanding fines. He was unable to do so and was told that he was being arrested. The man was standing in the entrance to the kitchen area. He was formally cautioned and replied that he would not go with the police. The man was holding a cup of coffee and was told to put it down, which he did. Then the two officers stood either side (the officer's crewmate standing inside the kitchen area) and took hold of his upper arm. When the interviewee took hold of the man's arm the officer remarked that it was then that he became aware of the man's physical strength and realised that he had the potential to resist. The man immediately tensed and resisted. However, the officers had no difficulty manoeuvring him from the entrance to the kitchen into and across the sitting room. Meanwhile the third officer was dealing with the woman who was being verbally abusive towards the police and throwing some household items (tape cassettes and cuddly toys) although not directly at police, more in rage. The officers escorted the man out of the flat and into the stairwell where they had to turn left along a short passageway towards the stairs.

The man grabbed the banister rail at the top of the stairs. The woman was behind them continuing to be abusive. So, the interviewee's colleague handcuffed the man's right wrist and pulled him away from the banister so that he faced the wall. The man continued to struggle, and the officers were having difficulty applying the second cuff even with the assistance of the third officer.

Then the woman grabbed the interviewee's baton and pulled it from its holster. This caused the officer to break away from the handcuffing and retrieve his baton from the woman. He said to the woman, 'Give it back', to which she replied 'No'. So, he stepped forward grabbed the baton and yanked it from her hand. Throughout this exchange the baton remained retracted. One of the officers then radioed for assistance from other officers. The interviewee placed his baton back in its holster and resumed assisting with handcuffing the man and once this was achieved the officers took the man briskly down the stairs. The man was not complying and they virtually carried him, supporting his weight between them. The third officer was behind them protecting their backs. The woman did not follow down the stairs.

It is precisely the authority and the capacity to back it up with force if necessary that distinguishes police officers from others whose working environment is often other people's homes. Case study 5.5 contrasts starkly with 5.4 for here social workers are unable to exert any control over those present in the house of a client who aggressively expressed their negative attitude to the presence of the social worker.

Case Study 5.5: Smoke blown into social worker's face

The interviewee – a newly qualified social worker – was visiting a client with a colleague (an assistant social worker) who would be taking over her case whilst the interviewee was on annual leave. The client was a heroin addict and her home was often filled with people who were themselves drug addicts. The interviewee found it 'a very threatening environment'.

Upon arrival the two social workers found the sitting room was occupied by three or four other women who were animatedly talking, laughing and joking. The client was standing and busying herself in the middle of the room. The interviewee knew some of those present, but not a 'large black girl' who the interviewee described as 'a well-built girl' with braided spiky hair. The atmosphere of 'chaos' was one that the interviewee found unnerving.

The interviewee sat perched on the arm of a chair near the door, whilst her colleague sat on the opposite side of the doorway on the arm of a sofa. The interviewee introduced her colleague to the client. The client raised the perennial issue of her desire to move to another town some distance away so that she could be near to her family. Throughout this conversation, the others present in the room kept up their own conversations, laughing and joking.

The interviewee and client were discussing the details of the transfer to another local authority, when without warning the young black woman who had been sitting to the right-hand side of the interviewee leapt from the sofa on which she had been sitting and pushed her face into that of the interviewee. The young black woman said quite aggressively, 'Are you from fucking Social Services are you?' The interviewee replied that she was. The woman then added, 'You a fucking social worker are ya?' Again the interviewee replied that she was. The woman was now pacing back and forth in front of the interviewee, picking things up from a small table and putting them down in a way that led the interviewee to conclude that she was winding herself up. However, the woman was now between the interviewee and the doorway, effectively blocking the exit. The woman was obviously getting increasingly angry. Meanwhile, everyone else in the room had gone quiet and was watching this woman. The interviewee was thinking to herself, 'She's going to go for me. She's going to go for me' and felt trapped. The woman stared at the interviewee and again thrust her face into that of the interviewee, now literally spitting with rage. She yelled, 'I was with Social Services and it was fucking crap.' Another guest intervened, telling the woman to 'sit down and behave'. For a couple of seconds the woman paced agitatedly around the centre of the room, but then walked across the room and threw herself histrionically into a chair. Whilst sitting down she continued to fiddle with things that came to hand in an agitated manner and continued to look angrily at the interviewee. The interviewee was utterly taken aback and unable to respond. She felt confused, trying to figure out what had prompted the outburst. Throughout the eruption the interviewee's colleague had sat quietly watching what was happening. She later confessed that she too thought it 'was all going to blow' and was quite shocked.

Shortly afterwards the social worker and her colleague departed.

Unlike the pair of police officers, these two social workers felt unable to command the situation. Instead, they became victims of one of the other guests who seized the initiative.

Isolation

Case study 5.5 is unusual in as much as there were two social workers present. Normally, social workers make home visits alone and because of staffing shortages find it difficult to find a companion even when they believe there is a potential danger. Being alone in a threatening environment is known to elevate levels of fear (Killias 1990). Thus, when the young social worker was confronted by the teenage son of her client wielding an airgun (Case study 4.10) it was, in part, the fact that she was unaccompanied that lent additional menace to the incident. So too, the CPN who visited the personality disordered man with the appearance of a 'thug' and an aggressive German Shepherd dog as a companion (Case study 4.3); and the psychiatric social worker who found herself intervening between the son with Asperger's syndrome and his mother (Case study 3.9). In each of these instances, it was the sense of isolation that exacerbated the feeling of vulnerability.

Escape

Related to the problem of isolation is the ability to escape. Thus, the social worker who realised too late that her client was drunk and unwilling to allow her to leave was unable to escape by her own efforts (Case study 3.10). In another situation a social worker found herself talking to a client who suffered from a psychiatric condition that compelled her to hoard almost everything. As the two women sat talking, the client's son appeared in the only channel left between the rotting garbage piled high inside the sitting room. The young, physically well-built young man launched a tirade of abuse as he slowly advanced down the channel towards the social worker. She reported that as this situation unfolded the young man appeared physically to grow larger until he filled the space available. Eventually, the young man's mother intervened, pleading with him to desist and he abruptly left. Again, whilst there was no direct attack, blocking the only exit proved very intimidating.

However, it is even possible that a social worker or mental health professional finds him or herself unintentionally trapped without the client being aware of it. This is graphically illustrated in Case study 5.6 when a mental health worker visited a patient who had been referred by his GP because he was suffering anxiety.

Case Study 5.6: Paedophile fantasies

The door to the small terrace house was opened by a middle-aged man dressed as a 'biker'. His hair was long but thinning and tied in a pony-tail; he wore a black 'heavy metal' tee-shirt and jeans; he was considerably overweight and perspired freely. The man greeted the interviewee warmly, for he had been expecting a CPN to visit, and he invited her into the house. The CPN was a woman in her 40s and experienced in mental health. Walking ahead of the interviewee he led the way down a narrow flight of stairs and into a crowded basement kitchen. The room stank of stale cooking and the interviewee found the atmosphere quite oppressive. The man invited her to sit on the only chair that was visible in the kitchen and once she had done so the man pulled a folding chair from beneath a table in the centre of the room and placed it down without artifice in the only space that remained – directly in the doorway.

After brief preliminaries the interviewee asked the man to describe his symptoms. The man began explaining that he had begun experiencing vivid and distressing paedophile fantasies about the son of a friend of his. He believed that his desires were reciprocated by the boy, but he was anxious about the consequences for his friendship with the boy's father.

As the man spoke, the interviewee gradually realised that he must be referring to the son of a friend of her family. She was familiar not only with the boy but also with his parents. Normally, she would have terminated the conversation once this realisation dawned, but she found herself in an acute dilemma. For by the time that she came to this realisation the man was graphically describing his fantasies about the boy and was becoming increasingly agitated. He was now sweating profusely and hyperventilating. The interviewee wondered how he might respond if she indicated that she was personally acquainted with the boy and his parents. Moreover, she was acutely aware that she was effectively trapped within this tiny and crowded kitchen. She was confident that the man had not intended to confine her, but by unfolding the chair and placing it in the doorway leading to the stairs, that is what he had unwittingly achieved. Since the kitchen was in a basement, there was no external door or windows that offered any realistic prospect of escape.

The interviewee felt that she had no alternative but to remain in the kitchen listening to the man's increasingly graphic description of his lustful thoughts towards this boy. If this was not disagreeable enough, she found his inferences of how the boy reciprocated his attentions even more offensive. She felt herself wanting to repudiate what the man was saying and offer information that would contradict his views, but that would reveal her personal knowledge of the boy. The man became increasingly agitated and so did she as her anxiety grew. All of this was exacerbated by the sweltering heat in the kitchen.

Several times she tried gently to terminate the conversation, but each time the man insisted upon giving further detailed information about his fantasies. Again, she felt unable to press him too strongly to conclude the conversation for fear of the consequences, although she freely admitted that at no point did the man say or do anything threatening. The interviewee simply did not know how he would react, especially if she inadvertently disclosed her familiarity with the boy's family.

An interview that would normally last 30 minutes developed into a 90 minute marathon. Eventually the man came to a conclusion. The interviewee seized the opportunity and said that she would need to consult the man's GP about possible treatment. The man led her up the stairs and to the front door, where he thanked her effusively for being willing to listen. She bade farewell, went to her car, drove a short distance before pulling up to calm down and collect her thoughts.

Time

Just as people can feel isolated in space so too they might feel isolated in time. Certainly this was the impression given by several A&E interviewees who tended to depict the early hours of the morning as a forbidding time when A&E staff were virtually alone besieged by hordes of young people sporting injuries acquired during the course of drunken excess. Many of the case studies previously documented occur against a background of rowdy waiting rooms and incessant pressure to treat drunken young people.

Environmental stress

Demand

The nighttime is not alone in producing conditions that are conducive to stress. Several A&E staff prefaced their accounts of individual encounters by drawing attention to the pressure under which they were functioning at the time, trying to find sufficient beds in which to accommodate the flow of patients entering A&E. An encounter with a truculent patient may act as the proverbial 'last straw' in such circumstances and assume a significance that it might not otherwise have attracted. It has been generally observed that there is a correlation between the frequency of hostile incidents and staff morale, especially in the hospital service (Jenkins *et al.* 1998).

Public order

Police officers suffer these kinds of pressures like their counterparts in the caring professions, but they are uniquely exposed to a particular kind of environmental stress – the policing of public order. So far we have considered encounters that can readily be considered in isolation, such as attending a 'domestic' quarrel. Often these encounters conclude with the arrest of a hostile person. However, policing soccer matches injects a quite distinct additional dimension that is experienced as particularly stressful. Even when serious or sustained violence does not erupt, the prospect that it might unpredictably 'kick off' can prove quite intimidating. This was the fate of a police inspector in charge of two Police Support Units totalling more than 40 officers at a railway station awaiting the arrival of 'away' supporters. He felt quite relaxed as a large group of well-behaved supporters arrived and began making their way to the stadium. Then suddenly there was a scuffle as a small group of 'home' supporters made a brief 'hit and run' attack on the away fans. Before the police could react, the 'home' supporters were walking nonchalantly away from the scene. Thereafter the inspector felt himself to be on tenterhooks trying to anticipate any further trouble and safeguarding against it.

On other occasions the police may find themselves caught in the midst of a sustained battle between large gatherings of rival supporters, as did one officer who accompanied colleagues in a personnel carrier to a soccer match in a nearby town. He describes long periods of inactivity punctuated by unpredictable and incomprehensible violence in the midst of frightened, appalled and incredulous onlookers.

Other public order incidents can occur more or less spontaneously, which serves to elevate the feeling that one is dealing with chaotic and threatening events. Arguably, it also undermines discipline as officers react under the influence of what they refer to as 'red mist'.

Case Study 5.7: Taxi driver dispute

On the day in question the interviewee (a sergeant with 12 years' service) came on duty at 10 pm and was informed at the briefing that there would be a protest by taxi drivers at 10.30 pm about the arrest of one of them the previous night amid allegations of assault by police. However, there was no contingency plan for policing or monitoring this event. He was deployed along with a more senior sergeant and several PCs in a personnel carrier. The evening began quite busily and as the personnel carrier went along a major road in the town to an urgent call, it encountered 'a huge mass of people' congregating in the road and obstructing the traffic. As the personnel carrier neared the obstruction, members of the predominantly Asian crowd began chanting and shouting at them. Items – he thought plastic bottles – were thrown at the personnel carrier. The senior sergeant radioed control room to advise them of the situation and his fears that it might lead to disorder. The interviewee and others on board the carrier then became aware that the police-dog van following about a minute or so behind the carrier had been physically stopped by the crowd. The dog handler had radioed 'in quite a panic', reporting that someone had put a placard on his windscreen and this had almost caused him to have an accident. The officers in the personnel carrier did not intervene.

The crew of the carrier dealt with the call to which they had been en route pretty quickly and the senior sergeant decided that the carriers should return to where the crowd had gathered and impose some order and move the obstructions. Upon their return to the scene, the officers debussed and began inspecting vehicles and arranging for their removal by their owners/drivers. There was a lot of verbal abuse and a lot of potential for escalation. The dog handler also attended and recognised the person who had placed the placard on his windscreen. There was an altercation and the man was arrested for a public-order offence. The arrested man shouted and 'made the most of the incident'. There was then a 'push and pull' among a crowd of about 20. As soon as the prisoner was placed in the van, it was perceived that the situation was in danger of further escalation, so the senior sergeant decided that the officers should withdraw.

Almost immediately, the officers on the carrier were deployed to protect the police station to which the protesters had gone. Upon arrival it was apparent that sufficient officers were present to cope with the situation. A man was arrested and others surged forward, to which police responded by drawing their batons and forming a belt cordon. Then things quietened down: 'racial equality managers' and senior officers arrived at the scene, and some negotiation with and among the crowd commenced. During this period of 'stalemate' both the protesters and the police 'stood around' for some considerable time.

Then there was a further incident: a police car en route to a call had become involved in a minor collision with a taxi near the railway station. The protesters at the police station departed and headed for the railway station. Made aware of what had happened by radio transmissions, the senior sergeant decided that the personnel carrier would attend the railway station despite directions from the control room to the contrary. As the carrier approached the railway station the interviewee could see two cars (which turned out to be taxis) blocking the road. The interviewee decided to mount the pavement and go around the blockage. As they did so, he saw a number of people surrounding two officers who had their batons drawn in the defensive position and were fending people off in an attempt to keep them at a distance. Just as the carrier came to halt near this fracas there was an eruption of violence in which one officer was pushed and the other was struck in the face with a punch. Without any command, the carrier crew debussed and went straight into the crowd to assist their colleagues. The interviewee identified the man who had punched one of the officers. This man had backed away from the general skirmish; the interviewee pursued this man, grabbed him and ended up grappling and fighting on the ground. Other officers came to his assistance and the man was arrested and put in the 'cage' at the rear of the carrier.

Once this incident had been dealt with, the interviewee became aware that another large group had gathered around a second personnel carrier a little nearer the station where someone else had been arrested. This crowd was surging towards the carrier and officers at the rear of the carrier were pushing people away. The interviewee and other officers ran to their assistance.

At that stage officers were acting separately in small groups or as individuals under no command. The senior sergeant quickly assembled officers into a cordon across the front of this second carrier and curving around to the side on which there was a sliding door to stop people getting into it. Some officers wore helmets, others caps, but the interviewee and most of the carrier crew were wearing no headgear of any sort. The interviewee did, however, take hold of his baton in his right hand in the defensive position, using his left hand to fend off members of the crowd. People in the crowd were very hostile, volubly abusive and he saw colleagues struck and kicked by members of the crowd.

He vividly remembered and often repeated during the interview how much noise, hostility and aggression was forthcoming from the crowd. He likened the noise to a hollering in the manner of a Native American war-cry. All he could see was a 'sea of faces' shouting and chanting and screaming, many of them 'contorted with rage'. He said that he was familiar with chanting and shouting at soccer matches, he had attended major politically contentious public order events, but he had never experienced such hostility at such close quarters before. The noise caused him apprehension since the tactics taught for public-order situations were not applicable in this situation. For instance, it was impossible to hear the radio and receive commands.

The next incident to occur was a scuffle to his right, but he was satisfied that there were enough officers dealing with the situation. Then a man whom he had pushed away a moment before and had been trying to push through the cordon, appeared in his peripheral vision holding a belt wrapped around his raised fist with a large silver buckle exposed. He thought, 'Fuck! That's for me!' and as he did so the man swung the buckle, hitting him behind his left ear. It took him completely by surprise and he had no time to react or defend himself. The man immediately began to retreat into the surrounding crowd, walking backwards and still facing the officer, but obstructed by the pressure of other members of the crowd. The interviewee said that in that instant he lost self-discipline and he stepped out of the cordon a couple of yards in pursuit of his assailant. His sole focus was on the thick white woollen pullover that his assailant was wearing. He paid no heed to other aspects of the assailant's appearance and later could not identify the assailant by sight from among those arrested and taken to the station. The officer lunged at him, grabbing the pullover at chest height with his left hand, determined not to allow the man to escape. He was still carrying his baton in his right hand in the defensive position. As he held on to the man he could feel himself being punched and kicked, but he felt little pain. Moreover, he has no recollection of the crowd noise during this moment. He had his chin tucked into his upper chest, his eyes were closed and he was holding on to the man but also trying to pull the man towards him and downward. Another officer grabbed the interviewee around the waist and pulled him and the assailant back behind the cordon, resulting in the assailant lying face down on the ground. Meanwhile the cordon had pushed the crowd a few yards further away from the station and so he found himself with his assailant and the colleague some distance behind it. The man still had the belt wrapped around his hand, and he felt compelled to remove it from him – he thinks out of fear. The assailant was then cuffed using the other officer's handcuffs. The two officers then placed the assailant in the rear of the carrier in which the interviewee had arrived (not the one he and his fellow officers were protecting). The interviewee described this as being relatively unproblematic, with little resistance from the assailant.

The cordon, having pushed the crowd away from the station, succeeded in dispersing it. However, there was then another violent confrontation opposite the station near some shops. Again, officers had begun acting separately in different groups with little coordination – 'as the crowd dispersed, so the line dispersed'. The latest violent confrontation began when officers attempted to arrest a very muscular African-Caribbean man that led to a struggle involving possibly six officers. The interviewee felt that there was no organisation and he didn't know what to do and where to go. A cordon then formed, he was unsure how, and the man was placed in a carrier and taken away. His most vivid recollection was of the crowd acting with concerted hostility and outnumbering the police (who by now amounted to 20 or so officers), by three or four to one. Throughout the events of that evening, he said that he feared that the police were likely to 'get a beating'. Afterwards, the crowd remained protesting, but now peacefully.

Although the interviewee was seriously assaulted, it was the *context* within which the assault occurred that gave it its full significance. The noise and hostility emanating from the crowd and the lack of organisation on the part of the police led to the fear that the latter 'would receive a beating'.

Policy

One of the issues raised by officers' accounts of public-order operations is their feeling that they are unwarrantably constrained by official policy. One officer commented *inter alia* that he would be required to complete a form detailing his use of force during the incident that he described. He also remarked how the 'paperwork' associated with using CS spray was a strong disincentive to using it. It is noteworthy that the officer who was threatened by a man wielding a loaded shotgun explained her abstention from using CS spray by saying 'It would get me into trouble' (Case study 3.1).

This reveals a wider issue of the policy context within which incidents occur, for staff in all four professions felt strongly that they were unsupported by senior management and organisational policy. A&E staff declared repeatedly that they could not use force even in self-defence and doubted the effectiveness of security screens and other target-hardening measures. They also alleged that management would not pursue prosecutions against those who assaulted staff. One interviewee described how a man who seriously assaulted him was only prosecuted through the action of his staff association. Some staff assaulted in residential care situations claimed that policies forbidding the use of physical restraint exposed them to needless injury. These allegations receive some support from the National Audit Office report that expresses concern 'that some strategies might conflict with staff's legal rights to defend themselves, but the majority of trusts had not subjected their policy to legal review' (National Audit Office 2003b: 16). Social workers and mental health professionals also claimed that staff shortages obliged them to make potentially dangerous home visits alone. They also invidiously compared the refusal to equip frontline staff with mobile phones with the provision of such devices to senior managers.

Not only did staff in all four professions feel unprotected by management, they felt actively threatened. This gave added force to the threats of some adversaries to complain about their conduct, because they felt that management would pursue such a complaint with vigour.

Conclusions

This chapter has documented how context can exacerbate the sense of threat and menace, but it also demonstrates how specific such contexts are. A&E staff have the benefit of working within their 'own territory', but in the middle of the night they find themselves isolated and vulnerable. Police officers share with social workers and mental health professionals a working environment in other people's homes, but police have the coercive authority that social workers and mental health professionals lack. Operating in a public-order context is unique to police and is associated with distinctive sources of anxiety and menace.

Chapter 6

The moral dimension of workplace violence

Introduction

An understandable reaction to the title of this chapter would be to scream that of course workplace violence has a 'moral dimension'! Clearly 'violence' is morally wrong, indeed it is criminal assault. Even threatening violence normally amounts to a criminal offence. So, violence in the workplace must be wrong. Surely there is nothing to explore! Well, yes there is. For what is striking about the data collected as part of this project is that whilst all the interviewees responded to the same invitation to describe incidents in which they suffered 'violence, intimidating or threatening behaviour,' the severity of the episodes described varied enormously. Equally varied were the interviewees' reactions to the incidents including their responses to describing them in interview. Some interviewees were eager to describe their encounters, whilst others were much more reticent, often claiming that they had not really suffered from violence. In some cases the interviewee's response to describing the incident was sufficiently severe (for instance, hyperventilating) that the interviewer offered to terminate the interview – an invitation invariably rejected. Yet, there was no apparent connection between the objective seriousness of the episode and the severity of the interviewee's reaction. The off-duty police officer whose nose was broken in a violent struggle with a youthful shoplifter terminated his account with the humorous recollection of how his fiancée had rebuked him for getting himself into this scrape, whereas some interviewees exposed to non-injurious altercations showed far more adverse reactions.

It has long been acknowledged in research on violence generally that there is no simple correlation between the gravity of an assault and the severity of the victim's reaction to it: crime surveys have revealed that young men seem to take violent victimisation more or less in their stride (Aye Maung 1995, 2003; Hough and Sheehy 1986; Pease 1988). Nor is this disparity between objective and subjective reaction restricted to crimes of violence. As Maguire and others note, it is clear that psychological reactions to property offences can be surprisingly severe (Maguire 1980, 1982; Maguire and Corbett 1987). Maguire remarks of residential burglary, 'Ostensibly a property offence, interviews with victims consistently reveal that it [is] regarded much more as a personal offence by those who experience it' (1985: 549). This suggests that the meaning attributed by victims to their experience is crucially important to understanding their reaction to it.

So what makes an incident 'serious' in the view of our interviewees? This is the question that this chapter seeks to address. However, before turning to the evidence from our interviews, we should note that this was not an issue that this research was designed to examine, it simply arose as a conundrum during the course of the fieldwork. Therefore it was not something that was systematically inquired into; like all the interview material in this research it arose from interviewees' unprompted recollections.

Reactions to violence and threats

The diversity of reactions can be considered at two levels: the occupation collectively and the individual. It has already been noted that police officers suffered the most serious physical violence and previous chapters have illustrated the severity of some of these assaults and many more could have been cited. Mental health professionals also suffered quite serious assaults and threats, and so too did some social workers. Surprisingly (given the public attention that it has received) A&E staff tended to suffer fewer serious physical assaults and interviewees had to reach further back into their memories to recall occasions when they felt jeopardised. Yet, the severity of reaction failed utterly to reflect this distribution of objective seriousness. Indeed, considered at the occupational level, police officers tended to be quite phlegmatic even about seriously injurious encounters. Social workers and mental health professionals were less phlegmatic, but nonetheless tended to take violent encounters pretty much in their stride. A&E staff, by contrast, were much more sensitive to their exposure to any aggression. For instance, the male nurse who was assaulted by the partner of the woman with lacerated arms (Case study 3.4) explained that he suffered flashbacks and nightmares and had been obliged to take time off work following the assault. Even after the aggressor had been prosecuted and a lapse of nearly two years since the assault, he still felt unsafe at work and wondered how much longer he could continue.

To be assaulted by a physically muscular man could be unnerving to anyone, but some A&E staff regarded episodes that were virtually devoid of threat and menace as 'violent'. This reveals the underlying moral dimension of the offence caused. The nurse in Case study 6.1 was among the first to volunteer to be interviewed and confessed that she remained very angry about what had happened.

Case Study 6.1: Abusive female patient

A woman in her early 20s was admitted to A&E by ambulance in the early hours of the morning, having been found in a collapsed state. She was dressed in 'party clothing' and was heavily made up, but the make-up was now smudged and her clothing was dishevelled and bore the remains of vomit. The ambulance crew did not know who had called the ambulance; they had found the woman lying unconscious. They also indicated that she had been verbally abusive towards them.

The woman was taken to a cubicle where she was now awakened. The interviewee introduced herself by her first name, asked the woman for her name and for details of what drugs she had taken because she appeared to be under the influence of drugs and/or alcohol. However, the woman turned her head away from the interviewee and refused to answer. The interviewee repeated her question, explaining that it was important to know what the woman had taken in order to help her. The woman then became abusive saying 'Fuck off Sherlock!' The interviewee said, 'OK, fine, but we really do need to know what you've been taking.' Again, the woman replied with 'Fuck off, Sherlock! Leave me alone. What's it got to do with you?' The interviewee replied that she wouldn't be in trouble and the police wouldn't be called, but they needed to know for her own safety what she had taken.

The woman's response was to repeat 'Fuck off Sherlock' and to bury her head in the pillow and go to sleep. The interviewee was anxious to find out if she had taken any drugs, for if not she would have been content to allow the woman to sleep off the effects of the alcohol.

However, when the interviewee tried to take a blood sample for analysis the woman refused to straighten her arm. Because of the woman's non-compliance, the interviewee took the view that she would be unable to take a blood sample and so she left the cubicle and found the doctor (who had yet to see this patient) and asked what he wanted the interviewee to do. She explained to the doctor that the woman was non-compliant, but he said that it was necessary for a blood sample to be taken. So the doctor accompanied the interviewee back to the cubicle where the interviewee introduced the doctor and explained that it was important for them to take a blood sample. The woman was now lying on her side and appeared to be trying to sleep. The interviewee attempted to hold the woman's arm still and straight so that the sample could be taken by the doctor, but again the woman resisted yelling 'Get off! Get off!'

The doctor briefly examined the woman, looking into her eyes and asking her what she had taken, but the woman again refused to answer. The doctor took the view that she was aware of where she was and if she was able to fight the medical staff she was fit enough to go home. So, he decided that she should receive no more treatment and be allowed to leave as early as possible. The interviewee felt angry with the woman by this stage, because she was refusing to allow the interviewee to do her job. She found it objectionable that they were 'having a bit of battle' whilst trying to treat this woman.

The doctor then left the cubicle, leaving the interviewee to write up the notes. The interviewee left the cubicle and attended to other matters for a time to allow the woman to recuperate. She then returned to the cubicle. As she approached it a porter mentioned to her that the woman had urinated on the floor. As the interviewee walked into the cubicle the woman was climbing back on to the trolley leaving a puddle of urine on the floor. The interviewee felt very angry at this behaviour and said, 'I can't believe what you've just done, you disgusting person. You could at least have asked and we'd have got you something to go to the toilet.' The woman responded by saying, 'Fuck off!' The interviewee used some incontinence pads to mop up the urine.

The interviewee replied, 'Well, the doctor says you can go home now. So come on! Please get your clothes on and go home.' The woman's response was to say, 'Fuck off. Leave me alone. I'm staying here.' The interviewee left the cubicle and went round to the nurses' station where she said to the nurse-in-charge, 'I can't believe what that girl in there has done. She's peed on our floor. She got up and peed on the floor!' The nurse-in-charge was busy and said over her shoulder, 'Oh well, she can go anyway can't she? Well, better get her out of here.'

The interviewee returned to the cubicle and said, 'There's nothing wrong with you. We don't want you in our department. You've been abusive since you've been here. You've defecated on our floor. This is an Accident and Emergency department and you don't need to be here. So please put your clothes back on and leave our department!' The woman made no reply, but appeared to be sleeping. So the interviewee reached forward to adjust the trolley so as to sit her up. As the woman came into the sitting position she lashed out with her right fist and struck the interviewee in the middle of the chest. The interviewee's reaction was one of shock at this and she pushed the woman back against the trolley backrest using her right hand. She now felt extremely angry, albeit that the blow was not painful. She shouted at the woman 'Don't you dare! Don't you dare hit me! Right, that's it. Please put your clothes on and get out of here!' At that moment the charge nurse came around to the cubicle and said, 'Leave it, leave it. Let me just get the police.'

The interviewee left the cubicle; the police attended and escorted the woman from the A&E.

Within each profession there were those individuals who reacted phlegmatically to hostile episodes and others whose response was more adverse. Whilst police officers generally tended to be more phlegmatic, some were not. This is illustrated by Case study 6.2, in which a community constable was merely taunted by a youth he was seeking to arrest.

Case Study 6.2: Taunted by youths

The interviewee was a male officer in his mid-40s who had worked as a community constable for the previous four years. He did not consider this incident to have been 'violent', but it was 'difficult'.

It occurred at around 9 pm on a cold, dark, damp evening and arose from the reported theft of a moped. The owner of the moped had taken it to show a friend and whilst there a mutual acquaintance had been allowed to ride the vehicle a short distance, but instead he rode off on the moped without permission. The officer had gone to see the family (who were well known to the interviewee) and the father identified the thief by name. The interviewee was joined by a woman officer who was driving a police patrol car. The two officers and the father and brother of the aggrieved moped owner went in separate vehicles to an address where it was thought the thief could be found. As the two vehicles arrived at the address, the suspect and some acquaintances ran off but were eventually sighted on the forecourt of a nearby petrol station. The officer arrested the suspect and placed him, handcuffed, in the rear of the police car. This situation defused almost immediately.

As the police car drove off en route for the police station, with the father and brother following behind, the suspect in the rear of the police car volunteered the information that a youth walking along the footpath had been with him when they had stolen the moped. The patrol car pulled up a few yards in front of second suspect and the officer alighted in order to arrest him. The youth had obviously seen the patrol car, but the officer felt that he was so cocky that he was not at all 'fazed' by this turn of events. He describes this lad as 15 years old, 'extremely cocky' and 'very abusive' and 'involved in quite a lot of crime'. The woman officer immediately radioed for assistance because they would need at least another car in which to convey the second suspect to the police station. Adding to her problems, the first suspect ceased being compliant.

The interviewee took hold of the second suspect and told him he was being arrested for the theft of the moped, but the suspect started to struggle immediately. He denied the offence and kept shouting 'Let go of me! Let go of me!' The interviewee said that he was holding him in order to stop him 'doing anything silly'. A group of around 10 other lads gathered around and this distracted the officer. The group consisted of young lads, aged between 14 and 17/18 who were known to the interviewee as local kids associated with anti-social behaviour in the neighbourhood.

The suspect broke free of the interviewee's grasp and ran off across the road. The interviewee ran after him, aware that the suspect was much younger and fitter than he, so his aim was not to attempt to catch the young man but to keep him in view whilst awaiting the arrival of other officers. He doubted whether he would have been able to catch the young man under any circumstances and had he tried he would have ended up looking 'even more stupid' than he already did. He was also anxious about the presence of the group of lads who might intervene if he arrested the youth, so he had drawn his baton as a precaution.

The youth did not attempt to escape, but instead taunted the officer by beckoning the officer to 'come and get me' and then ran off whenever the officer got close enough. The suspect made no determined attempt to escape, which, in the view of the officer, he could have done at any time. Instead, he ran around a large grassy verge on the offside of the police car and a narrower grassy verge on the nearside. The group of youthful onlookers were jeering and taunting. At one point the suspect ran through where this group were standing. As the interviewee attempted to follow, they had literally closed ranks to bar his path. The interviewee barged his way through them, which was accompanied by shouted complaints that he had assaulted them. The interviewee felt that the suspect was 'taking the piss', something he found frustrating and humiliating.

After what the interviewee estimated was five minutes or so, a police personnel carrier arrived and the suspect was arrested. He could still have escaped had he wanted to, but he waited for the carrier to arrive ('playing the hard man') and the officers piled out and arrested him. The group of 10 spectators remained at the scene during the arrest and jeered and taunted, but dispersed when officers walked towards them.

By this time a number of local residents had come out of nearby houses and were abusive and complaining. The interviewee inferred that these residents, knowing the officer as a figure in the community, saw him helmetless chasing the suspect and assumed that the suspect had stolen the officer's helmet for a prank. These neighbours seemed to resent the arrival of a large number of officers in a personnel carrier in order to arrest the suspect. One of the most vocal of the residents had had his van broken into on several occasions and the owner/resident was drawing invidious comparisons about the number of officers available to assist the interviewee to deal with this relatively minor incident and the inability to prevent offences being committed against himself. It was the attitude of local residents that stuck vividly in the mind

> of the interviewee. He felt humiliated that this group of residents were egging on the suspect and making comments about the interviewee's inability to catch him. He felt in retrospect that he had been lured into providing a spectacle.

This incident was not alone: two other community constables referred to similar situations where they were not physically threatened, but nevertheless found the experience deeply humiliating. One of them chased two underage riders of a motorbike on his pedal cycle. Amazingly he was able to catch the motorbike, but was then surrounded by children who taunted him. He found himself in danger of losing either the motorbike or his own cycle to the encircling children since he found it impossible to retain hold of them both. The other community constable recalled an incident in which local youths sat on a parked car that they had wrecked and dared him to arrest them, secure in the knowledge that the owner was too intimidated to give evidence against them. So frustrated was this officer that he admitted to having threatened the boys himself and then feeling guilty for this unprofessional lapse.

The moral contract of professional service

Some interviewees suffered serious physical assaults but remained phlegmatic, whereas others experienced less serious attacks and yet were profoundly disturbed by them. Why? The answer to this puzzle lies not in the material conditions of work, but in the implicit moral contract between professionals and their respective clientele. To explain this, consider a recurring source of confrontation within A&E. It is normal medical practice not to stitch a wound over a possible fracture site, for the obvious reason that it may be necessary to gain direct access to the fracture in order to treat it, especially if it is a cranial fracture. In the early hours of the morning it is not uncommon for young men to present themselves at A&E with serious head wounds suffered during drunken brawls. Nursing staff, following normal medical practice, routinely refer such men for cranial X-rays to establish whether or not they have suffered a skull fracture, before stitching the wound. This entails more or less lengthy delays whilst X-rays are taken and the diagnosis confirmed. Many young men, particularly if they are intoxicated, have no wish to expend their time on this procedure and demand (more or less aggressively) that the nursing staff should stitch their head wound without an X-ray and allow them to leave. These confrontations are often experienced by nursing staff as unpleasant, intimidating and threatening.

It is not only the overt behaviour of the young men in such encounters that medical staff find objectionable. It is *also* their breach of the implicit moral contract between medical staff and patients. Sick and injured patients turn to members of the medical and nursing professions for their expertise and care. This implies subordination of the patient to the professional, since the former entrust themselves into the care of the latter. Professionals expect that patients will defer to their professional judgement and comply with the treatment regimen. As the interviewee in Case study 6.1 remarked, she 'hates it' when patients refuse treatment; she regards it as 'something of a challenge'. Shouting obscenities not only displays aggression that might threaten actual violence, but tramples underfoot the professional self-respect of medical staff. As this interviewee also said to the nurse-in-charge, 'I can't believe what that girl in there has done. She's peed on our floor. She got up and peed on the floor!' Perhaps one of the reasons that A&E departments are so widely thought to be particularly dangerous and violent places is that medical staff, who dedicate their professional lives to helping people at times of their most acute need, seem the last people who *deserve any hostility* from those they treat.

The moral contract between police officers and those whom they arrest is utterly different: people are only rarely arrested in their own interests; it is the wider public interest that is being served. Policing is an imposition on those who are most directly its recipients, not a service. Many suspects comply with their arrest, but if they do not they are coerced. When the young woman in Case study 6.1 resisted attempts to take a blood sample she acted like some suspects do when they resist handcuffing. Whereas police would have overpowered a resisting suspect, the medical staff were obliged to relent in the face of this denial of consent. Police officers were not surprised when suspects resisted however much they dislike being hurt, but medical staff are *affronted* by the refusal of patients to comply. Whereas A&E staff were deeply offended by the obscenities uttered by patients, police officers regarded it as part of their job – 'You get used to it'.

What discomfits and disturbs police officers is not resistance, but the kind of humiliation suffered by the community constable (Case study 6.2), for this brings police *authority* into question, and authority is the moral basis of the relationship between police officers and the public (Waddington 1999). Moreover, community constables are supposed to have a less anonymous and more agreeable relationship with residents in the locality. They see themselves *serving* identifiable interests, not some amorphous 'public'. In short, they feel they *deserve better* and resent the disrespect meted out by young people; hence the community constable's humiliation at being *publicly* ridiculed by the group of youths in Case study 6.2.

Social workers – especially those involved in child protection (as most interviewees were) – enjoyed a very similar relationship with their clients as that of the police to suspects. Social work clients rarely entrusted themselves into the care of social workers. Much more commonly, the intervention of social workers was an unwelcome imposition – a threatening intrusion into the lives of clients designed to serve the interests of a child or a wider public. Insofar as clients deferred to the instructions of their social worker, it was under the threat of severe sanctions. Often, confrontations arose because social workers were taking some kind of coercive action: removing children from the family, refusing to return them from care, restricting contact between child and parents, or continuing institutional confinement. Accordingly, social workers have much lower expectations of how they will be treated by clients than A&E staff have about how they should be treated by patients.

> Perhaps in some respects we should not be so surprised at the level of violence encountered by social work staff. They do after all, as Stephanie Petrie points out, 'have more personal power to intervene in people's lives and liberty than any other professional, including the police'…Social workers have come to expect the exercise of their powers to meet with hostility in these circumstances…Social workers, in addition to…statutory powers, have significant powers to facilitate or deny clients access to a number of resources. (Norris and Kedward 1990)

Like police officers, social workers had low expectations. They appreciated that they were not welcomed by their clients and often represented something of a threat. Whilst they might have felt vulnerable on many occasions, they could appreciate why clients reacted to their interventions with hostility. Conceptualising the problem of violence and hostility in this way helps to resolve Rowett's (1986) anomaly – that assaulted staff often felt the assault was both unpredictable but also understandable. Predictability is a matter of fact (does one event regularly *follow* another?): often violence and hostility were unpredictable, thus enhancing feelings of vulnerability. Yet even an unpredictable outburst could prove 'understandable' if a social worker could empathetically appreciate why their client felt *justified* in becoming hostile.

Mental health professionals also have lower expectations, because they accept that their patients may not have the *capacity* to enter into a mutual moral contract. A deluded schizophrenic visited by mental health professionals in order to be committed to a psychiatric hospital cannot be expected to respect the expertise of a mental health professional or the latter's commitment to the patient's welfare. So, a suicidal patient who chased a trio of mental health professionals from her home with a knife could not be *blamed* for doing so, however frightening the experience might have been. Indeed, the interviewee was rather shocked when police with shields were called in to overpower the girl.

Malice

There is one intriguing twist that adds weight to this argument. On several occasions mental health interviewees mentioned that their adversary in the incident had been diagnosed as suffering from a mental illness, but they disputed the accuracy of the respective diagnoses, suggesting instead that the patient was 'personality disordered'. The distinction between these two categories revives the traditional difference between 'mad' and 'bad'. A person suffering a mental illness, such as schizophrenia, cannot be blamed for their offensive and dangerous behaviour, whereas a 'personality disordered' patient is not 'ill' but 'wicked' and therefore could be held morally responsible for their actions. Whatever the diagnostic significance of this distinction, its moral significance for interviewees was apparent – it allowed them to blame the patient for inflicting harm (see also Akerstrom 2002; Hinsby and Baker 2004).

'Personality disordered' people act *maliciously* and that transforms the moral status of their actions. Yet, the attribution of malice had wider significance for caring professionals. It was common for both groups of health professionals, during the formal interview and in casual conversation alike, to remark that they were familiar with being struck and abused. The important point here was that this was offered as an explanation for why they *did not include such incidents among those they deemed to be 'violent'*. Accident and emergency staff referred to occasions where deranged elderly people, psychiatric patients and even drug addicts lashed out and could cause injury without malice (see also Mayhew and Chappell 2003). For instance, staff accepted that drug addicts who had overdosed might lash out involuntarily as an antidote was administered. However, this was quite different to a drug addict wilfully becoming angry or aggressively demanding treatment. A drug addict who has overdosed is not morally responsible for the physiological reaction to the antidote, but *is* responsible for having taken drugs that reduce inhibition. A telling comparison is to be found in the attitude that A&E interviewees took to people acting under the influence of alcohol. In no case did an interviewee mention drunkenness as an excuse for behaving unacceptably. What explains this exclusion? Perhaps it is that staff regard simply getting drunk as morally culpable. So, when the drunken young woman climbed down from the trolley in an A&E cubicle and urinated on the floor (Case study 6.1) this prompted far more moral outrage on the part of the nurse than the blow that the patient struck to the nurse's chest.

Deranged patients may need to be treated with caution lest they unintentionally inflict injury, but this does not evoke moral censure. Thus, despite the injuries sustained by the nurse attacked by the elderly senile patient, her first reaction was to reassure the man who rescued her that the elderly patient was not responsible for his actions (Case study 3.5). The young man of Far Eastern appearance who suddenly launched into a display of martial arts (Case study 4.6) frightened the nurse who was in the triage room with him, but his actions were regarded by the nurse as not at all reprehensible, unlike many more incidents that were potentially less injurious.

There were revealing exceptions to the tolerance shown to the mentally ill. One of these is documented in Case study 6.3 in which homophobic remarks made by a mentally ill patient waiting in A&E for committal to a psychiatric hospital lost none of their moral turpitude.

Case Study 6.3: Homophobic comments

The interviewee, a young male nurse, became aware of a male patient in the room immediately opposite the cubicle in which he was treating a patient. This room was used to locate patients with psychiatric problems. It was no larger than any other cubicle, but was enclosed and had a door rather than curtains. What had attracted the interviewee's attention was that the patient in the room was swearing with increasing audibility. The patient that the interviewee was treating at the time indicated some distaste for what could be heard. The interviewee was also aware that there was a young girl in the waiting area with her parents, an elderly woman in a wheelchair and others who might feel distressed. The interviewee felt that he should ask the man in the room to be quiet.

The interviewee entered the room, where he found an African-Caribbean man sitting alone talking to himself and swearing. The man was 'big' (6' 2" or taller), he was very broad and dressed casually in his own clothes. The nurse asked the man if he could keep his voice down. The man's response was to place his finger over his own pursed lips in a sign that he would be quiet. Satisfied with this response, the nurse left the room and returned to treating his patient, who asked, 'Can't you have him removed?' The interviewee made no response and carried on treating the patient.

However, it was not long before the man began again to swear and use obscenities in an even louder voice than before. So, the nurse again crossed to the room and standing in the doorway asked the man to be quiet, saying 'Look. I've asked you nicely to be quiet. Now will you please be quiet?' The man became verbally aggressive towards the nurse, refusing to comply with the nurse's requests for him to be quiet. Whereas before he had been abusive about people generally, he now directed his abuse at the nurse. He said that the nurse was a 'faggot' and he would not be ordered around by such a person. As he was being abusive, the man stood upright. The nurse was standing immediately adjacent to the door which was open. The man then began to walk towards the nurse who had his back to the door. He continued to be abusive and the nurse found this very threatening. The nurse stepped backwards out of the room and turned slightly to his left. The man walked in front of him, turning away from where the nurse stood and exited through the waiting room door.

Case study 6.3 involves moral identities beyond those of the professional/client relationship. Gay men and lesbians are uniquely vulnerable to homophobic insults and by calling the nurse 'a faggot' the man in the room invoked that moral identity. In doing so he vitiated the tolerance normally extended to people suffering mental illness.

Receptionists and volunteers

Viewing the experience of interpersonal hostility through a moral lens not only explains why professionals reacted as they did; it also explains the sensitivity to hostility exhibited by receptionists and volunteers. In all three services, professionals suggested that receptionists should be interviewed on the grounds that they were particularly exposed to aggression and violence by patients and clients. Whilst numbers are inevitably small, it was striking that when receptionists were interviewed, the incidents they recounted were among the least severe. It must be said that this might be an artefact of the research design, for all interviewees were asked to recount only the most *recent* hostile encounter. If receptionists were exposed to a more or less constant barrage of hostility, this might predispose them to recalling recent and not particularly severe encounters. However, one of the most severe reactions was suffered by a receptionist at the A&E in circumstances that hardly bore comparison with aggression and violence displayed towards nursing staff. This receptionist had been on duty throughout a night shift when the waiting room became particularly rowdy. A mentally ill man waited some considerable time for an ambulance to convey him to the local psychiatric hospital, causing him and his family increasing distress and leading the latter to demand that the receptionist arrange for a more urgent response from the ambulance service. Later, a drunken man expressed his frustration at what he regarded as the insufferable delay in receiving treatment to his fractured foot by hurling chairs around reception. The receptionist withdrew from the reception desk and was placed in no danger by either episode and yet she took extended sick leave because of stress following this experience. In other cases receptionists recounted incidents in which they were rebuked for failings in the service provided by the organisation. Case study 6.4 documents one such example, the impact of which upon the receptionist should not be underestimated.

Case Study 6.4: Humorous abuse

A patient had been treated in A&E and the computer recorded that they had been 'discharged'. However, the patient had not left the site, but was waiting for a relative to collect them. Unfortunately, when the relative arrived at reception, the receptionist on duty (not the interviewee) interpreted the 'discharged' status as meaning that the person had left A&E and told the relative this. The relative had then returned home, only to find on his arrival that the person he had gone to collect was still in A&E. So, he retraced his journey to A&E.

By the time the relative returned to A&E the interviewee had relieved the receptionist previously on duty. The department was quite busy, with a great many waiting patients. The noise level in the waiting room was correspondingly high. Apart from herself there was a colleague and a clerk in reception.

A respectable looking middle-aged man approached reception. He appeared to be agitated, but the interviewee could not hear him at first because he was not speaking into the microphone. She said to him, 'Sir, I can't hear you, could you speak into the microphone?' At this his agitation turned to anger and he shouted that he had just driven 20 miles to and from the A&E because of the inefficiency of the department. He became red in the face and began spluttering with rage. The interviewee replied that she had only just that moment come on duty and didn't know what he was talking about. She asked him to explain the situation more fully and the man explained what had happened. The receptionist said that she would go and find his relative and would get back to him. As the interviewee walked into the treatment area she was intercepted by her colleague who had inadvertently misled the man previously. Her colleague was very apologetic, but the interviewee brushed her apologies aside and they cooperated in finding the missing relative.

The patient was found and reunited with his relative. The interviewee returned to the reception desk, whereupon the patient's relative approached the desk and began shouting that this wasn't the way to run an efficient service; he wasn't at all happy, he'd suffered a lot of needless stress. He asked whether the people running the department knew who was and was not in A&E and it didn't reflect well on the people in the department. He asked whether there were any dead bodies 'lying out back', suggesting that they should go and check because they plainly had no idea who was and was not in the department. He added that hospital staff could not 'organise a piss-up in a brewery'. This verbal tirade was accompanied by hand-waving and finger-pointing. The receptionist apologised for the mistake, but added that her colleague had been correct in saying that 'according to the computer' the patient had been discharged. She repeated the apology and said that she hoped that now he had been reunited with his relative all would be well. The man then retorted that 'you haven't heard the last of this' and threatened the receptionist personally that he would be complaining about her conduct to her manager and the Trust. The receptionist said that if that was what he wanted to do, then he was free to do so.

The interviewee appreciated the reason for the man's anger. This was a problem that had occurred before and to which the attention of managers had been drawn by staff.

Receptionists were not alone in their enhanced sensitivity to abuse, but were joined by volunteers who also reacted adversely to relatively mild expressions of hostility. One example is documented in Case study 6.5.

> **Case Study 6.5: Abuse of a volunteer**
>
> The interviewee (a woman with a pronounced Irish accent) was a volunteer who had supported an elderly woman whom she described as very bitter and uncharitable towards others, especially vulnerable people. The elderly woman had previously taken an overdose and the first time the interviewee met her she was recovering in intensive care. The woman was very disappointed that her suicide attempt had not succeeded. The interviewee began visiting the client frequently to offer support, including helping to keep the house clean, which was beyond her normal duties but she tried to help as much as possible.
>
> Then the woman took a second overdose, but the interviewee discovered her on one of her visits and was able to alert the ambulance. As a result of this second attempt the woman was now an in-patient in the local hospital. The interviewee visited her in hospital. Upon arrival the interviewee popped into the ward office to tell them who she was and whom she was visiting. The nurses indicated to her that the woman had been 'playing up'. The interviewee went to the woman's room and immediately the woman launched an unprovoked anti-Irish tirade. A couple of nurses were walking along the corridor outside the room, heard the 'torrent of abuse' and came into the room to see what was happening. The elderly woman was accusing the interviewee of passing herself off as a social worker, when in fact she was only a cleaner and a 'skivvy'. The nurses told the elderly woman that she should not be talking this way. The nurses advised the interviewee to leave and have nothing to do with the woman. Later that day the interviewee spoke to her supervisor, who told her not to visit the elderly woman again.
>
> A little later the elderly woman was moved to a nursing home and the interviewee and a colleague visited her in order to take her some personal items. When they arrived at the nursing home the elderly woman was in a lounge with four staff and 6–8 other patients. When the two women entered the lounge the elderly woman again launched into an offensive tirade, pointing at the interviewee and saying loudly, 'This lady doesn't have any qualifications. In fact, she's a domestic help and is here under false pretences.'

The interviewee found these slurs very hurtful. What shocked her was that the elderly woman could be so hateful towards her. The interviewee found this more intimidating than more overtly violent incidents. She had worked with insane people in the past and experienced difficult situations, but she found this the most shocking.

In another case, a social work student who had volunteered to spend her summer vacation working at a drop-in centre for disadvantaged parents and their children asked a couple of mothers to help clear the debris created during the morning by children playing, but they had flatly refused her request. Other mothers had ostentatiously assisted the social worker and indicated their disapproval of the refusal by the pair of mothers. Nevertheless, the student was so disturbed by the experience that she began to doubt (and at the time of the interview remained doubtful of) her suitability as a social worker and voluntarily entered into psychotherapy in an effort to resolve her feelings of inadequacy.

These reactions are consistent with the notion of a moral contract. Receptionists are among the least well paid of employees in the public sector and, in A&E, they work inconvenient hours. They are also among the least influential in determining general policy issues and treatment decisions, yet it is to them that patients and clients complain because they are the most visible representatives of the hospital, mental health trust or Social Services. Volunteers are unpaid or receive very poor recompense for working in uncongenial conditions for the good of others. They too have little or no influence over the circumstances that might irk patients and clients. In other words, they simply do not *deserve* ill-treatment of almost any kind. Experiences that might be considered unpleasant and disagreeable aspects of the job of professionals acquire much more negative moral force when lowly paid employees or volunteers are exposed to them.

Restoring the moral balance

Even when people are hostile, the moral universe can be restored by apology and restitution. This is illustrated by an incident in which a young and very slightly built female social worker visited a recovering heroin addict with a record of violence. The man had won custody of his young son and had resolved to kick his habit in order to fulfil his responsibilities as a father. The social worker had begun to establish a positive professional relationship with the man, whom she admired for his dedication to his son. However, neighbours had contacted the Social Services Department to report what they considered to be inappropriate behaviour on the part of the father. The social worker visited him to discuss these allegations. Sitting opposite him in his sitting room, she could see him becoming visibly angry. Suddenly, he sprang to his feet and the social worker formed the view he was barely able to maintain control of his anger. He told her to leave immediately, which she did. This explosion of anger frightened her, especially when she was obliged to pass by him on her way to the exit. However, shortly afterwards the man telephoned the social worker to apologise for his behaviour and thus transformed this otherwise frightening encounter into something with which the social worker felt able to cope. Since the incident the professional relationship has been restored.

Offence can also be mitigated by an aggressor offering a plausible explanation for their anger. Thus, a man who had been angry at being kept waiting for a replacement plaster cast on his broken ankle was perfectly agreeable once the nurse began applying the replacement cast. During the application of the plaster, he had explained that he was a single parent anxious to be on time to collect his two children from school. He had become alarmed at the prospect of being kept waiting. The plaster-nurse took this explanation as an acknowledgement that he had been wrong to be angry with her colleagues and amounted to offering a plea of mitigation. This was sufficient to restore the moral universe and she was quite happy to treat the man and chat amicably with him.

Management

The moral contract between professionals and their clientele does not exist in isolation, but is just one component of a network of moral obligation. Notable in this context are the relationships of the professionals to superiors and to colleagues. The antagonism felt for senior management in police forces in many jurisdictions is well documented (Reuss-Ianni and Ianni 1983), but staff in caring professions seem to share much the same view of their superiors (Paterson *et al.* 1999). For instance, McLean *et al.* note that

> ...studies have drawn attention to some of the shortcomings in policies and procedures. These include gaps in the provision of training, lack of management support, lack of communication

between staff at different levels, failure to follow up incidents, absence of mechanisms to monitor procedures and lack of post-incident support for staff. (McLean *et al.* 1999)

Noak *et al.* examined policy documents of hospitals and concluded that 'this study highlighted some clear omissions of key areas in the policies examined' (2002: 400). Jenkins *et al.* (1998) point to the absence of policies on hostility and violence in A&E departments, as well as the low rate of prosecutions against those victimising staff. The suggestion that managerial commitment to protecting their staff from violence is limited to 'jumping through (bureaucratic) hoops' is given credence by the report of the National Task Force Against Violence to Social Care Staff (2001), whose authors remark: 'training people to complete risk assessments is not the same as providing resources needed in view of assessments that some duties are high risk'. Littlechild (1995) attributes the under-reporting of violent incidents to the belief among social workers that they will receive little or no support from management (see also Edwards *et al.* 2001). O'Beirne *et al.* (2003) found probation officers deeply resentful towards the deafness of senior management to their demands for improved security. Rowett (1986) found that only about half of the assaults reported by his respondents were followed by a managerial response that was judged to be satisfactory by the victim. Brady and Dickson (1999) note that 'in 1996, a security conference aimed at NHS managers was cancelled due to a lack of interest'. The interviewees in this research tended to echo these complaints (see Chapter 5).

However, there was a difference between the four professions in how they viewed their *immediate* supervisors and co-workers. Staff in A&E were much more critical of management at all levels than were either mental health professionals and, still less, social workers and the police. This is surprising, since attention has already been drawn to the investment that hospital management had made in providing security for A&E staff in stark contrast to the jeopardy in which mental health staff, social workers and police routinely found themselves.

The reason for the differences lay not in what management did to *protect* staff, but in how they *responded* to any hostile episode. It was common for social workers to remark that in the aftermath of the incident they were anxious to return to the office where they would share their experience with colleagues and receive the support of local managers. The latter might reassure the aggrieved professional that the offending client or patient would be removed from their individual caseload and reallocated to another colleague and/or that home visits would be withdrawn. The literature on work-related violence frequently recommends thorough debriefing of those exposed to hostility (Brady 1999; Grimwood and La Valle 1993; Jenkins *et al.* 1998; Matthews 1998). For instance, Brady considers that de-briefing has the following benefits:

> The describing of the events while they were still fresh in the mind helps to give a more objective review before the emotions around them colour the memory. It puts them into the correct perspective, with the part that each element played in the total situation. Describing the feelings experienced helps to ventilate them before the emotions of anxiety, weakness and failure, if there, become repressed and so undermine the worker's self-confidence later. It will help prevent the aggressor taking on ogre-like proportions in the memory. When the feelings are of confidence at having dealt with a severe problem successfully, they will be reinforced still further. The devising of an alternative strategy, if that is needed, will help counteract feelings of helplessness and anxiety about what to do the next time. (Brady 1993: 68–9)

All of this may be valid, but it is striking how it is a *response* to a threatening experience rather than its prevention that has such therapeutic value. We are tempted to observe that it is a little like closing the proverbial stable door after the horse has bolted!

It is our contention that in addition to any psychological benefits (Matthews 1998) debriefing also has *moral* value. When co-workers make tea, gather round the aggrieved worker, listen to their story and sympathise with them, and when local management takes action (even if it is retrospective), this affirms that the professional is indeed a *victim* of unacceptable conduct and is *entitled* to feelings of fright and anger. In other words, debriefing is an opportunity to validate the employee's status as the *innocent victim of unacceptable conduct*. In contrast to this, a managerial response that hostility on the part of clients is part and parcel of the job and something that must be tolerated amounts to a *denial of victimhood*. This communicates the view that one has no right to feel outraged at what has happened and no entitlement to receive sympathy and consideration. Some of those who exhibited the most severe reactions during the course of interviews also said that it had been the first opportunity they had had to tell a (hopefully) sympathetic listener what had happened. Recounting what had taken place provides an opportunity for shared moral outrage and expressions of sympathy for the plight of a colleague, thus restoring the moral universe.

It is instructive that among the most severe reactions to hostile experiences were cases in which mental health professionals and social workers were denied such a response. In all three cases the professional found, or feared they would find, themselves being accused of misconduct by formidably articulate and vindictive patients or clients. These adversaries did not (or did not *only*) attack the individual physically, but used or threatened to use the complaints process so that the organisation itself attacked that person's professionalism. By doing so they threatened to reverse the moral equation: it was the professional who found themselves actually or potentially cast in the role of the offender and their adversary who donned the mantle of 'victim'. In all three services it was the failure of senior management to support staff who were the recipients of complaints that was the principal reason for distrust.

Peers

Whilst many interviewees praised the support of their peers, there were occasions when they felt that their colleagues had let them down. Perhaps the most dramatic example of that was the policewoman threatened with a loaded shotgun (Case study 3.1). When dispatched to the incident she reminded the control room that she was single-crewed and was reassured that there was no threat. She later discovered that the original call *had* made reference to a gun and that this was displayed on the computer screen in the control room as a flashing warning. In addition, she felt that her immediate supervisors and more senior officers paid little attention to her welfare in the aftermath of this trauma. Finally, the decision of the Crown Prosecution Service to reduce the seriousness of the charge to a technical firearms offence and the light sentence imposed by the court merely confirmed her view that the criminal justice system cares little for the welfare of police officers. However, this was a solitary, if dramatic, example of police officers feeling let down by peers (and others).

Social workers and mental health professionals more often felt that they were allowed to venture into potentially dangerous situations without adequate warning. The social worker who found himself threatened by the convicted-killer boyfriend of a client (Case study 4.11) did not discover until after the event the full criminal background of the man. The boyfriend had claimed to have a long career of criminal violence, but the social worker did not know whether this was truth or fantasy until after the episode when he discovered that the Probation

Service were fully aware of the boyfriend's past. Equally, the police did not respond with the urgency that the social worker believed was appropriate when the husband of the woman she was accompanying to court attacked them both in the street (Case study 5.2). Moreover, bystanders failed to intervene as the two women fought their way along a high street. Nor did bystanders assist the nurse who was being attacked by the senile elderly man (Case study 3.5). In the view of the nurse *the elderly patient* was not culpable – because he was demented – but the bystanders were to blame for their inactivity.

On the other hand, when colleagues and counterparts in other agencies *do* assist at time of need, they receive the thanks and admiration of those in jeopardy. Thus the nursing sister was immensely grateful to the police for their speedy response to the incident when two young men tried to break their way into the treatment area (Case study 3.12).

Caring professionals regard themselves as part of a moral community forming a network of moral obligation. When others fail to fulfil that obligation, they too are culpable. However, in this 'moral economy' management owe the greatest duty and are often found wanting.

Duty

The moral contact was not one-sided: professionals felt, usually very strongly, that they were morally obligated to help their patients, clients and vulnerable third parties despite this exposing them to otherwise avoidable hazards. A young casualty doctor initially refused to treat a drunken man who had punched him a glancing blow. However, when other staff prevailed upon the man to offer an undertaking to behave, the doctor completed his examination and prescribed treatment, mainly because there was no one else available to do it and he knew that the man needed treatment. He concluded that it was expedient to treat the man as quickly as possible and have him leave the department. On other occasions patients who discharged themselves were re-admitted as soon as they changed their minds, despite having behaved badly during the initial examination or treatment. Of course, this creates the danger that violence and hostility are tacitly tolerated because it is expedient in the short term to do so.

Even police officers found themselves constrained by this obligation. Thus, when the officers attended the scene of utter destruction created by the tenant engaged in an angry dispute with his landlord (Case study 3.11), they felt duty-bound to venture into the stairwell to offer assistance to the tenant who had injured himself and was now calling for help. It was when he tried to ignite the carpet that he vitiated this aspect of the moral contract and transformed himself into an antagonist.

'I deserved it'

For obvious reasons, interviewees rarely selected incidents in which they had acted improperly so as to fully justify hostility towards them. One exception to this is instructive. It was a social worker who, upon seeing a client in the street, approached her in an attempt to make an appointment that he had been trying to arrange for some time, but which the client was steadfastly avoiding. When the woman reacted aggressively to his approach, he realised that his actions had been 'out of order' and accepted responsibility for what proved to be an embarrassing and discomfiting encounter.

Conclusion

The 'moral dimension of violence' has profound implications for the vexed issue of what should count as 'violence'. If a person feels they do not deserve even the mildest rebuke, their reaction might be as severe as that of another person who has been subjected to an objectively more ferocious attack, but one that they consider to be deserved or, at least, understandable. Vulnerability, therefore, might better be conceived in terms of a person's exposure to *undeserved hostility* rather than any objectively measurable level of aggression.

   The moral dimension of victimisation has been recognised previously, albeit obliquely. In his pioneering study of the victims of burglary, Maguire (1980, 1982) notes that what victims found most unsatisfactory about the police response to their reporting this offence was the impression given that the officers did not care. Activities such as 'dusting' for fingerprints played little role in apprehending offenders; however, 'these actions can to some extent be regarded as a kind of "ritual", but this does not mean that they have no value' (Maguire 1980: 272). That value is moral, for quoting Wright (1977), Maguire agrees that: 'What offends people's instinctive sense of rightness is that the response is insufficient, rather than that it is insufficiently hurtful to the offender' (p 272). He continues, 'there is the desire for recognition of the offence as a significant event about which "something should be done"'(p 273). In other words, victims feel that they *deserve* better treatment. To have their victimhood acknowledged might go some way to restoring the moral universe, just as victimised caring professionals valued management and colleagues 'shutting the stable door' by expressions of sympathy and concern.

Chapter 7

Taming the violent workplace?

'Violence?'

The central issue throughout this book has been the definition of violence. We showed in Chapter 1 how an 'inclusive' definition of violence has become established by a wide range of individuals and organisations with an interest in the subject. We also raised the prospect that such a definition may be an ideological construct that fuels a worldwide 'moral panic' about violence at work. Elsewhere (Waddington *et al.* 2005) we have identified three ways in which the inclusive definition is applied. The first is methodological: if we are interested in how people experience and understand their experiences (as has been the purpose of this book), then it makes sense to use the most inclusive definition possible. If people believe that they have been exposed to violence, then 'violence' is what they have been exposed to. If, however, we wish to make an objective assessment of how much violence is occurring, who suffers most and how it is distributed, then this approach presents a problem, for what people label as 'violence' might vary. This leads to the second type of definition, which is analytical. This definition seeks to distinguish various aspects of the phenomenon that we call 'violence'. It was to this that we addressed ourselves in our earlier article.

The third approach is normative and is employed by campaigners and policy-makers. Whereas the analytical imperative is to define and differentiate in pursuit of clarity, normative discourse encourages as broad a definition of violence as possible. Political mobilisation is facilitated when the problem is perceived to be widespread. We are in the territory of social movements here in which trade unions and staff associations seek to 'frame' the issue so as to enhance protection for their membership (Gamson and Meyer 1996; Klandermans 1997, McAdam 1996; Snow and Benford 1992). Regulatory agencies also have a vested interest in broadening the definition as a vehicle for extending their powers. It is to this debate that this chapter is devoted. What are the practical implications of our research? We will suggest that an inclusive definition, whilst it has some advantages, also creates practical and normative problems.

The 'dog' that did not 'bark'

Before proceeding to review and discuss the research outlined in the preceding chapters, let us just note in passing a significant absence. There was virtually no evidence that when asked about violence any of our interviewees considered reporting instances of bullying and harassment from colleagues or superiors. This contradicts the view that bullying and harassment *within* the workforce is the source of most violence and menace (Bradley 1992; Carroll 2003; Denenberg and Braverman 1999; Ishmael and Alemoru 1999; McMillan 1995) and supports Mayhew and Chappell's conclusion that 'bullying was only a small proportion of all events reported by the interviewees' (Mayhew and Chappell 2003: 29). In our sample, only once did an interviewee raise the question of whether the violence the researchers referred to included internal bullying. By the time that interview was conducted, most of the sample had already been interviewed and it was decided to steer the interviewee away from issues of bullying and harassment.

Is there a problem?

As noted in Chapter 1, concern about violence at work has been fuelled by egregious incidents of the most severe violence and a plethora of surveys claiming to reveal the previously hidden extent of the problem. The weakness of those surveys (and it is an inherent weakness in the survey methodology) is that it relies upon respondents' own definitions of what constitutes 'violence'. If those respondents are being sensitised to the dangers that lurk at work, then there is the prospect that the threshold at which they define 'violence' may be reduced, thus feeding growing concern in a self-reinforcing spiral. Since also survey estimates of 'violence' commonly conflate acts of physical violence with intimidation and abuse, there is the danger that the scale of the problem is inflated. These are all the ingredients for creating a 'moral panic'. So, is the growth of concern over workplace violence a 'moral panic' or a justified recognition of a serious problem? It is our view that the problem is not as it is so often portrayed, but it is still a serious problem and not a 'moral panic'.

Whilst it is our view that the problem is real and not overstated, it remains the case that it is a quite different problem to that presented by various interested parties. The problem is less one of danger of physical attack (although this danger does exist) and more a question of anxiety on the part of workers. This might be read as 'blaming the victim' – 'pull yourself together and get on with the job'! It is not! For there is ample reason for workers in the professions we studied to feel anxious. There are parallels here with the literature on fear of crime (Hale 1996). At first fear of crime was dismissed as an irrational and exaggerated response to crime, but as research has examined more closely who is fearful about what, so the rational basis of fear has come to be appreciated. One of the earliest contributions to this growing appreciation is of direct relevance to the issues examined in this book. It is the observation that there is a strong association between exposure to so-called 'incivilities' and fear of crime (Hough 1996; Maxfield 1984). More recently, this observation has been incorporated into the theory of 'signal crime' (Innes 2003; Innes *et al.* 2004). Innes argues that some (but not all) crimes send 'signals' to the wider public about the condition of their neighbourhood or even the society in which they live. In other words, crimes can have a meaning other than their legal status. Many murders go unremarked, but others (such as the abduction and murder of 3-year-old Jamie Bulger by two young boys) can engender or perhaps focus otherwise inchoate perceptions. A vandalised bus shelter can come to symbolise the suspicion that 'no one cares'. Incivilities matter because they give experiential credibility to media reports of more serious incidents (Smith 1984).

Turning to our own data, the signal that is transmitted by the largely low-level threatening and otherwise disagreeable conduct that our interviewees described is one of their own *vulnerability*. If a drunken client can physically prevent her social worker from leaving her house (Case study 3.10), or a fellow guest can launch an unprovoked tirade (Case study 5.5), or injured patients in A&E can repeatedly and aggressively demand treatment, then the signal sent is that others might do much more. This is why the question of *who* commits the act is so important. For if the client's boyfriend who casually remarked that he could stab the social worker sitting a few feet away had recently served a term of imprisonment for manslaughter (Case study 4.11), or if the young man with the appearance of a 'drug-dealer' repeatedly declined to remain in the cubicle assigned to him – whilst his adversary in the fight that had resulted in his injuries lies near to death nearby (Case study 4.5) – then the amplitude of the 'signal' is massively enhanced.

Managing 'signal' incidents

In their pioneering study of work-related violence, Poyner and Warne (1988) argued persuasively that first and foremost it is necessary to 'recognise the problem'. They had in mind the situation they found to be commonplace of obviously violent incidents not being recorded and, therefore, going unaddressed by supervisors and management. Since this report was published, risk-management strategies invariably include 'identifying the risk' (see for example the NHS risk-management framework reproduced in National Audit Office 2003b). Many might consider this to be a statement of the blindingly obvious, but our analysis suggests that it is the elusive nature of 'the problem' that proves so challenging. Management must recognise that 'the problem' lies more often in the meaning that staff give to incidents, rather than in the objective characteristics of the incidents themselves.

Help is at hand, again from the 'signal crime' perspective. For this theoretical framework underlies a practical approach to law and order on the streets – 'reassurance policing' (Crathern 2005). Police are now officially encouraged to appreciate that objective indicators of crime are insufficient: by most counts, the actual incidence of crime has declined significantly over the past dozen years. The practical (and this case, political) problem is that the public do not believe it: fear of crime continues to remain high. Under the 'reassurance policing' initiative, what police officers are encouraged to do is to understand the communities they police sufficiently well to appreciate the signals that people are detecting in their environment. Then, the police are obliged not only to do whatever they can to reduce or eliminate those sources of negative signals, but also to be *seen to do so*. A covert operation that has the effect of reducing burglary in an area is likely to have much less impact on public reassurance than a high-profile intervention that achieves the same impact, or even perhaps less. We are in the domain of perceptions here. If people *believe* a problem has been reduced then they are likely to feel reassured; if they remain unaware that a problem has actually been reduced, reassurance is unlikely to blossom.

As we discussed in the previous chapter, violent, threatening and abusive incidents are viewed through a moral lens. The workers we interviewed craved reassurance every bit as much as people on crime-ridden estates. As Wilson and Kelling (1982) pointed out many years ago, the presence of dilapidated property, rubbish-strewn streets, abandoned vehicles and disorderly people gives the impression that 'nobody cares' and that impression liberates lawlessness. So it is in the workplace: staff need to feel that *somebody cares – really!* The good news for managers is that such caring comes cheap. As we also noted in the previous chapter, management has generally been regarded as poor at conveying the impression that they do care – something that our research (with minor qualification) echoes. The signal sent to many workers is that administrative arrangements ostensibly aimed at addressing problems of workplace violence are mere form-filling (Kedward 2001; Lehane and Carver 2003). It is hardly any surprise, therefore, that forms are so rarely completed (National Audit Office 2003b).

This amounts to a catastrophic management failure when 'closing the stable door once the horse has bolted' is a cheap and easy means of showing that management cares! All it takes is a little attention to the plight of the staff member and expressions of concern. From what our interviewees told us, and other interviewees have remarked to other researchers, management, instead of moderating the 'signal' sent by the incident, often succeeds in amplifying it – adding needless insult to existing injury. Dismissing incidents that distress and disturb staff as just 'part of the job' proclaims loud and clear that 'nobody cares'.

Not all appropriate management responses are as cheap. There are clearly resource implications in ensuring that home visits are undertaken by pairs of staff whenever there is the suspicion that problems might arise. However, we question the ethics of underfunded public services functioning by allowing dedicated staff to bear the 'costs'. We do not accept that the dangers and difficulties that accompany the care of the mentally ill in the community should be converted into anxiety and stress suffered by mental health professionals whose vulnerability is needlessly enhanced by making home visits to patients known to be potentially dangerous. Likewise, if the '24-hour economy' seeks commercial gain from encouraging alcohol-fuelled excess on the part of its clientele (Hobbs *et al.* 2003), then surely it is appropriate that these companies should pay for the cost of providing A&E staff with as much 'security' as the pubs and clubs in which young people acquire their inebriation. It is increasingly accepted by governments that the costs of material pollution should be incorporated into the price of products. For instance, the costs of disposing of car tyres should be borne by tyre manufacturers and passed on to customers. Perhaps the same principle should be applied to the '24-hour economy'.

Zero tolerance

One initiative that appears to take seriously the 'signal' sent by incidents and the managerial response to them has been the adoption of 'zero tolerance' policies.

> In the latter part of 1999, Ministers developed the NHS Zero Tolerance Campaign in England across the spectrum of government departments, with the aim of tackling the issue of violence and intimidation against NHS staff. (Gournay 2001)

The NHS has not been alone: other health services worldwide have done much the same (for example in Queensland; see Queensland Nurses' Union 2000). Staff now appear to have the reassurance that if they are victimised, management will take firm action against perpetrators. Coyne (2001) argues that a policy of prosecuting offenders will prevent such incidents being swept under the carpet and will force health authorities to address problems.

However, evidence is already emerging of an implementation gap:

> while most NHS trusts have promulgated the policy of zero tolerance ... translating theory into practice has proved difficult for some. In particular, while there is no central data on prosecutions, staff surveys show that prosecutions are rare. Although all trusts were required to assess the need for a policy on withholding treatment by April 2002 ... In practice, most trusts have found it difficult to implement. (National Audit Office 2003b: 5)

It is tempting to attribute such failure to spineless managers, but the problem goes deeper than that, for even when a case is thought sufficiently serious to refer to the police, prosecution follows in less than half those cases.

It is not spineless managers that are the problem, but the 'zero tolerance' policy itself – a quick-fix, 'get tough' policy that fails to consider what 'zero tolerance' would, in practice, be applied.

Whittington notes that 'the emphasis of government policy seems to be upon physical violence directed against staff' (Whittington 2002: 820). However, physical violence is only a small part of the problem, and if our data are any guide it is rarely sufficiently serious to justify prosecution, albeit that when egregious acts of serious violence are not prosecuted with the vigour they deserve, this too sends a 'signal' very clearly that 'they don't care'.

The real pervasive problem is one of 'incivility': ubiquitious use of obscenities; passive acts of non-compliance, such as the bejewelled young man with the appearance of a drug-dealer who declined to wait in the cubicle assigned to him (Case study 4.5); or a patient who demonstrated anger like that of the tattooed 'hardman' who leapt to his feet (Case study 4.3). Then there are others whose offensive actions are slight by any objective appraisal: the young lad who taunted and humiliated the community constable (Case study 6.2), or the young woman who urinated on the floor of an A&E cubicle (Case study 6.1). Zero tolerance shown towards such minor incivilities could not amount to much. The same would go for those who occasionally inflict material damage in the course of displaying their rage. Even if restitution for the damage was demanded, how would zero tolerance be shown towards the fear and alarm that such displays evoke in those who witness them?

Complaints

There are three issues that starkly expose the limits of zero tolerance. In this section we will consider allegedly malicious use of complaints processes, whilst in the following sections we will consider the problems of prejudice and the profile of the clientele. Malicious use of complaints processes comes in two forms: first, clients, patients and suspects who calculatedly use or threaten to use official complaints procedures to coerce staff into complying with their wishes or to exact revenge. Undoubtedly, there are those who do abuse complaints processes for malicious purposes, but the problem is that this cannot be ascertained with certainty until the complaint has been fully investigated. As the case of Dr Harold Shipman – the physician credited with being Britain's most prolific serial murderer – illustrates, even apparently absurd complaints made against well-regarded professionals can be entirely justified (Smith 2005). In the past, academics and campaigners have legitimately criticised public authorities (especially the police) for dismissing too readily complaints made against their personnel.

The problem is that staff find the process of investigation hugely threatening – as if the organisation itself has turned upon them when all they believe they have done is to serve that very same organisation (what Diamond [1997] describes as 'administrative assault'). Staff in all four services complained vociferously that their respective organisations took complaints against them far more seriously than their own complaints against clients, patients, or suspects. And it is bound to be so: for if an investigation is to be conducted thoroughly then those who conduct it must remain neutral and objective. This amounts to maintaining distance between themselves and the staff who are complained against. Failure to do so might itself be grounds for bringing an official complaint against the investigator. Hence, the investigator, who in many instances may also be the manager, cannot offer support and sympathy for the person complained against, for to do so might be taken as indicating favouritism.

In the well-trodden terrain of police complaints processes many commentators have wryly observed that given the low probability that a complaint will be substantiated, police officers have little to fear. What this fails to appreciate is that anxiety is aroused not only by the probability of the consummation of the threat, but also the value of that which is threatened. In the case of all four occupations represented here, it was people's careers that were jeopardised and for devoted professionals it was also their sense of self. As we have mentioned previously, one CPN likened it to 'being violated'.

Secondly, there are occasions when clients, patients and suspects become enraged justifiably or at least understandably. Here the angry person can be legitimately criticised for the *way* in which they express their annoyance at sub-standard service, but not for feeling annoyed in the first place. Zero tolerance could be exhibited towards patients who bang on the reception security screen and yell obscenities at the staff whilst demanding treatment. However, any response to such behaviour will, at the very least, be mitigated by the knowledge that patients may have waited several hours for treatment and are understandably at the end of their tether. For these reasons, it is highly improbable that any hospital would take retribution against the patient's relative who humiliated the receptionist after being sent on a needless round trip (Case study 6.4). In consequence, staff would again feel that they were not being supported.

However, suppose that effective action *could* be taken to suppress the more offensive expressions of annoyance, whether justified or not. The implication of that would be that malicious yet articulate and well-connected adversaries would still be able to intimidate staff because they expressed themselves in ways that were not overtly objectionable, whilst inarticulate thugs would be precluded from expressing justifiable annoyance through the limited means at their command. In other words, it would yet again privilege social and cultural capital as it did in the case of the mother of the arguably autistic child who threatened the career of the social worker (Case study 3.13), because she 'knew her way around the system'. As Whittington observes, '"zero tolerance"…could eventually lead to an abuse of patients' right to express appropriate annoyance and irritation with an inadequate service' (Whittington 2002: 820).

Prejudice

This brings us to the vexed issue of prejudice touched upon briefly in Chapter 4 in the context of the implicit racism of Case study 4.5. As the interviewee in this case freely confessed, what made the bejewelled youth who declined to remain within the cubicle so threatening was not only that the man's erstwhile adversary was struggling for life in the resuscitation room, but also that he was *black*. It was race that greatly contributed to him 'looking the part'. This was far from a solitary example: the youths who tried to batter down the doors into the treatment area were also black (Case study 3.12); so too was the man whose partner had lacerated her arms (Case study 3.4). In these cases and others, race and the prospect of being accused of racism were a prominent theme. This clearly undermines the victimhood of the interviewees, who felt intimidated by these patients, for the question arises whether they would have felt equally intimidated had the person been white.

The issue goes to the heart of the 'signal crime' approach, for 'signals' are not only transmitted, they must be *received and understood* in order to have their impact. The 'receiver' of any 'signal' might be prone to distortion and the imagery associated with racism represents precisely that kind of distortion. The remedy, therefore, lies in 're-tuning' the 'receiver' rather than enforcing 'zero tolerance' against the signal transmitted. Threatening, intimidating and even abusive behaviour is likely to lie, to some extent, in the eye of the beholder. This extends beyond race and racism, although that is its most egregious manifestation. The tattooed 'hardman' was fearsome because his shaven head, muscular torso, far-right tattoos and large dog also evoked forbidding imagery (Case study 4.3). The nurse's response to the homeless jaundiced drug addict who scratched at his sores was stimulated in part by the image he presented and indeed he claimed that he was receiving discriminatory treatment on precisely these grounds (Case study 4.4). Moreover, the attribution of malice to some patients and disputed psychiatric diagnoses could also discriminate against some people. Coyne cites evidence from an experimental study in which British and Canadian nurses were shown videos portraying fictional disturbed patients. It found that nurses were more likely to recommend police action where they attributed the disturbance to personal choice rather than mental illness. Coyne continues: 'It is feasible that those patients who are prosecuted are those patients who are dislikable or considered to be in some way "to blame" for their violence, particularly personality disordered patients or patients with a history of substance misuse' (Coyne 2001: 142).

Difficult people

What unites the four occupations in our research is that their clientele is disproportionately composed of people with difficulties. Research among the police reveals that much of their work is conducted with people who lack economic, social and cultural capital. It has been estimated that the *majority* of arrestees suffer some significant psychological impairment (Gudjonsson *et al.* 1993; Gudjonsson 1994). Those who attend A&E are seeking emergency medical treatment for injuries and illnesses that are likely to provoke anxiety and distress both to themselves and their companions. Social workers and mental health staff spend their professional lives trying to help and protect those who have difficulty helping and protecting themselves. Given the profile of their clientele it seems reasonable to infer: (a) that members of all four professions will be disproportionately exposed to people who are likely to be disagreeable or worse, and (b) that if these professionals do not engage with these potentially disagreeable people, then who will?

> Prosecution of patients for acts that could be considered as symptomatic of their condition (impulsiveness, low threshold for frustration, responses to psychotic stimuli, agitation and the consequent reaction to obstructions to their desires) is a controversial area. (Coyne 2001: 143)

'Zero tolerance' creates as many problems as it solves. It is unlikely to reassure staff because there are many circumstances in which it cannot or should not be implemented. The 'signal' that such non-implementation is likely to send to staff is that once again management rhetoric is hollow.

Handling difficult people better

Difficult people pose a significant unavoidable occupational hazard, which, like similar hazards in other walks of life, must be handled. How can police officers, emergency medical staff, social workers and mental health professionals be helped to handle better the difficult people they encounter in the course of their work?

There is no shortage of advice for staff in these professions: training manuals abound (Bibby 1994, 1995; Brady 1993; Braverman 1999; Dorset Social Services 1992; Grenyer *et al.* 2004; Kerber 1999; Leadbetter and Trewartha 1998; Mason and Chandley 1999; National Association of Social Workers 1996; O'Keefe and Mennen 1998; Owens and Keville 1990; Rowett, Colin and Breakwell 1992; Royal College of Nursing 1998; Shepherd 1994). All of them emphasise prevention and de-escalation. This meshes with a growing realisation in police circles that assessing whether force is used justifiably requires an appraisal not only of the immediate threat posed by the suspect, but also whether an officer had acted wisely in finding him or herself in the situation where force had become necessary at all (Klockars 1996). Research for the Police Complaints Authority (Police Complaints Authority 2003) suggested that certain tactics employed in armed operations may themselves create the conditions in which the armed officers confront a threat sufficient to justify opening fire. This tacitly endorses Binder and Scharf's (1980) argument that recourse to the use of force is usually the terminal stage in a *process* of interaction during which it may have been possible to avoid such an outcome. The same assumption lies behind the manuals of guidance offered to members of the caring professions: control the encounter and nothing untoward need occur.

It is our contention that whilst these manuals and similar advice may contain some valuable lessons, they grossly overestimate the extent to which it is practically possible to avoid difficult encounters. It is obviously better if professionals avoid finding themselves in circumstances that are conducive to violence and aggression. Certainly in retrospect it is tempting to identify moments at which any of the encounters considered in this book could have been steered towards a less confrontational outcome. The social worker who unwittingly entered the home of the drunken client and then found herself imprisoned by the woman (Case study 3.10) and the CPN who found herself effectively detained in the basement kitchen as the 'biker' revealed his paedophile fantasies (Case study 5.6) would doubtless both agree that it would have been wiser not to enter the premises at all. The practical problem is that such episodes develop through successive imperceptible steps, as the officer who accompanied the suspect to A&E found to his cost (Case study 3.2). Initially, the man was compliant, even amiable, then as he became progressively agitated the officer responded by first remonstrating with him; then allowing him to walk off whilst remaining in pursuit; upon finding themselves in a reasonably secluded location, reaching out to attract his attention; then finding the man behind him and himself in a neck-hold. The whole point of the emphasis on a *process* of interaction is that minor actions are taken without knowledge of the reactions that might follow. After all, if it was otherwise then no game of chess would ever come to a conclusion – and playing chess is a good deal simpler than dealing with the vagaries of difficult people.

Whilst any of us can retrospectively identify such moments, none of us can claim with certainty that had the professional acted differently then confrontation would have been avoided. To do so would be a counter-factual. It is perfectly possible that had the social worker declined to enter the drunken client's home or the CPN refused to remain in the basement kitchen, either situation could easily have spun more rapidly and disastrously out of control. No one is blessed with sufficient prescience as to foretell the manifold outcomes of any specific action taken in the course of interaction because how others respond is conditioned by how *they* perceive and understand what is happening.

Apart from the limits to predictability imposed by the process of social interaction, dangers might arise entirely unexpectedly. When two social workers visited a youthful couple of drug addicts because of concerns raised by neighbours about the welfare of their two infant children, there was no realistic prospect of them anticipating that the couple's drug supplier would arrive and demand payment during the course of the unheralded social work visit. All four professions operate within a milieu of social and personal disorder, chaos, dilapidation and crime. In doing so, they are inevitably exposed to unpredictable dangers.

Even where danger is anticipated it might be impossible to avoid. Social interaction is routinely facilitated by parties to it conducting themselves in accordance with normative expectations. Visiting someone in their home places the visitor in the position of a 'guest' to which are attached a plethora of normative expectations, one of which is to wait to be invited to enter and cede to the householder the right to direct where one might sit. Hence, it may have been regrettable that when he visited the client whose boyfriend was a convicted killer the social worker found himself sitting far from the door whilst the boyfriend casually spoke of stabbing him, but there was no realistic alternative. The social worker could hardly enter the sitting room and direct who should sit where and had he done so then he may have antagonised the boyfriend and placed himself in greater jeopardy. Of course, police officers do precisely this. They walk into private homes and breach rules of etiquette by remaining standing, separating parties if expedient and determining who talks when, but they do all this from a position of coercive authority. Social workers and mental health professionals seek to have a different, closer and more trusting relationship with their clients that undermines such an approach. Indeed, it is even questionable whether the cautious, calculating and defensive posture that so many manuals of guidance recommend is compatible with an open and trusting relationship.

Equally, whilst emphasis is frequently given in manuals of guidance to avoiding provocation and de-escalating conflict, this is not always possible or even proper. There are aspects of the roles of all four professions that are unavoidably provocative. Winstanley and Whittington note that 'the delivery of unpleasant or aversive stimuli such as giving injections or wound care, or making the patient do things they would rather not is an integral part of the nursing role' (2004: 9) and is likely to provoke an aggressive response. Nurses refuse to stitch wounds over potential fracture sites for compelling clinical reasons. This can provoke drunken young men into acts of aggression that could be avoided by subordinating clinical judgement to patient demands, but to do so would be improper. Social workers and mental health professionals could avoid provoking their clients by subordinating the welfare of those it is their duty to protect (for instance, children at risk) to their own comfort and safety. Police officers could avoid many hazards by retreating from confrontations, but their duty is to intervene in precisely such circumstances.

Of course, to observe that these professionals have a duty to act in ways that the recipients of their actions may find inconvenient, unpleasant and aversive, does not absolve professionals from performing those actions so as to minimise their negative aspects. However, not all interventions occur in circumstances of the professional's choosing, as the off-duty officer found to his cost when he apprehended the youths he suspected of shoplifting (Case study 3.3). As he conceded, it was probably imprudent of him to initiate an encounter with the three shoplifting suspects whilst dressed in paint-spattered clothing and not in possession of a police warrant card. However, since he was not in possession of a mobile phone either, had he merely followed the trio he would have had no means of summoning assistance. The choice he faced was to do *something* or do *nothing* and he felt duty-bound to intervene, hoping that he could convince the trio to return to the shop to resolve the matter informally. When they refused he felt compelled to disclose that he was a police officer and attempt to arrest at least one of them. The combination of duty and circumstances can and does sometimes box professionals into the proverbial corner.

These are not the only occasions where professional staff knowingly expose themselves to danger because they feel duty-bound to do so. The woman police officer who attended the scene of destruction wrought by an enraged tenant (Case study 3.11) was not obliged to venture into the stairwell and climb through the precariously balanced jumble of trashed household items in response to the tenant's cries for help. She did so because she considered it her duty.

Even when threat is anticipated, stress cannot be avoided. The CPN who was warned about her patient's homicidal fantasies was able to prepare for their next encounter with careful attention to her own safety (Case study 4.14). Yet, this was achieved at significant emotional cost. Believing that another person desires to inflict physical injury or death is stressful in itself. Making preparations lends reality to those beliefs and the damage is done.

Whilst staff who expose themselves to danger would doubtless welcome as much protection as can be made available, our interviewees were aware that danger came with the job. Perhaps what they expected was to have their courage and commitment recognised and valued. There has been much debate in the health literature about the relationship of violence to more general work-related stress. Certainly, exposure to violence and abuse is frequently identified as a stressor, but it is not alone. Some authors suggest that changes in health service management in many parts of the world are responsible for creating additional stress for health professionals (Di Martino 2003; Gillespie and Melby 2003).

Getting real

There is little evidence that any of the training regimes so freely prescribed actually work (Grenyer *et al.* 2004; Mayhew and Chappell 2003; National Audit Office 2003b): little wonder, for hardly any attention is paid to examining the actual problems which training aspires to remedy. Instead, as the NAO report on the Health Service remarks, 'Training programmes were largely "off the shelf" and the syllabi were based more on the experience and preference of the trainers than a rational analysis of training needs'. A glaring example of this is to be found in the training given to police officers in how to use their defensive equipment.

It will not have escaped the attention of many readers that contemporary police officers are equipped with an array of weaponry: longer batons that often incorporate a 'side-handle'; rigid handcuffs; and incapacitant sprays. What was notably absent from police officers' recollections of violent encounters in our research was recourse to the use of the weapons they carried: the use of batons or CS was rare. Along with the accumulating paraphernalia of 'arrest and restraint' has come training in its use. However, this training is based upon a fundamental misconception of the circumstances in which police officers use force. Invariably, training sessions envisage that the officer is *attacked* and is obliged to use their weaponry in self-defence. The evidence from our interviews with officers was that this was rare. As one police interviewee – a sergeant with many years' experience – explained, only twice in his career had he been *attacked.* All the other violent encounters that he had experienced could have been terminated by his abandoning his efforts to arrest his assailants. 'All I needed to do was to hold up my hands and say "Go on then, off you go" and that would have been the end of it.' Violent encounters for most police officers consist of trying to overpower someone (usually a young man) who is struggling to free himself. This does not minimise the scale of the problem, for in such struggles injuries can occur, as they did to the off-duty officer who arrested the youthful shoplifters (Case study 3.3). However, so far as we can determine, training is not given in how officers should deal with such situations, beyond the rather stereotyped catalogue of officially approved holds that can be applied.

Blaming the victim

One of the most pernicious aspects of policy on workplace violence is the implicit blaming of the victim. Training programmes and advice manuals that emphasise how violence can be prevented and aggression de-escalated leave the impression that if staff are victimised it is because *they* are incompetent (McLean *et al.* 1999). No wonder then that staff decline to report even the more serious episodes of violence and hostility for fear that it will reflect adversely upon their professional competence (O'Beirne *et al.* 2004).

Reasons given by staff for not reporting incidents include concern that the incident might be viewed as a reflection of their inability to manage the incident, not wanting the attention any action might bring and forms being too complicated or inappropriate for recording what happened. (National Audit Office 2003b: 2)

Moreover, by emphasising training, responsibility is pushed down the management hierarchy. Mayhew observes:

The available evidence suggests that the preventive strategies that are most likely to decrease the risk of occupational violence have not been widely adopted in the health industry. That is, the occupational violence preventive interventions that are higher up the OHS 'hierarchy of control' have tended to be ignored, and only lower-order strategies adopted (e.g. training). (Mayhew 2003: 4)

The NAO report on the Health Service (2003b) drew attention to how staff shortages had resulted in chronic failures by NHS Trusts to comply with Health and Safety legislation and increase the risk of accidents. These are not the province of the competence of staff, but basic resource issues that are supposedly the responsibility of management.

Taking workplace violence seriously

The twin emphases on 'zero tolerance' and training in how to handle (and especially defuse) volatile encounters are spurious 'quick fixes' for what our data demonstrate are in reality complex, multifaceted and sometimes subtle problems. This approach is facilitated by the 'inclusive definition of violence' which allows the discourse that surrounds this issue to shift its focus as expedient. Whittington identifies how different definitions are employed by different agencies:

Whilst the emphasis of government policy seems to be upon physical violence directed against staff, policy statements from other bodies include a much wider range of patient behaviours within their remit. The Royal College of Nursing, for instance, suggests that violence includes abuse, threats, the inducement of fear and the application of force. (Whittington 2002: 820)

Whilst the propagation of the inclusive definition has mobilised policy-makers by revealing the extent of the problem, it has let them off the hook. Thus, 'zero tolerance' can be presented as a robust solution to the problem of workplace violence, but only addresses its most egregious manifestations. Likewise, the provision of training discharges organisational obligations for 'due diligence', whilst entirely unproven in its effectiveness.

If workplace violence is to be taken seriously, the first step is surely to 'recognise the problem', as Poyner and Warne (1988) recommended so long ago. What our data demonstrate is that 'the problem' is unlikely to yield to any 'quick fix'; that is why we abstain from making recommendations. Dealing with this problem will require policies every bit as subtle as the problem itself. One size will not fit all.

Meanwhile, what are policy-makers to do? Well, they can ensure that whenever the horse has bolted, the stable door is secured by supporting their staff. This is particularly so in those cases where complaints have been made against staff, or the staff fear that complaints may arise. Procedures that follow a twin-track of investigating complaints vigorously, on the one hand, whilst offering support, on the other, should not be beyond managerial imagination.

References

Ackroyd, S. and Hughes, J. (1992) *Data Collection in Context*, 2nd edition, London: Longman.

Akerstrom, M. (2002) 'Slaps, punches, pinches – but not violence: boundary-work in nursing homes for the elderly', *Symbolic Interaction* 25(4): 515–536.

Aromaa, K. (1994) 'Work-related violence as escalatory interaction', in R. Bast-Pettersen (ed.) *Research on Violence, Threats and Bullying as Health Risks among Health Care Personnel*, Reykjavik: Nordic Council of Ministers.

Aye Maung, N. (1995) *Young People, Victimisation and the Police: British Crime Survey Findings on Experiences and Attitudes of 12 to 15 Year Olds*, London: HMSO.

Barnard, M. A. (1993) 'Violence and vulnerability: conditions of work for streetworking prostitutes', *Sociology of Health and Illness* 15(5): 683.

Bibby, P. (1994) *Personal Safety for Social Workers*, London: Suzy Lamplugh Trust.

Bibby, P. (1995) *Personal Safety for Health Care Workers*, London: Suzy Lamplugh Trust.

Binder, A. and Scharf, P. (1980) 'The violent police-citizen encounter', *Annals of the American Academy of Political and Social Science* 452: 111–121.

Bradley, V. (1992) 'Workplace abuse, unrecognised emergency department violence', *Journal of Emergency Nursing* 18(6): 489–490.

Brady, C. (1999) 'Surviving the incident', in P. Leather, D. Beale, C. Lawrence, C. Brady and T. Cox (eds) *Work-Related Violence: Assessment and Intervention*, London: Routledge.

Brady, C. and Dickson, R. (1999) 'Violence in health care settings', in P. Leather, D. Beale, C. Lawrence, C. Brady and T. Cox (eds) *Work-Related Violence: Assessment and Intervention*, London: Routledge.

Brady, E. (1993) *Coping with Violent Behaviour: A Handbook for Social Work Staff*, Harlow: Longman.

Braverman, M. (1999) *Preventing Workplace Violence: A Guide for Employers and Practitioners*, Thousand Oaks: Sage.

Brennan, W. (2001) 'Having words: verbal abuse at work. The various theories and research on verbal violence towards people at work are examined', *Safety and Health Practitioner* 19(10): 36–39.

Brewer, J. D. (1990) 'Sensitivity as a problem in field research', *American Behavioral Scientist* 33(5): 578–593.

British Dental Association (1997) *Violence at Work*, London: British Dental Association.

British Medical Association (2003) *Violence at Work: The Experience of UK Doctors*, London: Health Policy and Economic Research Unit, British Medical Association.

Brown, R., Bute, S. and Ford, P. (1986) *Social Workers at Risk: The Prevention and Management of Violence*, London: Macmillan.

Budd, T. (1999) *Violence at Work: Findings from the British Crime Survey*, London: Home Office Research Development and Statistics Directorate.

Budd, T. (2001) *Violence at Work: New Findings from the 2000 British Crime Survey*, London: Home Office Research Development and Statistics Directorate.

Budd, T. (2003) *Alcohol-related Assault: Findings from the British Crime Survey*, London: Home Office.

Bute, S. (1994) 'Violence to social workers', in T. Wykes (ed.) *Violence and Health Care Professionals*, London: Chapman and Hall.

Campbell, R. and Kinnell, H. (2001) '"We shouldn't have to put up with this": Street sex work and violence', *CJM* (42): 12–13.

Carroll, V. (2003) 'Verbal abuse in the workplace: How to protect yourself and help solve the problem', *American Journal of Nursing* (March): 132.

Chappell, D. and Di Martino, V. (2000) *Violence at Work*, Geneva: International Labour Office.

Cherryman, J. and Bull, R. (2001) 'Police officers' perceptions of specialist investigative interviewing skills', *International Journal of Police Science and Management* 3(3): 199–212.

Choongh, S. (1997) *Policing as Social Discipline*, Oxford: Clarendon.

Choongh, S. (1998) 'Policing the dross: a social disciplinary model of policing', *British Journal of Criminology* 38(4): 623–634.

Church, S., Henderson, M., Barnard, M. and Hart, G. (2001) 'Violence by clients towards female prostitutes in different work settings: questionnaire survey', *British Medical Journal* 322(7285): 524–525.

Cicourel, A. (1964) *Method and Measurement in Sociology*, New York: Free Press.

Cohen, S. (1972) *Folk Devils and Moral Panics*, Oxford: Martin Robertson.

Construction Law (2000) 'Partnering in a rough, tough world. Even acrimonious divorce work did not prepare the young Jan Middleton for the insults, posturing and threats of violence which typified construction litigation "without prejudice" meetings', *Construction Law* 11(7): 6–7.

Cooper, C. L., Hoel, H. and di Martino, V. (2003) *Preventing Violence and Harassment in the Workplace*, Dublin: European Foundation for the Improvement of Living and Working Conditions.

Coyne, A. (2001) 'Should patients who assault staff be prosecuted?', *Journal of Psychiatric and Mental Health Nursing* 8: 139–145.

Crabb, S. (1995) 'Violence at work: the brutal truths', *People Management*: 25.

Crathern, C. (2005) *NRPP: National Reassurance Policing Programme*, London: Home Office.

Croner Employment Digest (1997) 'Violence at work – what is the employer's potential liability?', *Croner Employment Digest*: 1–3.

Curbow, B. (2001) 'Origins of violence at work', in C. Cooper (ed.) *Violence in the Health Sector, ILO/WHO Report*, Geneva: ILO, WHO.

Cutler, B., Penrod, S. D. and Martens, T. K. (1987) 'Improving the reliability of eyewitness identifications: putting context into context', *Journal of Applied Psychology* 72: 629–637.

Davies, M. G. and Thomson, D. M. (1988) *Memory in Context: Context in Memory*, Chichester: Wiley.

DeClercq, N. (2000) 'Violence at Work. By Duncan Chappell and Vittorio Di Martino', *Labor Studies Journal* 25(3): 105–106.

Denenberg, R. V. and Braverman, M. (1999) *The Violence-Prone Workplace: A New Approach to Dealing with Hostile, Threatening, and Uncivil Behavior*, Ithaca, NY: ILR/Cornell University Press.

Denton, M., Zeytinoglu, I. and Webb, S. (2000) 'Work-related violence and the OHS of home health care workers', *Journal of Occupational Health and Safety Australia and New Zealand* 16(5): 419–428.

Diamond, M. A. (1997) 'Administrative assault: a contemporary psychoanalytic view of violence and aggression in the workplace', *American Review of Public Administration* 27(3): 228–247.

di Martino, V. (2003) 'Relationship between work stress and workplace violence in the health sector', *Workplace Violence in the Health Sector*, Geneva: International Labour Office.

Dorset Social Services (1992) *Dealing with Violence: Guidelines for Staff when Faced with Violent or Aggressive Behaviour During their Work*, Dorchester: Social Services Department, Dorset County Council.

Dunkel, J., Ageson, A. T. and Ralph, C. J. (2000) 'Encountering violence in field work: a risk reduction model', *Journal of Teaching in Social Work* 20(3/4): 5–18.

Eastley, R., MacPherson, R., Richards, H. and Mian, I. H. (1993) 'Assaults on professional carers of elderly people', *British Medical Journal* 307: 845.

Edgar, K., O'Donnell, I. and Martin, C. (2003) 'Tracking the pathways to violence in prison', in R. M. Lee and E. A. Stanko (eds) *Researching Violence: Essays on Methodology and Measurement*, London: Routledge.

Chemist and Druggist (2004) 'PDA examines level of support. An online survey will be used to ask pharmacists who have experienced violence at work about what levels of support employers provide after an incident of violent behaviour', *Chemist and Druggist* (6444): 6–7.

Edwards, D., Burnard, P., Coyle, D., Fothergill, A. and Hannigan, B. (2001) 'A stepwise multivariate analysis of factors that contribute to stress for mental health nurses working in the community', *Journal of Advanced Nursing* 36(6): 805–813.

Elston, M. A., Gabe, J. P., Denney, D., Lee, R. and O'Beirne, M. (2002) 'Violence against doctors: a medical(ised) problem? The case of National Health Service general practitioners', *Sociology of Health and Illness* 24(5): 575–598.

European Agency for Safety and Health at Work (2002) *Violence at Work*, Luxembourg: Office for Official Publications of the European Communities.

European Agency for Safety and Health at Work (2003) *Prevention of Violence to Staff in the Education Sector*, Bilbao: European Agency for Safety and Health at Work.

European Commission (1998) *Sexual Harassment in the Workplace in the European Union*, Directorate-General for Employment, Industrial Relations and Social Affairs.

Farrugia, S. (2002) 'A dangerous occupation? Violence in public libraries', *New Library World* 103(1180): 309–319.

Findorff-Dennis, M. J., McGovern, P. M., Bull, M. and Hung, J. (1999) 'Work-related assaults: the impact on victims', *American Association of Occupational Health Nursing Journal* 47: 456–465.

Fisher, R. P., Geiselman, R. E. and Amador, M. (1989) 'Field test of the cognitive interview: enhancing the recollection of actual victims and witnesses of crime', *Journal of Applied Psychology* 74: 722–727.

Fletcher, D. (1997) 'Nursing is "dangerous" occupation', *The Weekly Telegraph*, London.

Foddy, W. (1993) *Constructing Questions for Interviews and Questionnaires: Theory and Practice in Social Research*, Cambridge: Cambridge University Press.

Foust, D. and Rhee, K. J. (1993) 'Incidence of battery in an urban emergency department', *Annals of Emergency Medicine* 3: 583–585.

Freyne, A. and Wrigley, M. (1996) 'Aggressive incidents towards staff by elderly patients with dementia in a long-stay ward', *International Journal of Geriatric Psychiatry* 11: 57–63.

Gallagher, J. (1999a) *Protect Us from Harm: preventing violence at work*, London: TUC Health and Safety Unit.

Gallagher, J. (1999b) *Violent Times. A health and safety report: TUC report on preventing violence at work*, London: TUC Health and Safety Unit.

Gamson, W. A. and Meyer, D. S. (1996) 'Framing political opportunity', in D. McAdam, J. D. McCarthy and M. N. Zald (eds) *Comparative Perspectives on Social Movements*, Cambridge: Cambridge University Press.

Gates, D., Fitzwater, E. and Meyer, U. (1999) 'Violence against caregivers in nursing homes: expected, tolerated and accepted', *Journal of Gerontological Nursing* 25(4): 12–22.

Geiselman, R. E. and Padilla, J. (1988) 'Cognitive interviewing with child witnesses', *Journal of Police Science and Administration* 16(4): 236–242.

Gerberich, S. G., Church, T. R., McGovern, P. M., Hansen, H. E., Nachreiner, N. M., Geisser, M. S., Ryan, A. D., Mongin, S. J. and Watt, G. D. (2004) 'An epidemiological study of the magnitude and consequences of work related violence: the Minnesota nurses' study', *Occupational and Environmental Medicine* 61(6): 495–503.

Gerberich, S. G., Church, T. R., McGovern, P. M., Hansen, H. E., Nachreiner, N. M., Geisser, M. S., Watt, G. D. and Ryan, A. D. (2001) 'Occupational violence: Minnesota nurses' study', *The 129th Annual Meeting of American Public Health Association Oct 21-25*, Atlanta, Ga.

Giga, S. I., Hoel, H. and Cooper, C. L. (2003a) 'Violence and stress at work in the performing arts and in journalism', *Working Paper*, Geneva: International Labour Office.

Giga, S. I., Hoel, H. and Cooper, C. L. (2003b) 'Violence and stress at work in the postal sector', *Working Paper*, Geneva: International Labour Office.

Gilbert, D., Guerrier, Y. and Guy, J. (1998) 'Sexual harassment issues in the hospitality industry', *International Journal of Contemporary Hospitality Management* 10(2/3): 48–53.

Gill, M. and Hearnshaw, S. (1997) *Personal Safety and Violence in Schools*, Norwich: HMSO.

Gillespie, M. and Melby, V. (2003) 'Burnout among nursing staff in accident and emergency and acute medicine: a comparative study', *Journal of Clinical Nursing* 12: 842–851.

Golding, A. M. (2000) 'Violence at work', *Health and Hygiene* 21(4): 152–153.

Goode, E. and Ben-Yehuda, N. (1994) *Moral Panics: The Social Construction of Deviance*, Oxford: Blackwell.

Gournay, K. (2001) 'The recognition, prevention and therapeutic management of violence in mental health care: a consultation document prepared for the United Kingdom Central Council for Nursing, Midwifery and Health Visiting', London: National Task Force on Violence Against Social Care Staff, Department of Health.

Graham, S. (2000) 'When violence comes to work', *Safety and Health* 161(2): 28–33.

Grenyer, B. F., Ilkiw-Lavalle, O., Biro, P., Middleby-Clements, J., Comninos, A. and Coleman, M. (2004) 'Safer at work: development and evaluation of an aggression and violence minimization program', *Australian and New Zealand Journal of Psychiatry* 38(10): 804–810.

Grimwood, C. and La Valle, I. (1993) 'Beware of the client', *Community Care*: 15.

Gudjonsson, G. H. (1994) 'Psychological vulnerability', in D. Morgan and G. Stephenson (eds) *Suspicion and Silence: The Right to Silence in Criminal Investigation*, London: Blackstone.

Gudjonsson, G., Clare, I., Rutter, S. and Pearse, J. (1993) *Persons at Risk During Interviews in Police Custody: The Identification of Vulnerabilities*, London: HMSO.

Guerrier, Y. and Adib, A. S. (2000) '"No, we don't provide that service": the harassment of hotel employees by customers', *Work Employment and Society* 14(4): 689–706.

Hadfield, P., Lister, S., Hobbs, D. and Winlow, S. (2001) 'The "24 hour city" – condition critical', *Town and Country Planning* 70(11): 300–302.

Hale, C. (1996) 'Fear of crime: a review of the literature', *International Review of Victimology* 34: 79-150.

Harvey, H. D., Fleming, P. and Mooney, D. (2002) 'Violence at work: an initial needs assessment for the environmental health department as a health promoting workplace', *Journal of Environmental Health Research* 1(1): 41–49.

Health and Safety Executive (1996) *Violence at Work: a guide for employers*, Sudbury, Suffolk: Health and Safety Executive.

Health and Safety Executive (1997) *Violence and Aggression to Staff in Health Services*, London: HSE Books.

Health Services Advisory Committee (1987) *Violence to Staff in the Health Services*, London: Health and Safety Executive.

Healy, J., Brennan, P. C. and Costelloe, J. P. (2002) 'Violence at work: a major radiographic issue', *Radiography* 8(2): 85–90.

Heritage, J. (1984) *Garfinkel and Ethnomethodology*, Cambridge: Polity.

Hinsby, K. and Baker, M. (2004) 'Patient and nurse accounts of violent incidents in a Medium Secure Unit', *Journal of Psychiatric and Mental Health Nursing* 11: 341–347.

Hlebovy, D. (2000) 'Violence in the workplace', *Nephrology Nursing Journal* 27: 631–633.

Hobbs, D., Hadfield, P., Lister, S. and Winlow, S. (2002) '"Door lore": The art and economics of intimidation', *British Journal of Criminology* 42: 352–370.

Hobbs, D., Hadfield, P., Lister, S. and Winlow, S. (2003) *Bouncers: Violence and Governance in the Night-Time Economy*, Oxford: Oxford University Press.

Hoel, H. and Einarsen, S. (2003) 'Violence at work in hotels, catering and tourism in Norway', *Sectoral Activities Programme Working Paper*, Geneva: International Labour Office.

Hoel, H., Sparks, K. and Cooper, C. L. (no date) *The Cost of Violence/Stress at Work and the Benefits of a Violence/Stress-Free Working Environment*, Geneva: International Labour Organization.

Hogh, A., Borg, V. and Mikkelsen, K. L. (2003) 'Work-related violence as a predictor of fatigue: A 5-year follow-up of the Danish Work Environment Cohort Study', *Work and Stress* 17(2): 182–194.

Hollin, C. R. (1981) 'Nature of the witnessed incident and status of interviewing variables influencing eyewitness recall', *British Journal of Social Psychology* 20: 295–296.

Hough, M. (1996) *Anxiety About Crime: Findings from the 1994 British Crime Survey*, London: Home Office.

Hough, M. and Mayhew, P. (1983) *The British Crime Survey: First Report*, London: HMSO.

Hough, M. and Sheehy, K. (1986) *Incidents of Violence: Findings from the British Crime Survey*, Vol. 20, London: Home Office Research Bulletin.

Illsley, B. (1997) 'Violence at work: the experience of women planners in Scotland', *Gender and Scottish Society: Polities, Policies and Participation*, Edinburgh: Unit for the Study of Government in Scotland, University of Edinburgh.

Incomes Data Services (2000) *Violence at Work*, London: Incomes Data Services.

Innes, M. (2003) '"Signal crimes": detective work, mass media and constructing collective memory', in P. Mason (ed.) *Criminal Visions: Media representations of crime and justice*, Cullompton: Willan.

Innes, M., Lowe, T., MacKenzie, H., Murray, P., Roberts, C. and Twyman, L. (2004) *The Signal Crimes Perspective: Interim Findings*, Guildford: University of Surrey.

Irving, B. and Hilgendorf, L. (1980) *Police Interrogation: the Psychological Approach*, London: HMSO.

Ishmael, A. and Alemoru, B. (1999) *Harassment, Bullying and Violence at Work: A practical guide to combating employee abuse*, London: The Industrial Society.

Isotalus, N. (2002) 'Prevention of physical violence at work', *African Newsletter on Occupational Health and Safety* 12(1): 12–14.

Isotalus, N. and Saarela, K. L. (1999) 'Increasing violence in customer service work as a new risk: an example concerning pharmacies', in J. Rantanen, S. Lehtinen and K. L. Saarela (eds) *Safety in the Modern Society*, Helsinki: Finnish Institute of Occupational Health.

Jenkins, M. G., Rocke, L. G., McNicholl, B. P. and Hughes, D. M. (1998) 'Violence and verbal abuse against staff in accident and emergency departments: a survey of consultants in the UK and the Republic of Ireland', *Journal of Accident and Emergency Medicine* 15(4): 262–265.

Journal of Environmental Health Research (2002) 'Violence at work: an initial needs assessment for the environmental health department as a health promoting workplace', *Journal of Environmental Health Research* 1(1): 41–50.

Kedward, C. (2000) 'Local authorities and violence to social work staff: Towards a common framework', *Managing Community Care* 8(5): 28–34.

Kedward, C. (2001) *Local Authorities and Violence to Social Work Staff: Towards a Common Framework*, London: National Task Force on Violence Against Social Care Staff, Department of Health.

Kerber, B. A. (1999) 'Keep it cool: Steps to identify and defuse work-site violence', *Credit Union Management* 22(8): 30-31.

Killias, M. (1990) 'Vulnerability: towards a better understanding of a key variable in the genesis of fear of crime', *Violence and Victims* 5: 97–108.

Klandermans, B. (1997) *The Social Psychology of Protest*, Oxford: Blackwell.

Klockars, C. B. (1996) 'A theory of excessive force and its control', in W. A. Geller and H. Toch (eds) *Police Violence: Understanding and Controlling Police Abuse of Force*, New Haven, Conn.: Yale University Press.

Kloss, D. (2003) 'Violence at work', *Occupational Health Review* 103: 40.

Kohnken, G., Milne, R., Memon, A. and Bull, R. (1999) 'The cognitive interview: a meta-analysis', *Psychology, Crime and Law*, 1–35.

Kurtz, S. P., Surratt, H. L., Inciardi, J. A. and Kiley, M. C. (2004) 'Sex work and "date" violence', *Violence against Women* 10(4): 357–385.

Leadbetter, D. and Trewartha, R. (1998) *Handling Aggression and Violence at Work: a training manual*, Lyme Regis: Russell House

Lee, R. M. and Stanko, E. A. (eds) (2003) *Researching Violence: Essays on Methodology and Measurement*, London: Routledge.

Lehane, M. and Carver, L. (2003) 'Hurt feelings', *Nursing Standard* 19 November: 19.

Leyden, G. (1999) 'Reducing violence to teachers in the workplace', in P. Leather, C. Brady, C. Lawrence, D. Beale and T. Cox (eds) *Work-related Violence: Assessment and Intervention*, London: Routledge.

Lister, S., Hadfield, P., Hobbs, D. and Winlow, S. (2001) 'Accounting for bouncers: occupational licensing as a mechanism for regulation', *Criminal Justice* 1(4).

Littlechild, B. (1995) 'Violence against social workers', *Journal of Interpersonal Violence* 10(1): 123–130.

Local Government Management Board (1991) *Violence at Work: issues, policies and procedures: a case study of two local authorities*, Luton: Local Government Management Board.

Macpherson of Cluny, S. W., advised by Cook, T., Sentamu, T. R. R. D. J. and Stone, R. (1999) *The Stephen Lawrence Inquiry*, London: HMSO.

Maguire, M. (1980) 'The impact of burglary upon victims', *British Journal of Criminology* 20(3): 261–275.

Maguire, M. (1982) *Burglary in a Dwelling*, London: Heinemann.

Maguire, M. (1985) 'Victims' needs and victim services: indications from research', *Victimology: An International Journal* 10(1-4): 539–559.

Maguire, M. and Corbett, C. (1987) *The Effects of Crime and the Work of Victim Support Schemes*, Aldershot: Gower.

Mason, T. and Chandley, M. (1999) *Managing Violence and Aggression: a manual for nurses and health care workers*, Edinburgh: Churchill Livingstone.

Matthews, L. R. (1998) 'Effect of staff debriefing on posttraumatic stress symptoms after assault by community housing residents', *Psychiatric Services* 49: 207–212.

Maxfield, M. (1984) *Fear of Crime in England and Wales*, London: HMSO.

Mayhew, C. (2003) 'Preventing violence against health workers', *Worksafe Victoria Seminar*, Victoria.

Mayhew, C. and Chappell, D. (2003) 'Workplace violence in the health sector – a case study in Australia', *The Journal of Occupational Health and Safety – Australia and New Zealand* 19(6).

McAdam, D. (1996) 'The framing function of movement tactics: strategic dramaturgy in the American civil rights movement', in D. McAdam, J. D. McCarthy and M. N. Zald (eds) *Comparative Perspectives on Social Movements*, Cambridge: Cambridge University Press.

McCurry, P. (2000) 'In the line of fire. As the incidence of violence at work increases, are directors aware of their legal obligation to look after their staff?', *Director* 54(3): 98–103.

McLean, J. (2000) 'Violence against social services staff', *Evaluation for Practice Conference*, University of Huddersfield.

McLean, J., Brockmann, M. and Foster, G. (1999) *Violence against Social Care Workers*, London: National Institute for Social Work.

McMillan, I. (1995) 'Violence. Losing control: The results of an NT survey into bullying at work', *Nursing Times and Nursing Mirror* 91(15): 40.

Memon, A. and Bull, R. (1991) 'The cognitive interview – its origins, empirical support, evaluation and practical implications', *Journal of Community and Applied Social Psychology* 1(4): 291–307.

Memon, A., Bull, R. and Smith, M. (1995) 'Improving the quality of the police interview: can training in the use of cognitive techniques help?', *Policing and Society* 5(1): 53–68.

Memon, A., Holley, A., Milne, R., Kohnken, G. and Bull, R. (1994) 'Towards understanding the effects of interviewer training in evaluating the cognitive interview', *Applied Cognitive Psychology* 8: 641–659.

Memon, A., Vrij, A. and Bull, R. (1998) *Psychology and Law: Truthfulness, Accuracy and Credibility*, London: McGraw-Hill.

Milne, R. and Bull, R. (1999 *Investigative Interviewing*, Chichester: Wiley.

Mullen, E. (1997) 'Workplace violence: cause for concern or the construction of a new category of fear', *Journal of Industrial Relations* 39(1): 21–32.

Myhill, A. and Allen, J. (2002) *Rape and Sexual Assault of Women: the extent and nature of the problem. Findings from the British Crime Survey*, London: Home Office Research, Development and Statistics Directorate.

National Association of Probation Officers (1989) *Violence Against Probation Staff – Prevention, Monitoring and Response*, London: National Association of Probation Officers.

National Association of Social Workers (1996) Committee for the Study and Prevention of Violence against Social Workers Safety Guidelines (revised March), *Professional Social Work*.

National Audit Office (2003a) *A Safer Place to Work: protecting NHS hospital and ambulance staff from violence and aggression*, London: Stationery Office.

National Audit Office (2003b) *A Safer Place to Work: Improving the management of health and safety risks to staff in NHS trusts*, London: National Audit Office.

National Task Force Against Violence to Social Care Staff (2001) *Safety at Work Training Survey – Social and Health Care Staff*, London: National Task Force on Violence Against Social Care Staff, Department of Health.

National Union of Public Employees (1991) *Violence in the NHS*, London: NUPE.

Newhill, C. E. (2003) *Client Violence in Social Work Practice: prevention, intervention and research*, New York: Guilford Press.

Noak, J., Wright, S., Sayer, J., Parr, A.-M., Gray, R., Southern, D. and Gournay, K. (2002) 'The content of management of violence policy documents in United Kingdom acute inpatient mental health services', *Journal of Advanced Nursing* 37(4): 394–401.

Nolan, P., Dallender, J., Soares, J., Thompsen, S. and Arnetz, B. (1999) 'Violence in mental health care: the experiences of mental health nurses and psychiatrists', *Journal of Advanced Nursing* 30(4): 934–941.

Norris, D. and Kedward, C. (1990) *Violence Against Social Workers. The Implications for Practice*, London: Jessica Kingsley.

Nursing Standard (2005) 'Midwives most in danger of violence and harassment', *Nursing Standard* 5.

O'Beirne, M., Denney, D. and Gabe, J. (2004) 'Fear of violence as an indicator of risk in probation work', *British Journal of Criminology* 44(1): 113–126.

O'Beirne, M., Denney, D., Gabe, J., Elston, M. A. and Lee, R. M. (2003) 'Veiling violence: the impacts of professional and personal identities on the disclosure of work-related violence', in R. M. Lee and E. A. Stanko (eds) *Researching Violence: Essays on Methodology and Measurement*, London: Routledge.

Occupational Health (2001) 'HSE tackles violence at work. Executive takes action as gap in self-defence training for workers is revealed', *Occupational Health* 53(9): 6.

O'Connell, B., Young, J., Brooks, J., Hutchings, J. and Lofthouse, J. (2000) 'Nurses' perceptions of the nature and frequency of aggression in general ward settings and high dependency areas', *Journal of Clinical Nursing* 9: 602–610.

O'Connor, N. (2000) 'Violence at work', *Safety and Health Practitioner* 18(4): 68–69.

O'Keefe, M. and Mennen, F. E. (1998) 'Integrating content on violence into a social work practice curriculum', *Journal of Teaching in Social Work* 17(1/2): 81–100.

Owens, S. and Keville, H. (1990) *Safe and Secure: how to deal with potential violence at work*, St Leonards-on-Sea: Outset.

Paterson, B. and Leadbetter, R. (1999) 'Managing physical violence', in J. Turnball and B. Paterson (eds) *Aggression and Violence*, London: Macmillan.

Paterson, B. and Stark, C. (2001) 'Social policy and mental illness in England in the 1990s: violence, moral panic and critical discourse', *Journal of Psychiatric and Mental Health Nursing* 8: 257–267.

Paterson, B., Leadbetter, D. and Bowie, V. (1999) 'Supporting nursing staff exposed to violence at work', *International Journal of Nursing Studies* 36(6): 479–486.

Pease, K. (1988) *Judgements of Crime Seriousness: Evidence from the 1984 British Crime Survey*, RPU 44 edition, London: Home Office.

Pemberton, M. N., Atherton, G. J. and Thornhill, M. H. (2000) 'Violence and aggression at work', *British Dental Journal* 189(8): 409–411.

People Management (1998) 'Health and safety: "Human bomb" attack underlines growing risk of violence at work', *People Management*: 10.

Personnel Today (2001) 'Zero tolerance approach needed on violence at work. Firms are failing to meet legal obligations to employees attacked by clients', *Personnel Today*: 15–19.

Police Complaints Authority (2003) 'Review of shootings by police in England and Wales from 1998 to 2001. Report to the Secretary of State for the Home Department by the Police Complaints Authority pursuant to S. 79(1) of the Police Act 1996 Ordered by The House of Commons to be printed 30 January', London: Police Complaints Authority.

Poyner, B. and Warne, C. (1988) *Preventing Violence to Staff*, London: Health and Safety Executive.

Public Accounts Committee (2003) *A Safer Place to Work: protecting NHS hospital and ambulance staff from violence and aggression*, London: Stationery Office.

Py, J., Ginet, M., Desperies, C. and Cathey, C. (1997) 'Cognitive encoding and cognitive interviewing in eyewitness testimony', *Swiss Journal of Psychology* 56(1): 33–41.

Queensland Nurses' Union (2000) 'Zero tolerance to violence', *Queensland Nurses' Union*.

Reiss, A. J., Jr. (1987) 'The legitimacy of intrusion into private space', in C. D. Shearing and P. C. Stenning (eds) *Private Policing*, Newbury Park, Cal.: Sage.

Reuss-Ianni, E. and Ianni, F. A. (1983) 'Street cops and management cops: the two cultures of policing', in M. Punch (ed.) *Control in the Police Organization*, Cambridge, Mass.: MIT Press.

Rippon, T. J. (2000) 'Aggression and violence in health care professions', *Journal of Advanced Nursing* 31: 452–460.

Roach, L. (1997) 'Violence at work: On the role of legislation in protecting nurses from violence', *Nursing Standard* 12: 22–25.

Rogers, K. A. and Rogers, E. K. (1997) 'Violence at work: personal and organizational outcomes', *Journal of Occupational Health Psychology* 2(1): 63–71.

Rowett, C. (1986) *Violence in Social Work*, Cambridge: University of Cambridge, Institute of Criminology.

Rowett, C. and Breakwell, G. M. (1992) *Managing Violence at Work*, Windsor: NFER-Nelson.

Royal College of Nursing (1993) 'Approaching with care: violence at work', *RCN Nursing Update; Learning Unit 38*, London: Healthcare Productions for the Royal College of Nursing.

Royal College of Nursing (1994) *Violence and Community Nursing Staff. A Royal College of Nursing Survey*, London: RCN.

Royal College of Nursing (1998) *Dealing with Violence Against Nursing Staff: an RCN guide for nurses and managers*, London: RCN.

Royal College of Nursing/NHS Executive (1998) *Safer Working in the Community: a guide for NHS managers and staff on reducing the risks from violence and aggression*, London: RCN.

Ryan, K. K. (1997) 'Work zone or war zone? An overview of workplace violence', *Colorado Lawyer* 26(11): 19–28.

Safety Management (2001) 'Home Office violence at work survey published', *Safety Management* 12–13.

Scott, M. B. and Lyman, S. M. (1968) 'Accounts', *American Sociological Review* 33(1): 46–62.

Scottish Executive (2004) *Protecting Public Service Workers: When the customer isn't right*, Edinburgh: Scottish Executive.

Shepherd, B. (1997) 'Questions and answers in industrial relations. Violence at work', *Midwives* 110(1310): 68–70.

Shepherd, J. (ed.) (1994) *Violence in Health Care: A Practical Guide to Coping With Violence and Caring for Victims*, Oxford: Oxford University Press.

Simmonds, M. (2002) 'On the night shift in A&E', *Nursing Standard*: 20–21.

Smith, D. J. (2005) 'Shipman: the Final Report', *The Shipman Inquiry*, Crown Copyright.

Smith, S. J. (1984) 'Crime in the news', *British Journal of Criminology* 24(3): 289–295.

Smulders, P. G. W., Hesselink, D. J. K. and Evers, G. E. (2001) 'Violence, intimidation and discrimination at work in the European Union. An analysis of the 1996 European Work Environment Survey by the European Foundation for the Improvement of Living and Working Conditions', *Translations – Health and Safety Executive Library and Information Service*. HSE (16160; Sers I).

Snow, D. A. and Benford, R. D. (1992) 'Master frames and cycles of protest', in A. D. Morris and C. M. Mueller (eds) *Frontiers in Social Movement Theory*, New Haven, Conn.: Yale University Press.

Spokes, K., Bond, K., Lowe, T., Jones, J., Illingworth, P., N., B. and Wellman, N. (2002) 'HOVIS – The Hertfordshire/Oxfordshire Violent Incident Study', *Journal of Psychiatric and Mental Health Nursing* 9: 199–209.

Stanko, E. A. (2000) 'Victims R Us', in T. Hope and R. Sparks (eds) *Crime, Risk and Insecurity: Law and Order in Everyday Life and Political Discourse*, London: Routledge.

Stanko, E. A. (2003) 'Introduction: Conceptualising the meanings of violence', in E. A. Stanko (ed.) *The Meanings of Violence*, London: Routledge.

Stinchcombe, A. L. (1963) 'Institutions of privacy in the determination of police administrative practice', *American Journal of Sociology* 69: 150–160.

Sykes, G. M. and Matza, D. (1957) 'Techniques of neutralization', *American Sociological Review* 22: 664–670.

Thompson, N. (2004) 'Book review: Client violence in social work practice: prevention, intervention and research, by Christina Newhill', *British Journal of Social Work* 34(6): 927–928.

Thornhill, J. (2000) 'Risky business. Housing staff are getting used to dealing with violence at work. But they don't have to', *Housing*: 37.

Tolhurst, H., Talbot, J., Baker, L., Bell, P., Murray, G., Sutton, A., Dean, S., Treloar, C. and Harris, G. (2003) 'Rural general practitioner apprehension about work related violence in Australia', *Australian Journal of Rural Health* 11(5): 237–241.

Tulving, E. and Thomson, D. (1973) 'Encoding specificity and retrieval processes in episodic memory', *Psychological Review* 80: 352–373.

UNISON (1995) *Violence at Work: health service staff survey*, London: UNISON.

UNISON (1997) *Violence at Work: a guide to risk prevention for UNISON branches, stewards and safety representatives*, London: UNISON.

Upson, A. (2004) *Violence at Work: Findings from the 2002/2003 British Crime Survey*, London: Home Office.

Uzun, O. (2003) 'Perceptions and experiences of nurses in Turkey about verbal abuse in clinical settings', *Journal of Nursing Scholarship* 35(1): 81–85.

Vandenbos, G. R. and Bulatao, E. Q. (eds) (1997) *Violence on the Job*, Washington, DC: American Psychological Association.

Waddington, P. A. J. (1999) *Policing Citizens*, London: UCL.

Waddington, P. A. J., Badger, D. and Bull, R. (2005) 'Appraising the inclusive definition of "violence"', *British Journal of Criminology* 45(2): 141–164.

Weadick, T. (2001) 'Easy targets: the rising tide of violence at work', *Safety and Health Practitioner* 19(6): 23–27.

Wells, J. and Bowers, L. (2002) 'How prevalent is violence towards nurses working in general hospitals in the UK?', *Journal of Advanced Nursing* 39(3): 230–240.

Whittington, R. (2002) 'Attitudes toward patient aggression amongst mental health nurses in the "zero tolerance" era: associations with burnout and length of experience', *Journal of Clinical Nursing* 11: 819–825.

Wilson, J. Q. and Kelling, G. (1982) 'Broken windows', *The Atlantic Monthly*: 29–38.

Winlow, S., Hobbs, D., Lister, S. and Hadfield, P. (2001) 'Get ready to duck: bouncers and the realities of ethnographic research on violent groups', *British Journal of Criminology* 41(3): 536–548.

Winlow, S., Hobbs, D., Lister, S. and Hadfield, P. (2003) 'Bouncers and the social context of violence: masculinity, class and violence in the night-time economy', in E. A. Stanko (ed.) *The Meanings of Violence*, London: Routledge.

Winstanley, S. and Whittington, R. (2004) 'Aggression towards health care staff in a UK general hospital: variation among professions and departments', *Journal of Clinical Nursing* 13: 3–10.

Worden, R. E. (1996) 'The causes of police brutality: theory and evidence on police use of force', in W. A. Geller and H. Toch (eds) *Police Violence: Understanding and Controlling Police Abuse of Force*, New Haven, Conn.: Yale University Press.

Wright, M. (1977) 'Nobody came: criminal justice on the needs of victims', *Howard Journal* 16: 22–31.

Wynne, R. and Clarkin, N. (1995) 'Workplace violence in Europe – is it time to act?', *Work and Stress* 9(4): 377–379.

Index